THE COMING SOVIET CRASH

THE COMING SOVIET CRASH

— • • • —

Gorbachev's Desperate Pursuit of Credit in Western Financial Markets

JUDY SHELTON

THE FREE PRESS
A Division of Macmillan, Inc.
NEW YORK

Collier Macmillan Publishers
LONDON

The Free Press
A Division of Macmillan, Inc.
866 Third Avenue, New York, N.Y. 10022

Collier Macmillan Canada, Inc.

Printed in the United States of America

printing number

3 4 5 6 7 8 9 10

Library of Congress Cataloging-in-Publication Data

Shelton, Judy.
    The coming Soviet crash: Gorbachev's desperate pursuit of credit in Western financial markets / Judy Shelton.
      p.   cm.
    Includes index.
    ISBN 0–02–928581–X
    1. Bank loans—Soviet Union. 2. Loans, Foreign—Soviet Union.
3. Inflation (Finance)—Soviet Union. 4. Budget deficits—Soviet Union. 5. Soviet Union—Economic conditions—1976–   I. Title.
HG1642.S65S44 1989
332.1′753′0947—dc19   88–22787
                                                      CIP

To my husband G.L.

Contents

Acknowledgments

My initial interest in Soviet borrowing was sparked in May 1984 while doing research on global debt for Senior Fellow Martin Anderson at the Hoover Institution. Concerned about the lack of comprehensive statistics on Soviet indebtedness, I proposed to specifically analyze Soviet activities in Western financial markets and to determine the impact of Western capital on the Soviet economy. The research was generously supported by the Hoover Institution through a postdoctoral grant from the National, Peace, and Public Affairs Fellows Program, for which I am deeply grateful to Hoover Director W. Glenn Campbell. Additional funds were provided under the Title VIII program (The Soviet–East European Research and Training Act of 1983), administered by the Department of State, for which I am also appreciative.

Erwin A. Glikes, publisher of The Free Press, provided me with the opportunity to write a book on the Soviet Union's financial condition that would include political and economic policy implications for the West. Thanks are also due to my editor Grant Ujifusa for his insightful observations and comments. In addition, Laura Rosenfeld provided excellent editorial advice and guidance.

Among those who reviewed early drafts of the book and provided helpful suggestions, I would like to thank, in particular, Martin Anderson and Hoover Senior Fellow Henry S. Rowen. I also benefited greatly from discussions with Igor Birman, who played a pioneering role in bringing to light Soviet internal budget problems. Bevan Stein at the Organization for Economic Co-operation and Development (OECD) in Paris and T. R. G. Bingham at the Bank for International Settlements (BIS) in Basel were most helpful in explaining how individual country debt is monitored in the West.

Finally, I would like to thank my husband, Gil. His encouragement sustained me throughout this effort, and his evaluation of the manuscript at various stages served to improve the organization and presentation of the final product.

I am responsible, of course, for all remaining errors.

Introduction

The Soviets are now working very hard to obtain financial credits from the West. Why have they stepped up their borrowing from commercial banks? Why are they going after investment capital through joint ventures with private Western companies? What prompted their decision to issue sovereign bonds to Western investors—for the first time since tsarist times—and why are Kremlin officials suggesting that they would like to join the International Monetary Fund and the World Bank? The short answer is the correct one: They need the money.

Soviet vigor in the credit hunt shows just how badly they need the money. Never has it been easy for the Soviet government to admit it needs anything from the West, let alone something as basic as financial capital. Indeed, one of the proudest claims of the Soviet Union has been its long-standing assertion of economic self-sufficiency. Now to be forced to come to the West for financial help is to admit that socialism's blueprint has not delivered promised economic superiority, an admission, perhaps, that Marx and Lenin did not have all the answers or, to avoid such a blasphemy, that the Soviet people have been negligent in carrying out those two heroes' sacred dictates.

The latter is, of course, the only acceptable socialist rationale behind the effort to address the current Soviet economic crisis. It is what *perestroika*—rebuilding the Soviet economy—is about. General Secretary Gorbachev is not about to denigrate the founders of socialism; that would be wholly out of character. Instead, he genuinely believes that Lenin and his wise tenets offer the way to a truly productive industrialized economy. So the Soviet economy is performing so terribly not because socialism has any inherent faults as an economic system, but because certain basic operating units within the system have been allowed to drift away from the responsibilities given to them by the founders. In other words, too many of the state-owned enterprises that should be producing the revenues that underwrite the Soviet government have failed in their basic obligations. Now the system must be revamped to address the abuses that led to failure. This is the angle—that the system has gotten offtrack, not that the tracks were laid out wrong—from which Gorbachev can safely criticize the state of the Soviet economy.

The rationale also gives Gorbachev a way to approach the West without explaining in detail that the Soviet economy is very hard pressed to meet its own needs for consumption, fixed investment, and military spending. Yes, he admits, his country has suffered economic disappointments during the past decade. But just as capitalist countries have periods of expansion followed by recession, Gorbachev asserts that the Soviet Union is merely experiencing a temporary, though rather lengthy, period of stagnation. At some point in the future, perestroika will put the Soviet system back on track. In the meantime, during a period of transition, relief from arms competition would be most helpful. The West could no doubt use a breathing spell as well, Gorbachev adds. And while we're at it, why not expand the opportunity into a whole range of economic and financial relations between the Soviet Union and the West?

Perestroika is thus being promoted as the perfect backdrop for improved superpower relations, a time during which the Soviets will be so preoccupied with domestic economic problems that they won't have time to think aggressive thoughts. Not just Gorbachev but a number of observers in the West as well are pushing this line of analysis. What could be more innocent than wanting to reinvigorate the economy? Never mind that there is a direct relationship between Soviet economic strength and Soviet military power.

If the United States buys the notion that the Soviet situation is only temporary, not chronic, it is left trying to calculate just how much Soviet gratitude will be worth later when the system is back on track. If the United States cooperates today, the idea is that the goodwill created will translate into improved political relations tomorrow. That is consistent with the prevailing theory that because the Soviets will always be with us, it is better to stay in their good graces than to withhold financial help at a crucial time.

But just how desperate is the Soviet economic situation at this time? Is the system actually headed for collapse, as some people assert? If so, financial assistance from the West takes on a much more significant, perhaps even a pivotal, role.

It is one thing to make Western credit available if it is assumed that the Soviet economy will ultimately restore itself and that the objective is to win political points for helping it to do so. It is quite another to make the same credit available if it is assumed that our military and ideological rivals are engaged in a make-or-break struggle for economic survival. In the latter instance, much more is at stake.

Not that the U.S. government, or any other Western government, can exert complete control over Soviet access to Western credit, even if it tried. Because one of the oft-proclaimed virtues of Western democracies is the separation between private enterprise and public governance, capital controls imposed by government are seen as the highest form of interference in commerce. There is the disquieting fact, too, that Western governments themselves are major suppliers of credit to the Soviet Union; they are thus hardly in a position to ask bankers and businessmen to stop financing the Kremlin in the name of national self-interest.

Indeed, the Soviets do need the money. Long before it was apparent to most Western observers that the Soviet economy was deteriorating badly, Gorbachev was already laying the groundwork for the pursuit of Western credit. The correlation between Gorbachev's reign in the Kremlin and the escalation of Soviet borrowing activities in Western financial markets is striking. Within two years after Gorbachev took over in March 1985, Soviet debt to the West shot up from about $25 billion to over $37 billion, an increase of 50 percent.

During the same period, Gorbachev launched a campaign aimed at improving trade relations with Western Europe and Japan. He began handing out Soviet contracts for massive projects to Western firms, with the successful bidder expected to provide low-interest financing arranged through his government's trade credit program. Effective January 1987, Gorbachev took the unprecedented step of allowing Western businessmen to invest directly in the Soviet economy by way of joint ventures with Soviet enterprises. The terms are simple: Western firms provide the money, managerial expertise, and technology, while the Soviet Union supplies basic materials and labor.

Gorbachev also set his sights on bringing down barriers that blocked the Soviet Union from issuing sovereign bonds. In July 1986 he empowered Foreign Minister Eduard Shevardnadze to reach an agreement with Britain over outstanding tsarist debt. The Soviet Union succeeded in settling more than $800 million in claims by remitting less than $70 million and in the process obtained permission from the Bank of England to launch a Eurobond offering through the London capital markets. A similar agreement was reached with Switzerland, and in January 1988 the Soviet Union chose to float its first public bond offering on international capital markets out of Zurich.

Gorbachev's onslaught of financial maneuvers seems to have left the United States dazed. We know that the Soviets are hitting the financial markets from several angles at once, and we feel a vague alarm about how quickly they are becoming world-class debtors. There is recognition, too, that the intense activity by the Kremlin is connected to the deteriorating economic situation at home. But after superpower summits and arms control agreements, purely financial questions about the Soviet Union's creditworthiness and its internal budget crisis are being downplayed in the debate over East–West relations. The United States' preoccupation with heated and dramatic issues like the elimination of nuclear weapons and violation of human rights serves to nurture a subconscious make-loans-not-war attitude that none dare call détente.

Gorbachev, keeping to a plan to tap all possible sources of Western financial assistance, is eager to exploit the current frame of mind. He knows that the United States derives a measure of imperialistic glee from the prospect of exhorting the Soviet Union to do its bidding in exchange for financial and economic rewards. The challenge for Gorbachev is to work that to Soviet advantage. The fact that the seriousness of the internal budget situation facing the Soviet government is not fully appreciated in the West helps Gorbachev. So long as Westerners tend to underestimate how much financial incentive the Soviet Union has to seek accommodation, Gorbachev is prepared to tolerate a limited amount of meddling by American politicians on certain highly visible issues. But he fully intends to see that the Americans pay up for getting involved.

One purpose of this book is to bring to light, by scrutinizing the statistical and accounting data published by the Soviet government, the real state of the Soviet domestic budget while tracing its impact on the internal financial system. It is no secret in the West that the Soviet economy is in trouble, but not many outside observers have examined the Soviet system from a financial (as opposed to an economic) set of analytical yardsticks. The basic conclusion here is that the Soviet internal financial system is in decidedly worse shape than is generally assumed.

The other main purpose is to lay out the various ways in which Western financial capital is transferred to the Soviet economy. Commercial banks are often vilified for extending credits to Moscow. But bankers are just the most visible providers of funds among a group of discreetly low-profile participants. Then, too, it is not just the current methods of credit access that should interest us, but also the future opportunities the Soviets are vigorously pursuing. Not long ago, in fact, experts were speculating about when the Soviets might attempt to issue a Eurobond. Now that is a reality.

In short, Part I of the book tries to show *why* the Soviets need to borrow from the West, and Part II tries to explain *how* they are doing it. The logic here is that we must first understand why the Soviets need the money and how they are able to get it before we can talk about the extent to which the West—the United States in particular—should be party to the financing of the Soviet economy. This last question is treated in Part III.

At the heart of the matter is whether or not we are willing to contribute to the Soviet military capacity. If we assume that money is fungible and that savings to the Soviet economy in the manufacturing sector make more resources available to the military sector, we must acknowledge the risk to Western security interests. It follows that the United States has a responsibility to withhold credits—despite the protests of domestic businessmen and Western allies—because the West-to-East flow of financial capital constitutes *the transfer of a strategic resource.*

If, on the other hand, we regard Western financial assistance as something to be sold to the Kremlin, a cash cow whose price is negotiated by way of Soviet political concessions, we take it from the sphere of national security and put it on the bargaining table. Credit is something for which Gorbachev is willing to pay a lot, if forced, though he will most assuredly try to milk it through the fence. If Western financial aid is to be used as a lever for manipulating Soviet behavior, its potency must be maximized by restricting the movement of private capital to prevent unauthorized leakages to the Soviet Union.

These are, of course, matters of policy and administrative discretion. The objective here is to shed as much light as possible on the circumstances that are central to the debate over Soviet borrowing. Chief among them is the fact that the Soviet financial system is in desperate condition and that the Soviets are already borrowing heavily from various sources. That knowledge gives us proper perspective for evaluating political arrangements by which economic rewards from the West are exchanged for specific concessions by the Kremlin. The important thing to keep in mind is that any such deals are no tribute to Western diplomacy; they are being driven from the Soviet side. It is Gorbachev who, by holding out the possibility of reduced military tensions and increased emigration as bait, is coercing the West into providing the desperately needed financial help.

The Financial Condition of the Soviet Union

1

The Internal Budget Mess

To gain quick insight into the real state of the Soviet economy, we need only look at the financial statements on the internal Soviet state budget. If we concentrate on the revenues to the Soviet government, to determine where they come from and how they are calculated, we can then try to see how well they match up with Soviet government expenditures.

The internal budget documents serve as a shorthand guide for diagnosing a nation's economic vulnerabilities and prospects. It is like looking at a person's checkbook, not reviewing a list of his assets. For budget analysis, the goal is to find out whether or not a nation is financially viable as a going concern. Is there enough money coming in to cover expenses?

If a government takes in more than it spends, it has a budget surplus, which means more money can be devoted to capital investment or military spending, or that higher future levels of consumption are justified. If a government spends more than it takes in, it incurs a budget deficit, which must somehow be financed either out of internal savings or by borrowing abroad. In short, the relationship between revenues and expenditures determines whether or not a nation can move ahead confidently, knowing it has the internal resources to support its objectives.

For the Soviet Union, it is quite clear that the Kremlin would very much like to devote additional funds to capital investment. Gorbachev has publicly acknowledged the pressing need to modernize factories and revamp Soviet manufacturing processes to utilize high-technology innovations. It is also clear that Moscow intends to continue to mount a military challenge to the United States and to be ready, if necessary, to intensify spending to combat the threatened Strategic Defense Initiative. The Soviet government has likewise expressed its commitment to improving consumption levels for its citizens.

But all of that, of course, takes money. Unless the Soviets are running a significant surplus in the internal budget, they do not have the money required to do what they want to do. In that case, their choices are to incur a budget deficit, on the expectation that future growth in productivity will make up for temporary overspending, or to rely on the kindness of strangers by looking for money abroad. Neither is an attractive alternative to Moscow, because neither testifies to the competence of central planning. It is far preferable to achieve sufficient annual revenues through internal sources.

Which brings us back to the central question of whether or not the Soviet economy *is* generating enough revenues to meet the current spending requirements of the Soviet government—and in the process producing an adequate budget surplus to fund future expansion.

The key here lies in analyzing the make-up of the revenues themselves. Revenues to the Soviet government come mostly from the earnings of the state-run enterprises and cooperative organizations. Not much comes directly from members of the population. Westerners are usually surprised to learn that Soviet citizens do pay personal income taxes. But the bulk of total budget revenues, some 90 percent, is derived from the activities of the state and cooperative enterprises and organizations and is categorized as "receipts from the socialist economy."

Basically, the startup costs and working capital needs of Soviet enterprises are paid out of internal budget funds. After taking out some portion to cover certain operating expenses, the enterprises turn their revenues back over to the internal budget. That is in keeping with the socialist mode, which requires that the means of production be owned by the state. Accordingly, capital is assigned to Soviet enterprises by the government, and recipient enterprises are expected to fulfill their financial obligations to the state by contributing revenues to the government.

To make a rough comparison with the United States, American corporations and individuals provide revenues to the government's domestic budget by paying taxes, and from that money the government pays for military expenditures, social transfer payments, and fixed investment projects for improving the national infrastructure. But there are substantial differences, given the place of government in the two societies. In the Soviet Union, more than half of the national income flows through the internal budget,[1] as compared with the United States, where only about one quarter of GNP is represented in the domestic budget.

The internal state budget thus serves as the basic financial plan of the Soviet economy,[2] reflecting the pervasive role of government dictated by socialist doctrine. That enables us to infer a great deal about the health of the Soviet economy by analyzing the condition of the budget. It allows us also to make certain predictions about the future. If we in the United States think that budgetary imbalances foretell difficulties down the road for the domestic economy, then it follows that problems in the Soviet internal budget must carry even more ominous implications for the future of the Soviet economy.

Forever Balanced

Certain items of financial information in the Soviet Union, such as the size of debt outstanding, currency reserves, and the balance of payments, are regarded as state secrets. It is not difficult, however, to obtain fairly detailed financial statements on the Soviet internal budget showing the relationship between domestic revenues and domestic expenditures. The Soviet government has been publishing the information for decades and making it available in bookstores and libraries.

There are two publications, actually, that furnish data on the Soviet state budget, and both of them rely on statistics derived by the U.S.S.R. Central Statistical Administration, in Russian called the Tsentral'noye Statisticheskoye Upravleniye or TsSU. The first, put out directly by TsSU, is called the *National Economy of the U.S.S.R.: A Statistical Yearbook* (Narodnoye Khozyaistvo SSSR: Statisticheskiy Yezhegodnik).[3] It provides statistics on myriad economic topics, including, under the heading finances and credit, the internal state budget figures for various years. The second is put out under the auspices of the U.S.S.R. Ministry of Finances (Ministerstvo Finansov SSSR) and is called the *State Budget of the U.S.S.R.: A Statistical Handbook* (Gosudarstvennyy Byudzhet SSSR: Statisticheskiy Sbornik).[4]

There is strong correlation between the two publications, essentially because they are using the same statistics. For any given year, the amount listed for a particular category of revenues is the same for both. The main differences are that the first data set offers figures that have been liberally rounded off and leaves out minor revenue categories. In the second, the figures are presented in full detail, and the most trivial revenue categories are included.

At first glance, a Westerner is struck by a certain familiarity with the way the financial statements are structured. Revenues and expenditures are laid out in what appears to be standard accounting format with major categories marked by Roman numerals, lesser categories and subcategories with Arabic numbers or indented. In general, Soviet published statements on the internal state budget do not look very different from a corporate income statement for a Western firm.

Using the data supplied in either data set, we can quickly compare total revenues and total expenditures for any given year, going back for several decades. And here we find something remarkable: The Soviet budget is always balanced. According to the published information, revenues from the economy to the Soviet government have been coming in, year after year, at levels greater than those needed to cover government expenditures. Indeed, the Soviets have actually been achieving a budget surplus on a nearly permanent basis. That is, since 1940, there have been only three years—the war years 1941, 1942, and 1943—when the Soviet government was forced to spend more than it took in.

This rather surprising point was noted by Igor Birman in his book *Secret Incomes of the Soviet State Budget.*[5] Birman was born in Moscow, where he lived for forty-five years. He earned the Soviet equivalent of a Ph.D. in economics from Moscow State Economic Institute in 1960. He worked as a planner and a researcher, taught in various universities, and was a special correspondent of *Izvestiya* before emigrating to the United States in 1974.[6] Birman says it is quite strange that, even though Soviet economic plans are rarely fulfilled and despite serious difficulties in the Soviet economy, including years of great crop failures, the state budget regularly comes out with an excess of revenues over expenditures.[7]

Taking the relatively recent period since 1970, and pursuing Birman's investigative approach, Table 1.1 lists the annual revenues and expenditures for the Soviet internal budget as provided in the official government publications. The budget surplus, we can see, is evident throughout. The surplus is never very large, always a rather prudent figure. It ranges, as a percentage of total revenues, no higher than 3.38 percent (in 1981) and no lower than 0.57 percent (in 1986). This is remarkable in itself. A difference between revenues and expenditures that can be kept so rela-

TABLE 1.1. Published Soviet Budget Surplus (in millions of rubles)

Year	Revenues 1	Expenditures 2	Surplus Amount 3	Surplus % 4
1970	156,702.7	154,599.9	2,102.8	1.34
1971	165,956.1	164,151.5	1,804.6	1.09
1972	175,113.5	173,215.9	1,897.6	1.08
1973	187,775.8	183,980.0	3,795.8	2.02
1974	201,321.7	197,378.4	3,943.3	1.96
1975	218,768.9	214,520.7	4,248.2	1.94
1976	232,234.2	226,737.0	5,497.2	2.37
1977	247,819.3	242,790.2	5,029.1	2.03
1978	265,812.3	260,218.0	5,594.3	2.10
1979	281,531.4	276,370.4	5,161.0	1.83
1980	302,700.0	294,630.6	8,069.4	2.67
1981	320,635.2	309,793.7	10,841.5	3.38
1982	353,032.5	343,149.7	9,882.8	2.80
1983	357,919.1	354,265.0	3,654.1	1.02
1984	376,695.4	371,183.8	5,511.6	1.46
1985	390,602.5	386,469.3	4,133.2	1.06
1986	419,500.0	417,100.0	2,400.0	.57

SOURCES: Columns 1 and 2:
  1970–75, Gosudarstvennyy Byudzhet SSSR i Byudzhety Soyuznykh Respublik 1971–1975 gg.:Statisticheskiy Sbornik.
  1976–80, Gosudarstvennyy Byudzhet SSSR i Byudzhety Soyuznykh Respublik 1976–1980 gg.:Statisticheskiy Sbornik.
  1981–85, Gosudarstvennyy Byudzhet SSSR 1981–1985:Statisticheskiy Sbornik, pp. 4–5, 12–13.
  1986, Narodnoye Khozyaistvo SSSR za 70 let: Yubileinyy Statisticheskiy Yezhegodnik, pp. 628–29 (rounded figures).
Column 3: Column 1 less Column 2
Column 4: Column 3 divided by Column 1

tively small, yet so persistently on the plus side, implies a level of finesse in the art of central planning that approaches omniscience. After all, these are *ex post* results, not *pro forma* estimates.

The other interesting observation to be made is that the budget surplus, as a percentage of revenues, seemed to grow larger during the late 1970s and the beginning 1980s, even though it is widely accepted in the West that Soviet economic performance started to decline after 1975 and that the economy experienced only sluggish growth in the early 1980s. Matching revenues to expenditures was a close call, it seems, in 1986; still, a surplus was obtained. If the official figures are to be believed, then, the internal state budget is in solid enough shape, with revenues from the Soviet economy consistently managing to cover the expenditures of the Soviet government. One wonders what all the fuss is really about. Gorbachev's main task since coming to power has been to reform and revive the Soviet economy, but if it's not broken, we might ask, why fix it?

Using the budget figures from Table 1.1, we can see in Table 1.2 that the total revenues to the Soviet government have been growing at an impressive rate annually throughout the 1970s and into the 1980s, averaging just under 6 percent. There was a dramatic downturn in the percentage increase for 1983, following a surge in 1982, but more normal growth rates resumed in 1984 and 1985. In 1986, revenues grew by nearly 7 percent. With the internal budget remaining in such balance, the assumption is that there has been no inflation during this period. Thus the rise shown in the absolute numbers must represent a real, as opposed to a nominal, gain in revenues from the Soviet economy. That means the economy presumably has been producing solid increases in revenues throughout the period shown.

These figures, of course, have to strike us as too good. Perhaps the bothersome thing about a domestic budget always balanced and revenues always increasing is that it fits too well with the socialist paradigm. Among the oft-touted advantages of central planning is that imbalances between revenues and expenditures are not allowed to occur and that the economy produces a steady growth of revenues.

Socialist doctrine assumes that economic forces can be perfectly coordinated to maximize efficiency. Enlightened central management, socialists believe, permits sufficient revenues to be

TABLE **1.2.** Increase in Revenues to Budget (*in millions of rubles*)

Year	Revenues 1	Increase over Prior Year	
		Amount 2	% 3
1970	156,702.7	—	—
1971	165,956.1	9,253.4	5.58
1972	175,113.5	9,157.4	5.23
1973	187,775.8	12,662.3	6.74
1974	201,321.7	13,545.9	6.73
1975	218,768.9	17,447.2	7.98
1976	232,234.2	13,465.3	5.80
1977	247,819.3	15,585.1	6.29
1978	265,812.3	17,998.0	6.77
1979	281,531.4	15,719.1	5.58
1980	302,700.0	21,168.6	6.99
1981	320,635.2	17,935.2	5.59
1982	353,032.5	32,397.3	9.18
1983	357,919.1	4,886.6	1.37
1984	376,695.4	18,776.3	4.98
1985	390,602.5	13,907.1	3.56
1986	419,500.0	28,897.5	6.89

SOURCES: Column 1: Table 1.1, Column 1
Column 2: Increase in Column 1 over previous year
Column 3: Column 2 divided by Column 1

generated through productive activities to support the needs of the people and, at the same time, to maintain a government to oversee the military and capital investment needs of the country. Matching revenues to expenditures, especially in the consumption sector, serves to guarantee the stability of the national currency as well; if there is no deficit to finance, the government has no need to create unwarranted credit within the system. According to the Soviets, only *capitalist* societies are forced to contend with inflation.

Not having reconciled our own budget deficit, perhaps we can be accused of simply resenting the Soviet government for its evident success in budget management. But before we accept the Soviet financial statistics as accurate, we should indulge our suspicions by taking a closer look at the numbers themselves and the accounting concepts behind them.

It is not so much the expenditure side of the budget that should concern us. We can assume the Soviet government is spending at least as much as it is claiming in the official budget statements. The more pertinent question is whether or not the revenue side is being properly reported.

Is it possible that those responsible in the Soviet government bureaucracy for gathering the budget statistics and constructing the financial statements are more concerned with upholding socialist dogma than with supplying accurate data on the performance of the Soviet economy? If Western analysts are correct in their assessment that productivity in the Soviet Union declined precipitously during the last decade—and if Gorbachev himself is justified in his demands to implement drastic changes in the way the Soviet economy operates—then something is fundamentally wrong with the Soviet budget statistics, and that might radically alter our assessment of Soviet economic prospects.

Adding Up the Numbers

Since we want to analyze the revenues to the Soviet government from the economy, we need to follow Birman's earlier lead by working our way carefully through the statistical breakdown on revenues provided by the U.S.S.R. Ministry of Finances. Table 1.3 reproduces the financial statement on revenues to the state budget as it appears in *Gosudarstvennyy Byudzhet*, the more detailed of the publications on the domestic economy. The categories of revenue have been translated from Russian into English, of course, so we can understand their meaning. But the format of Table 1.3 is shown as it appears in the original Soviet documents, and the numbers for 1980 and 1985 are likewise taken directly from the published statements.

A figure denoting total revenues appears at the top of the table for each of the two years shown; below it are the breakdowns into lesser categories. We can see that the two principal categories of revenue to the Soviet government are designated as (I) receipts from the socialist economy and (II) receipts from the population. Interestingly, the Soviet government *does* differentiate between payments that come out of the enterprises and organizations sector and the revenues that are derived from individual members of the population—corporate versus personal taxes, in a sense. But a quick assessment of the relative contributions of category I and category II confirms that the latter doesn't sup-

TABLE 1.3. Soviet Budget Revenues (in millions of rubles)

	1980	1985
Total	302,700.0	390,602.5
Including:		
I. Receipts from the socialist economy	276,777.1	358,259.8
Of them:		
1. Turnover tax	94,108.7	97,716.4
2. Payments of state enterprises and economic organizations from profits	89,819.1	119,497.4
including:		
by branches of the national economy:		
industry and construction	56,013.7	76,739.7
agriculture	3,071.5	4,055.6
transportation	11,783.4	11,232.5
communications	1,919.5	3,444.0
housing and municipal services	3,287.6	4,710.6
trade	3,970.1	4,865.0
by types of payments:		
fee for fixed productive capital and working capital	29,182.6	38,127.8
free remainder of profits	43,987.1	47,114.1
fixed payments	424.7	5,157.3
deductions from profits and other payments	16,224.7	29,098.2
3. Income tax from cooperative and public enterprises and organizations	1,717.5	2,522.2
including:		
from *kolkhozy*	754.4	1,232.9
from cooperative enterprises and organizations and enterprises of public organizations	963.1	1,289.3
4. State social insurance revenue	13,957.0	25,381.5
5. Forestry revenue	477.7	825.1
II. Receipts from the population	25,922.9	32,342.7
Of them:		
1. State taxes from the population	24,511.4	30,017.5
including:		
personal income tax from the population	22,954.9	28,315.6
agricultural tax	261.0	231.2
tax on unmarried citizens and small family tax	1,295.5	1,470.7
2. Receipts from the sale of state loans and lottery revenue	890.3[a]	1,690.1

[a]This figure is given as two separate sources in 1980 statement.

SOURCES: 1980, *Gosudarstvennyy Byudzhet SSSR i Byudzhety Soyuznykh Respublik 1976–1980 gg: Statisticheskiy Sbornik*, pp. 10–11.
1985, *Gosudarstvennyy Byudzhet SSSR 1981–1985: Statisticheskiy Sbornik*, pp. 4–5.

ply a very high proportion of the total revenues accruing to the Soviet government.

It is worth doing the arithmetic, in fact, to verify that the two categories added together—receipts from the socialist economy and receipts from the population—equal the figure at the top for total revenues. A quick check reveals that everything is in perfect order; for both 1980 and 1985 the figures indeed add up to the given total, not just in general terms, but exactly, going one place beyond the decimal point. That kind of precision betokens an impressive commitment to accuracy on the part of Soviet statisticians. The numbers represent hundreds of billions of rubles, yet calculations are carried out to the nearest one hundred thousand rubles, which is like reporting the last dime on a six-figure deal.

Concentrating on category I, we can see in Table 1.3 that there are five major sources listed under the heading of receipts from the socialist economy: (1) turnover tax, (2) payments of state enterprises and economic organizations from profits, (3) income tax from cooperative and public enterprises and organizations, (4) state social insurance revenue, and (5) forestry revenue.

The first source listed, turnover tax, refers to money paid by Soviet enterprises to the state budget out of funds generated in the course of business, that is, by "turning over" goods from production to inventory or from inventory to sale, depending on the nature of the enterprise. It is akin to a value-added sales tax. During the late 1970s and very early 1980s, the amount of turnover tax paid by Soviet enterprises was the largest single source of revenues to the internal state budget. Since 1982, though, turnover taxes have been upstaged by payments of state enterprises and economic organizations from profits. In the financial statements, the figure for turnover tax is simply given outright under receipts from the socialist economy with no further breakdown.

The next source listed, representing payments of state enterprises and economic organizations from profits, is broken down in two different ways. First the composition of the total is detailed by the various "branches of the national economy" from which it is derived: industry and construction, agriculture, transportation, communications, housing and municipal services, and trade. Then the same total is broken down again, this time in terms of "types of payments" from profits: fee for fixed productive capital and working capital, free remainder of profits, fixed payments, and deductions from profits and other payments.

Looking more closely at the second breakdown by types of payments, we can add up the four amounts listed in Table 1.3 and verify that they add up to the total figure given for payments of state enterprises and economic organizations from profits. No discrepancy here; calculations reveal that the numbers add up to the required total figure—precisely. For both 1980 and 1985, the various categories of revenue under types of payments that constitute the overall figure for state enterprises and economic organizations from profits add up *exactly* to the right amount, again going one point beyond the decimal.

We might expect the same result in adding up the various categories of payments from profits as listed in the first breakdown, by branches of the economy. But when we do the arithmetic, we find that is not the case. Contributions from the six listed branches of the economy, added together, equal an amount significantly less than the amount shown for the total. That seems somewhat odd, given the taste for precision displayed in reconciling other statistics. One would at least think there would be an entry marked "other" to reflect implicit contributions from unnamed branches that bring the amount up to the total figure. If there were such an entry, it would constitute the third largest category in the breakdown of profits by branches of the economy for 1980 and the second largest for 1985.

When it comes to explaining where the payments from enterprises and economic organizations from profits are actually produced within the economy, then, the numbers come up short. But when it comes to explaining how the revenues are derived in terms of types of payments, the calculations come out perfectly. This leads us to look more carefully at the labels used in the breakdown by types of payments.

Soviet firms pay a fee for what is called fixed productive capital and working capital. The Soviet government assigns capital to state-run enterprises and economic organizations to fund current assets and pay for normal maintenance; this entry designates the fees paid by these firms for access to financing from the state. In addition to those fees, enterprises and organizations also remit to the Soviet government a substantial sum described in the breakdown as the free remainder of profits. It is not surprising that state-run firms would contribute profits to the internal budget, a practice in keeping with socialist doctrine; this is the largest category listed under the breakdown by types of payments for both 1980 and 1985. The next category, fixed payments, is an amount representing additional rents that must be remitted to the government in the case of "windfall" earnings. Finally, there is the somewhat mysterious category described as deductions from profits and other payments.

This last category would seem to be redundant. What kind of deductions from profits, over and above the amounts that have already been paid to the government, would provide an additional source of revenues to the budget? And what is meant by "other" payments? These payments are especially suspect because of the anomaly of using dual breakdowns to explain the total revenues from the payments of state enterprises and economic organizations from profits. Both breakdowns are ostensibly aimed at justifying the same total figure; yet the actual amounts produced by various branches of the economy are clearly inadequate to the task. Only by redefining the inputs according to types of payments is the appropriate number derived.

A skeptical accountant might wonder if the entry for deductions from profits and other payments contains an offsetting "plug" to bring the total up to the required amount. Could deductions from profits cover deductions against future profits that have yet to be realized? In other words, could they actually indicate advances *from* the budget, rather than contributions *to* the budget?

Laying our suspicions aside for the moment and moving on to the next principal revenue source listed on the Soviet financial statement under receipts from the socialist economy in Table 1.3, we again encounter a total figure broken down into component parts. Income tax from cooperative and public enterprises and organizations does not contribute much to revenues. Cooperatives and public enterprises are not state-run organizations *per se*; they operate on a so-called cost accounting basis, covering their own expenses with their own revenues and paying taxes to the Soviet government on the difference.

If we add the payments made by *kolkhozy* (agricultural collectives) to the payments made by the cooperative enterprises and organizations and enterprises of public organizations that perform various basic production and service functions, we obtain the exact total listed for this source of revenue for both 1980 and 1985, another demonstration of perfect accuracy in measuring revenues to the budget. It is not a very substantial total figure, to be sure, but accurate.

State social insurance revenue, the fourth source of revenues to the Soviet government in Table 1.3, makes a fairly large contribution to the budget, especially as compared to the previous entry. The inclusion of funds from the program, though, suggests a somewhat dubious accounting practice; these funds are shown as a revenue to the budget, but there is no corresponding entry on the expenditure side of the budget to show payments made in response to employee claims.[8]

The amounts indicated as coming from state social insurance revenue actually reflect withholdings from wages to establish pension-type funds to pay for employee vacations at tourist camps and mountain resorts as part of the benefits arranged through trade union organizations. In a sense, these withheld funds do function as a source of revenue to the government, because they can be tapped in the meantime. But to take idle funds into the budget as revenues makes it incumbent on the government to likewise record disbursement on the expenditure side. At any rate, the financial statement provides us only with a single total figure for state social insurance revenue, which we are asked to accept as given.

There is likewise nothing to calculate for forestry revenue, the last source cited under the heading of receipts from the socialist economy. The only questionable aspect of this entry is why it is listed. Its total contribution to the budget, as can be seen, is negligible. Yet it is given as one of the five main sources of revenue that make up total revenues from the socialist economy.

Having gained some familiarity with the various categories, it is appropriate to do one last perfunctory calculation to make sure that the five sources do add up to the total representing receipts from the socialist economy. For 1980, taking the actual numbers from Table 1.3, we add together the revenues from (1) turnover tax (94,108.7 million rubles), (2) payments of state enterprises and economic organizations from profits (89,819.1 million rubles), (3) income tax from cooperative and public enterprises and organizations (1,717.5 million rubles), (4) state social insurance revenue (13,957 million rubles), and (5) forestry revenue (477.7 million rubles), and find that the total from those sources comes to 200,080 million rubles.

But that cannot be right. The total figure for receipts from the socialist economy, as shown in the Soviet financial statement in Table 1.3, is a *different* number, a much higher number. According to Soviet accountants, the five sources in 1980 added up not to 200,080 million rubles but to 276,777.1 million rubles. Which leaves us with an unexplained gap of 76,697.1 million rubles.

Where did this amount—more than a quarter of the claimed total receipts from the socialist economy—come from? If we go through the same simple drill for 1985, again adding up the amounts given for each of the five categories of revenue listed under the heading of receipts from the socialist economy, we come up with an actual total of 245,942.6 million rubles, as against 358,259.8 million rubles claimed in the total figure, leaving an even bigger gap of 112,317.2 million rubles; for 1985, then, more than 30 percent of the total receipts from the socialist economy are left unexplained.

This is startling. Soviet financial statements appear to be properly straightforward, with Soviet accountants displaying tremendous diligence at totaling up numerous, relatively trivial amounts. Indeed, certain calculations suggest a near obsessive penchant for statistical detail. And yet they apparently feel no need whatever to acknowledge the inherent existence of additional revenues that amount to a huge contribution to total receipts from the socialist economy. It is inconceivable that Soviet accountants, who are so careful to include such inputs as forestry revenue, could overlook the massive discrepancy.

At the official Soviet exchange rate with the U.S. dollar, the amount of the unexplained revenues in 1980, some 77 billion rubles, is equal to about $125 billion. The unexplained revenues for 1985, 112 billion rubles, would translate into about $180 billion. Imagine the U.S. domestic budget with 30 percent of the revenues left unexplained; out of a total trillion or so, this would mean a gap of about $300 billion—roughly twice the amount of the entire U.S. budget deficit for 1987.

It is unlikely that the Soviet government considers the unexplained amounts a mere oversight. According to the expenditure side of the same published budget statement, the Soviet government spent 19 billion rubles on defense in 1985; the amount of unexplained revenues contributing to the total figure claimed for receipts from the socialist economy that year was nearly six times higher.

Here, perhaps, is a deliberate attempt to obscure the source of certain revenues to the internal budget, rather like the accounting treatment encountered earlier pertaining to payments of state enterprises and economic organizations from profits, in which the total figure was broken down in two ways. When you totaled up the revenues identified as coming from various branches of the economy, you got one figure; but when you added up the revenues described in terms of types of payments, including the ambiguous deductions from profit and other payments, you got another. This second, *larger* figure was the one that balanced with the total given.

The key to understanding the nature of the revenues to the Soviet internal budget from the socialist economy, then, does not require us to dig deeply into the various categories and subcategories to look for minor errors, but instead to step back from the individual sources and ask why a large unexplained gap exists between the sum of the revenues that can be specifically identified under receipts and the amount of revenues that are implicitly contained in the total figure claimed.

Why would the Soviet government refuse to identify what is clearly an important source of revenues to the budget, an amount that brings the total up to the required level? By required level, what is meant is the figure designating total receipts from the socialist economy, which, in combination with receipts from the population, results in an amount for total revenues to the Soviet internal budget that is just slightly higher than the amount representing total expenditures of the Soviet internal budget. In other words, an entry for total revenues that produces a budget surplus.

As we can see from Table 1.4, the existence of a gap is no isolated occurrence peculiar to the years 1980 and 1985. Indeed, Birman has identified such a gap in Soviet financial statistics going back to 1940 and continuing up to 1978.[9] During the most recent period, extending through the mid-1980s, the gap has become especially pronounced. Tracing the revenue statistics from 1970, adding up the individual sources from the socialist economy and comparing their actual total with the total amount claimed, we find that the unexplained gap in Soviet financial statements has generally been increasing annually in absolute terms. As a percentage of total receipts from the socialist economy, it has crept up from about 20 percent at the beginning of the 1970s to more than 30 percent in 1985.

What Is the Plug Figure?

One conclusion is clear: Soviet financial statements contain skillful discrepancies and omissions that disguise the true condition of the internal budget. When it comes to validating the most im-

TABLE 1.4. Gap in Claimed Budget Revenues from the Socialist Economy (in billions of rubles)

Year	Total Claimed From Socialist Economy	Identified Sources:[a]				Total Explained by Source	Gap	
		(1)	(2)	(3)	(4)	(5)		Amount	%
	1	2					3	4	5
1970	142.9	49.4	54.2	1.2	8.2	.5	113.5	29.4	20.6
1971	151.3	54.5	55.6	1.4	8.7	.5	120.7	30.6	20.2
1972	159.3	55.6	60.0	1.3	9.1	.5	126.5	32.8	20.6
1973	170.9	59.1	60.0	1.5	9.7	.5	130.8	40.1	23.5
1974	183.0	63.5	64.4	1.5	10.4	.5	140.3	42.7	23.3
1975	199.1	66.6	69.7	1.5	11.1	.5	149.4	49.7	25.0
1976	211.3	70.7	70.6	1.5	12.0	.5	155.3	56.0	26.5
1977	225.7	74.6	78.4	1.6	12.2	.5	167.3	58.4	25.9
1978	242.3	84.1	78.6	1.6	12.9	.5	177.7	64.6	26.7
1979	256.8	88.3	84.2	1.6	13.7	.5	188.3	68.5	26.7
1980	276.8	94.1	89.8	1.7	14.0	.5	200.1	76.7	27.7
1981	293.8	100.4	92.4	1.9	15.0	.5	210.2	83.6	28.4
1982	324.5	100.6	102.4	1.9	22.3	.8	228.0	96.5	29.7
1983	328.4	102.9	106.6	2.2	23.1	.8	235.6	92.8	28.3

1984	346.0	102.7	115.6	2.6	24.5	.8	246.2	99.8	28.8
1985	358.3	97.7	119.5	2.5	25.4	.8	245.9	112.4	31.4

[a]Identified sources:
(1) Turnover tax
(2) Payments of state enterprises and economic organizations from profits
(3) Income tax from cooperative and public enterprises and organizations
(4) State social insurance revenue
(5) Forestry revenue

SOURCES: Columns 1 and 2:
1970–75, *Gosudarstvennyy Byudzhet SSSR i Byudzhety Soyuznykh Respublik 1971–1975 gg.:Statisticheskiy Sbornik*, pp. 8–9.
1976–80, *Gosudarstvennyy Byudzhet SSSR i Byudzhety Soyuznykh Respublik 1976–1980 gg.:Statisticheskiy Sbornik*, pp. 10–11.
1981–85, *Gosudarstvennyy Byudzhet SSSR 1981–1985:Statisticheskiy Sbornik*, pp. 4–5.

Column 3: Sum of identified sources (1) through (5)
Column 4: Column 1 less Column 3
Column 5: Column 4 divided by Column 1 expressed as a percentage

portant source of revenue to the Soviet government, receipts from the socialist economy, the numbers do not add up. Yet in calculating total revenues for the Soviet internal budget, that is, receipts from the socialist economy and receipts from the population, the numbers add up perfectly. It is thus apparent that the published figures do indeed contain some kind of plug to bring the component revenues up to the required level. The plug amount is never identified, never acknowledged with an entry for "other," lest it bring to full light the immensity of the gap. We can only assume that the U.S.S.R. Central Statistical Administration, cooperating with the highest levels of the Soviet government, does not want to identify what the phantom source of revenue to the internal budget might be.

Our next task, therefore, is to determine what the plug *does* represent and whether it is a surrogate for legitimate revenues produced within the Soviet economy. As for the latter question, is it possible that there are specific revenue-producing entities in the Soviet economy whose contributions are not captured under the entries for turnover tax, payments from profits, or the other sources of funds listed in the breakdown on total revenues?

That seems doubtful. Why would there be additional revenues from additional internal sources that are not cited in the budget statement? By what rationale would they be omitted? Surely not because they would be trivial. If forestry revenue is not too trivial to include, it is clearly appropriate to list other genuine sources of revenue. It does not make sense, either, that the Soviet government would deliberately understate its revenues from the socialist economy or from the population. Since a figure for total revenues is claimed at the top of the financial statement, there is no reason to hide components in the breakdown. If some wellspring of legitimate revenues exists in the Soviet domestic economy, why not identify it explicitly?

Once again, we can glean some insight by looking at the big picture, rather than focusing on less pertinent tangents. If we think about the overall structure of the budget statement—the relationship between revenues and expenditures—we can begin to understand why the Soviet government finds it must supply a plug figure. Given the Soviet preoccupation with a balanced budget, we can readily comprehend what the plug amount represents.

For the most part, the expenditures of the Soviet government are a given. Throughout their history, the Soviets have demon-

strated that they are unwilling to cut defense spending even in
the face of severe budget constraints. Traditionally, consumption
has been the sector sacrificed to support higher-priority spending decisions, which has resulted in a Soviet standard of living
that barely meets the subsistence level among industrialized
countries. In the last decade, expenditures for fixed capital investment have likewise been cut to the bone, which has meant
that technological innovation in the Soviet manufacturing sector
has been seriously hampered.

The expenditure side of the internal budget can thus hardly be
adjusted downward. Clearly, to obtain a budget surplus, domestic revenues must come in high enough to cover the stated expenditures and more. Yet there is only so much in real revenues
from legitimate sources. To bring the total revenue figure up to
a level that would constitute a budget surplus *on paper*, the Soviet
government is forced to resort to pumping additional funds into
the budget. It does so in the classic manner: *by creating credit*.
That is, to preserve the budget surplus illusion, the Soviet government issues credits to supplement the level of receipts from the
Soviet economy. Those credits, disguised as revenues, are carried in the financial statement as if they represented genuine
contributions to the budget. What they are, instead, is a surrepti-
tious form of internal financing to mask the reality of inadequate
revenues.

When a government provides credit in excess of the amounts
supported by revenues, it creates money by simply printing it,
and there is no real value behind the claims asserted. So, obviously, extending credits to bring the receipts of firms up to some
required level does not in itself provide any genuine revenues
to the government. In the Soviet Union, the financing of firms
requires an outlay from the government and should be included
on the expenditure side of the budget. And that should be entirely supported by the legitimate revenues arising from the profitability of enterprises.

That is not just the narrow view of a capitalist. Soviet financial
authorities themselves maintain that the fundamental relationship between budget revenues and budget expenditures should
not be compromised:

Of the greatest importance for ensuring the stability of the
monetary system is the strict and consistent application in practice
of the principle of the *deficitlessness of the budget,* that is, the

prohibition of resorting directly or indirectly to the use of an
emission resource to cover any expenditures of the state budget
(including expenditures on financing the national economy).

This prohibition is connected with the fact that when using
emission to cover expenditures of the state budget that are not
balanced by revenues, the increase in the amount of money in
circulation can exceed the actual requirements of trade turnover
for means of circulation. In turn this will violate the economic law
of money circulation, will overfill the channels of circulation with
currency notes, and, as a result, will have an adverse effect on the
stability of money. In order not to permit a decrease in the
purchasing power of money, it will be necessary to withdraw from
circulation the excess currency notes, to implement a number of
measures for mobilizing monetary assets by some financial
methods, or to cut back some expenditures of the state budget.[10]

Accordingly, it is clear that the principles underlying monetary
stability are as applicable to managing the domestic budget of the
Soviet Union as they are for any other country. The use of an
"emission resource"—credit from the government to cover budget expenditures that are not otherwise supported by budget revenues—is a violation of the Soviet notion of a balanced budget.

So it would now seem clear that the gap is credit created by
the Soviet government to underwrite the level of expenditures in
the budget. And because that credit is embedded in the various
revenues from the socialist economy, it is not obvious where it
is concealed among the five sources listed, only that it is being
included as revenue when the total figure is calculated.

By process of elimination, though, we can assume that credit
extensions from the state are not part of the trifling forestry revenue. Also, we have discovered that revenue derived from state
social insurance is suspect in itself, so it is unlikely that additional credits are present in this entry, which is subject to the
scrutiny of trade unions. Of the three sources left, we can probably also disregard income tax from cooperative and public enterprises and organizations. Not only are the amounts involved
insubstantial, but those organizations are much less tied in to the
government than the state-run enterprises; accordingly, they do
not have access to the same kind of financing.

We are left with the state enterprises and economic organizations themselves; specifically, what they contribute in turnover
tax and what they contribute from profits. The amount of the

first is taken as a given, and calculations by the Foreign Demographic Analysis Division of the U.S. Department of Commerce suggest that the turnover tax figures in the budget are probably accurate.[11]

Therefore it appears that the supplemental revenues captured in the total figure relate directly to the operations of state enterprises and economic organizations, in short, to their profitability. Recall our earlier suspicions about revenues from so-called profits: The entry for "deductions from profit and other payments" seemed to contain a plug amount to bring the total up to the required level for the payments from state enterprises and economic organizations from profits. It now seems this same accounting technique is being employed, without labels this time, to bring the contributions from the listed sources of revenue up to the required total for receipts from the socialist economy. Credits from the state, it appears, are implicitly being construed as deductions from profit and used to balance the totals on the justification perhaps that they represent an offset against the future revenues expected to be generated by the recipient firms.

Thus, Soviet financial authorities are effectively claiming preemptive revenues in the budget statement. Whether or not they are convinced that the enterprises and organizations getting the credits are only experiencing temporary difficulties—that the credits will actually be covered by future contributions to the budget—is difficult to know. But their reluctance to identify the amounts explicitly as credits suggests a certain discomfort with the assumptions underlying the use of the plug.

At this point, the real story of the Soviet budget begins to come together. Declining economic productivity during the last decade *has* affected the level of revenues produced by Soviet state enterprises and organizations. And there has been a decided downturn in their profitability, their ability to generate a positive return on the capital assigned to them by the government. But rather than admit that Soviet firms are providing lower and lower revenues to the budget, the Soviet government simply makes up the difference, without acknowledging that the plug represents not additional unidentified revenues, but the advancement of credits. When Soviet firms fail to meet their financial obligations to the state, they are not forced into bankruptcy; instead, they are allowed to borrow the funds out of which to remit the requisite payments from profits back to the budget.

All of which shows that the supposed finesse exhibited by Soviet central planners is more a matter of making the numbers come out right in the budget statement than a demonstration of legitimately matching revenues to expenditures. Or as Birman concludes, consistent "budget profits" are the result of financial-statistical trickery.[12] In reality, Soviet expenditures are higher than budget revenues—that is, *real* revenues from the Soviet economy are not nearly sufficient to meet the current level of expenditures by the Soviet government. This means, of course, that the Soviets have not been producing balanced budgets after all. The notion of a consistent surplus in the Soviet internal budget is a fraud. The Kremlin is running a massive budget deficit.

Socialist ideology itself can provide no defense against the kind of budget crisis Soviet authorities are now forced to confront. The economic constraint that governs the management of domestic budgets is universally applicable: If expenditures cannot be supported by revenues, the difference must be financed. Soviet authorities have opted to finance their deficit internally by issuing credits, effectively borrowing against the future productivity of their own economy. In other words, the Soviet government is making loans to itself.

The inherent risk of running a deficit is that tomorrow's productivity gains may not be sufficient to compensate for today's spending excesses. So the Soviets are betting on an outcome that may never be realized, gambling against the prospect of a crash. At some point, the deficit itself becomes part of the problem; the monetary distortions it causes and the resulting imbalances between production and consumption choke off the needed productivity gains. The magnitude of the Soviet internal deficit, coupled with our observations of current Soviet economic problems, suggests that this point has already been reached.

The conclusion, then, is that the Soviet system is not self-supporting. The budget surplus that appears to provide the necessary funds for carrying out the future objectives of the Kremlin (increased defense spending, additional fixed capital investment, a higher standard of living) is merely an accounting fiction. Indeed, the revenues from the economy cannot even fund current needs.

Obscuring Reality

There's a certain irony here. The official Soviet financial statement is a sterling testimony to budget management; in fact, the economy is experiencing severe difficulties. If the budget statement accurately portrayed the relationship between expenditures and revenue, it might have been clear to Soviet authorities long ago that budget problems stemmed from the falling and inadequate profit contributions from state enterprises and organizations. The early focus could then have been on improving the return on the capital allotted to the firms, and restrictions could have been imposed against issuing unwarranted credits to enterprises that did not perform.

The whole idea, after all, of collecting statistics and organizing them into a financial statement is to create a management tool, a way to diagnose potential problems by spotting negative trends. In other words, instead of being suddenly confronted with a budget squeeze of crisis proportions and then forced to make wrenching economic choices under great pressure, financial analysis is supposed to highlight potential problems before they threaten the viability of the entire system.

But Soviet accounting practices serve to camouflage problems. If an outside analyst were to accept the published Soviet documents at face value, he would have to conclude that all is well in the domestic budget. That is the message of the Soviet financial statements, which is not consistent, of course, with what we know is going on in the Soviet economy. But without pinning down the source of illegitimate revenues to the budget, the analyst would have no way of reconciling obvious empirical fact with purported financial fact. They cannot be reconciled. Unmasking the Soviet deficit gives numerical validity to our suspicions.

Had we assumed that short of infiltrating the U.S.S.R. Central Statistical Administration it was impossible to get a fix on the Soviet internal budget, there would have been no point to our exercise. But we have learned that individual statistics are not tainted per se. It is the format in which they are presented that is deceptive. The financial documents are nothing if not consistent through the years, and therefore lend themselves to analysis, even if it means monitoring imputed amounts and looking for what is conspicuously omitted. Western observers are all too aware of the damaging effects of unbalanced budgets and primed to recognize the existence of a deficit in the Soviet domestic budget.

The question is: Are Soviet authorities themselves aware of the real status of the internal state budget? Would they knowingly convey the impression that the budget was healthy, even as they were in fact struggling to compensate for inadequate revenues by incurring a monumental budget deficit? There have been signs of growing friction between the Central Statistical Administration and Gorbachev. Some Western experts speculate that high-level bureaucrats in charge of official statistics may have conspired with conservative senior party members to cast a rosy glow on the Soviet economy. The objective would be to undercut Gorbachev's policies for radical reform in favor of preserving the *status quo*.[13]

Why would some party members want to conceal the budget realities? At stake is the wisdom of central planning and, more broadly, socialism as the only legitimate and effective road to economic health and prosperity. Assume, though, that Gorbachev is not only aware of the problem but willing to acknowledge the budget deficit publicly. In other words, he is prepared to tell his fellow Soviet citizens that their country has a huge deficit, the relative size of which would eclipse the U.S. budget shortfall. That would be shocking and blasphemous, for the U.S. deficit is regarded as the ultimate manifestation of capitalist mismanagement. So we can well imagine what more prudent members of the Politburo might counsel: Sensitive financial information must be withheld to preserve the sanctity of socialist doctrine and to maintain public belief in the competence of the Kremlin. Glasnost has not yet come to the U.S.S.R. Central Statistical Adminstration and the Ministry of Finances.

And yet the problem of the deficit is a reality. And to the extent that misleading financial statements bury the mistakes of central planning authorities, the problem will tend to grow worse. Before Gorbachev, it was possible to hide the reality and support the practices behind economic deterioration. Even if Gorbachev fully understands the grave problems that now grip the Soviet economy, others in the Soviet power structure would rather continue to delude the public, if not themselves, about the condition of the budget. Those officials will offer strong resistance to any proposal for restructuring the financial statements. They are unwilling to accept straightforward accounting if it means compromising the purported achievements of socialism or if it raises questions of personal competence.

At least one Soviet financial specialist has tried to redesign the financial statement to get at what is really going on. The editor-in-chief of the journal *Finansy SSSR* (Finances of the U.S.S.R.) made the following proposal:

. . . the set of budget revenues should be limited to four sections: Section I—Payments of State Enterprises and Organizations. Section II—Payments of State and Public Organizations. Section III—Payments of the Population. Section IV—State Credit.[14]

This is precisely the kind of reform needed to reveal the extent of deficit financing being carried out through the issuance of government-granted credits. The reform would create a clear distinction between credit and legitimate sources of revenue in the Soviet economy.

The editor's proposal was offered in 1976, just when productivity in the Soviet Union was beginning to sag. At the time, more state credit was injected into the economy to compensate for what was no doubt perceived as a temporary dip in revenues. But unlike the boom-or-bust cycles experienced by countries with market economies, the Soviet Union has yet to pull out of its long-standing decline. Hence, excessive issuance of state credit has become a permanent feature of a chronic economic situation. If Soviet authorities are waiting for a stellar year to reform the budget statement, they may still have a long wait. At current levels of Soviet economic performance, the reliance on state credit to balance the budget will continue.

In the meantime, we have to wonder, are the Soviets maintaining two sets of books? Is there a small coterie of Soviet officials, led by Gorbachev, who are privy to the details of the internal budget mess and who are guided by real, not manufactured, calculations of internal revenues? If the purpose of dual bookkeeping is to ward off any lapse of faith among ordinary Soviet citizens, we need not feel threatened but can only wonder at the gullibility of the population.

If instead the purpose is to deceive potential lenders in the West, we must question our own gullibility. Gorbachev does not strike most Western observers as the kind of person who would gladly suffer statistical tomfoolery, unless it suited his purposes. For their own protection, outside lenders should understand that the Soviet Union, far from being a paragon of financial virtue among sovereign borrowers, more closely resembles its fellow borrowers in the Third World, who are likewise having trouble reconciling revenues and expenditures. Soviet borrowing is particularly ominous because the government refuses to officially acknowledge the seriousness of the Soviet internal budget crisis and does not publish the *real* numbers. Potential lenders should insist on seeing both sets of books.

2

Economic Fallout

Now that we have determined that the Soviet domestic budget is carrying a massive deficit, we need to analyze the ways in which the condition is manifested in the Soviet economy. It is possible, once again, to make comparisons with the United States here, but only to a certain point. The economic fallout from running a deficit in the Soviet Union bears the unique stamp of socialist control. In the United States, it is fairly widely accepted that a budget deficit ultimately leads to inflation. The same holds true for the Soviet Union. It is also conceded, in the United States, that inflation means higher prices; indeed, the terms are practically used synonymously. But the actual definition of inflation is something a little different. What inflation really means, whether it occurs in the United States or the Soviet Union, is an increase in the volume of money and credit relative to available goods.

In a free market system, where prices adjust to reflect changes in the money supply, inflationary pressures are indeed manifested in the form of higher prices. More money means more dollars on the demand side of the equation, and suppliers respond by raising their prices accordingly. In the Soviet Union, though, where prices are set by the government and a vast number of basic foodstuffs and necessities carry artificially low prices as a matter of national policy, the inflationary pressures of a budget deficit are manifested in forms that are anathema to free market systems.

Before looking at how various symptoms of inflation are currently devastating the Soviet economy, we should be aware of the differences in the fundamental borrowing strategies of the U.S. government and the Soviet government. The United States, as a major participant in international financial markets, can borrow from external sources; foreign investors are willing to use their savings to finance the U.S. budget deficit. If that were not the case, and the United States were forced to finance the deficit internally, the effect of issuing excess amounts of government credit into the system would have a much more immediate and pronounced impact on the domestic money supply, and the inflationary pressures would therefore be more strongly felt.

The Soviet Union, meanwhile, is not a participant in the international credit markets. Because the ruble is not freely convertible into other currencies, Western investors cannot use it for anything other than to buy goods from the Soviet Union. While the Soviets can take out loans denominated in hard currency, they cannot apply the funds directly to ease the financial burden of an internal budget deficit. They can use hard currency only to make hard currency purchases. Indirectly, imports of Western goods may help to alleviate Soviet economic problems to the extent that they improve domestic productivity. But the inflationary effects of a Soviet deficit cannot be exported beyond Soviet borders. The Soviet monetary system is a closed one, and thus it must bear the full brunt of the financial distortion and turmoil caused by the creation of excess internal credit.

Gosbank: Caught in the Middle

The mechanism by which government-granted credits are released into the Soviet money supply is part of Lenin's legacy and his vision for transforming Russia's commercial banking system into a centralized accounting system under Soviet rule. Lenin felt that by making industry dependent on a central state-controlled source for initial capital and ongoing credits, it would be easier to direct the economic growth of the nation and allocate resources.

In the years just before World War I, Lenin was vehemently critical of the global banks that were operating throughout the world; he accused them of exploiting mankind by controlling the distribution of financial capital. Yet he also seemed to harbor a begrudging admiration for them. While he resented their use of monopolistic power in pursuit of capitalist aims, he saw that it could be employed very effectively to carry out his own ideas. Just prior to the October Revolution, he wrote:

> *Without big banks, socialism would be impossible.* The big banks *are* the "state apparatus" which we *need* to bring about socialism, and which we *take ready-made* from capitalism. . . . A single State Bank, the biggest of the big, with branches in every rural district, in every factory, will constitute as much as nine-tenths of the socialist apparatus. There will be country-wide bookkeeping, country-wide accounting of the production and distribution of goods; this will be, so to speak, something in the nature of the *skeleton* of socialist society.[1]

This vision became reality with the establishment of the Gosu-darstvennyy Bank, commonly called Gosbank, which literally means State Bank in Russian. Gosbank maintains supervisory authority over credit operations in the Soviet Union and is the sole issuer of cash. Under Gosbank are two other main banking agencies that fulfill specialized credit functions. One is Stroi-bank, charged with making domestic loans for capital investment, and the other is the Soviet Bank for Foreign Economic Affairs, which is the financial liaison with foreigners and carries out trade and other business activities involving hard currencies.

All the internal banking operations that take place in the Soviet Union fall under the purview of Gosbank; through it (and to a lesser degree through Stroibank) all state credit is issued into the Soviet economy. Gosbank maintains deposit accounts for enterprises and organizations operating in the socialist economy and, as part of its articles of foundation, Gosbank is accorded supervisory power over the financial and economic activities of Soviet firms. It is charged with overseeing their operations, ensuring that they are utilizing materials and labor according to plan and drawing down working capital as needed. Because Gosbank is empowered with such sweeping authority, it is essentially held responsible for the performance of the enterprises and organizations whose financial operations it governs, and herein lies a fundamental conflict of interest.

When state-run enterprises and organizations do not produce results that satisfy the expectations of central planners and create the necessary revenues for the internal budget, the onus falls on Gosbank officials to rectify the problem. For the state, the important thing is that the enterprises make their requisite contributions to the budget. Gosbank officials have the power to enable Soviet firms to do just that by advancing funds to them, raising the level of the deposit accounts maintained on behalf of the enterprise. That is altogether too great a temptation, because a firm's failure to make its payments to the government may lead to recriminations against Gosbank officials. In the sense, too, that Gosbank functions as the accounting and control apparatus for the Soviet government—the "skeleton" of socialist society—it sees itself as having an inherent obligation to ensure that the requirements of the budget are technically fulfilled.

Advances granted to Soviet firms by Gosbank represent a non-cash emission of credit. That is, Gosbank simply makes a bookkeeping entry to increase the amount of funds available to the firm as shown in its deposit account. Enterprises requiring credits over and above the amounts initially allotted to them can apply to Gosbank for the additional funds through a variety of programs. Although there have been attempts to maintain strict guidelines to limit the purposes for which supplemental credits can be issued, most of the stipulations have been subsequently broadened. Gosbank officials are generally prepared to accommodate a wide variety of rationales; firms have received loan advances under such labels as "interim" or "transitional" or "special" or "extraordinary" credits.[2]

Those various classifications do not disguise the fact that the recipient enterprises have failed to perform in accordance with the capital budgeting requirements imposed on them at the outset. Rather, it is an admission that they are operating unprofitably. Yet Gosbank officials have little choice but to grant requests for additional funding. To do otherwise would be to admit their own failure to supervise the operations of the firm properly. Some enterprises are required to supply revenues to the government based on accounting periods running as short as five days; if sufficient receipts are not on deposit in the account at the time of reconciliation, they must be advanced out of the firms' working capital. The depleted working capital must then, in turn, be replenished by banking authorities.

Not that Gosbank does not take some pains to ensure that enterprise managers prudently manage the financial resources made available to them. Gosbank officials do their best to make sure that funds are not dispensed for purposes inappropriate to the fulfillment of the production quotas imposed by central planning authorities. For example, enterprise managers are not allowed to use funds earmarked for buying materials to increase workers' wages. In fact, the wage payment system, which deals with cash, is kept strictly separate from the noncash accounting system, which permits enterprises to purchase materials from one another by making deposit level adjustments through Gosbank.

But whether enterprise managers ask for additional credits to cover obligatory payments to the Soviet government or because they need more money to buy extra materials or inventory, Gosbank can impose no real penalties against managers to discourage such requests. A Gosbank supervisor may threaten to restrict a firm's future access to credit, but what does he do when that firm becomes incapable of paying its turnover tax or fails to make some minimal contribution to the state budget out of its presumed profits? Gosbank officials cannot go over the heads of central planning authorities and force state-run firms into bankruptcy. So when sufficient pressure builds, Gosbank bureaucrats tend to give in, admonishing the enterprise chief to manage his operation more carefully in the future.

By bailing out unprofitable enterprises with more or less automatic credits, Gosbank is effectively sanctioning the perpetuation of inefficient production in the Soviet economy. It is one thing to supply financing to productive or potentially productive investment opportunities. It is quite another to furnish credits that raise the cost of production with no effect on output. In the latter case, Gosbank is merely subsidizing unprofitable enterprises; in the process, unwarranted credits are put into the system. The credit advances are thus more accurately described as grants, not loans, because they are seldom actually paid back out of revenues generated by more production or improved profitability.

What we are talking about are basically short-term credits to supplement the working capital of firms, to permit them to meet financial obligations to the government or to other enterprises. The interest rate Gosbank charges is quite low, normally about 6 percent. By socialist doctrine, that is not considered an interest rate but rather a fee paid for the use of capital (interest is viewed as a form of parasitic income extracted by capitalists). Firms are charged higher rates on loans past due, but their very delinquency belies their financial status; presumably they borrow additional amounts to pay off the higher interest rate. Here we should note that in most cases Gosbank officials do not vary the rate according to the perceived creditworthiness of the borrower or the potential economic return associated with the credit. The applicable rate is based on the formal characteristics of the loan, the particular industrial branch involved, or in some cases, the social target being pursued, none of which depends on the judgment of bank officials.[3]

To appreciate the extent to which credit now permeates the Soviet economy, Table 2.1 indicates the year-to-year increases in the level of outstanding short-term loans issued by Gosbank and Stroibank since 1970. As you can see, the amount of short-term credits in the Soviet economy increased from 104.7 billion rubles in 1970 to 426.4 billion rubles in 1985, more than a four-fold increase. During this same period, total Soviet budget revenues only increased two-and-a-half times. Thus short-term loans have become a much more prominent feature of the Soviet economy in terms of Soviet published statistics.

What is significant also is that a considerable portion of these short-term loans has been granted through Stroibank. Stroibank is the abbreviated Russian name for the All-Union Bank for the Financing of Capital Investment; a bank of that sort should not be issuing short-term credits. The traditional banking function initially assigned to Stroibank has clearly been stretched to meet the increasingly urgent need for supplemental short-term funds. The sudden major retraction shown for 1986 suggests an abrupt attempt to reverse the unhealthy practice, at least on paper.

Again, Western estimates indicate that the Soviet Union has experienced general economic stagnation since about 1975. The concurrence of two trends, then, declining productivity and rising levels of short-term credits, points to the conclusion that money is not being advanced to finance profitable investment opportunities or normal working capital needs. Instead, it reflects increasing subsidies for nonproductive enterprises. Gosbank is caught in the middle: In its dual role as operational supervisor of the state-run enterprises and comptroller of the budget, it must succumb to the pressure to paper over revenue shortfalls with more short-term loans and, in so doing, to flood the Soviet economy with excess credit.

TABLE 2.1. Short-Term Soviet Internal Credits (in billions of rubles)

	Granted by:			Increase Over Prior Year	
	Gosbank	Stroibank	Total	Amount	%
Year	1	2	3	4	5
1970	96.7	8.0	104.7	—	—
1971*	—	—	111.6'	6.9	6.2
1972*	—	—	120.9	9.3	7.7
1973*	—	—	134.7	13.8	10.2
1974*	—	—	149.3	14.6	9.8
1975	147.8	12.7	160.5	11.2	7.0
1976	161.5	15.9	177.4	16.9	9.5
1977	174.7	19.0	193.7	16.3	8.4
1978	182.4	23.7	206.1	12.4	6.0
1979	198.2	26.8	225.0	18.9	8.4
1980	222.0	39.4	261.4	36.4	13.9
1981	256.5	70.8	327.3	65.9	20.1
1982	280.4	74.5	354.9	27.6	7.8
1983	298.9	78.5	377.4	22.5	6.0
1984	316.5	86.3	402.8	25.4	6.3
1985	335.7	90.7	426.4	23.6	5.5
1986	325.7	30.9	356.6	−69.8	−19.6

*Total figure not broken down in Narodnoye Khozyaistvo for years shown
SOURCES: Columns 1 and 2:
   1970, 1980, 1985, 1986—Narodnoye Khozyaistvo SSSR za 70 let: Yubileinyy
   Slalislicheskiy Yezhegodnik, p. 634.
   1975, 1976, 1977, 1978, 1979—Narodnoye Khozyaistvo v 1980 g.:Statisticheskiy
   Yezhegodnik, p. 527.
   1981, 1982, 1983, 1984—Narodnoye Khozyaistvo v 1984 g.:Statisticheskiy
   Yezhegodnik, p. 579.
Column 3:
   1971, 1972, 1973, 1974—Narodnoye Khozyaistvo v 1975 g.:Statisticheskiy
   Yezhegodnik, p. 746.
For all other years—Column 1 plus Column 2
Column 4: Increase in Column 3 over previous year
Column 5: Column 4 divided by Column 3

Too Many Rubles

The Soviet government, in recent years, has not been oblivious
to declining productivity and reduced revenues. One of its responses has been to try to increase the productivity of labor. That
in itself is reasonable. But the Soviet government has gone about
it in a way that exacerbates the inflationary pressures in the
system.

   To provide workers with the motivation to be more productive, to work harder or longer, Soviet officials have sanctioned the use of monetary inducements. Increased wages and extra bonuses have been awarded by firm managers to try to get workers to increase output. But the very enterprises that have been the least productive—operating consistently at a loss, and forced regularly to appeal to Gosbank for credits—have been the ones most likely to turn to the stopgap solution of raising wages and offering bonuses in a desperate effort to get workers to produce more goods and more revenues. It is those same firms, too, that Gosbank has been the most eager to accommodate.

Increased wages are the primary means by which excess credits are turned into increased purchasing power in the consumption sector of the Soviet economy. When workers receive their wages, what were formerly bookkeeping entries to the deposit accounts of Soviet enterprises are transformed into currency. Changes in the deposit levels of enterprises reflecting advances from Gosbank are cashless transactions; the credits turn into rubles when they are paid out to workers as compensation for their labor. We should remember that except for the payment of wages and spending for consumption, cash is not used in the Soviet economy. When workers draw their salaries (the majority are paid twice monthly), Gosbank reduces the deposit account of the employing enterprise accordingly. Thus, the amount of currency in circulation is the direct result of the monetary wages and bonuses disbursed to workers and the rate of money turnover in the consumption sector.

Clearly, when increased wages induce workers to produce more, they are justified in the same way any other production expense might be. The total cost of production goes up, but if output likewise increases, no inflationary effect ensues. Indeed, if a marginal increase in compensation results in overall higher revenues to the firm, a real productivity gain is realized. The problems occur, of course, when wage increases are not matched by an increase in output. The wage increases then become strictly inflationary, because they translate into increased purchasing power without more goods available for purchase.

In the Soviet Union, excess purchasing power in the hands of the population is a quite literal concept. Since wages are paid in cash and consumer transactions are conducted on a cash basis, even those involving large consumer durables, monetary stability is maintained only when there is a consistent relationship between the amount of cash in circulation and the amount of con-

sumer goods available for purchase. Wage increases thus constitute a direct infusion of additional currency into the system,
which, if not absorbed by the introduction of additional goods,
are left as unmet claims against the Soviet economy.

If the inflationary pressures inherent in an increased money
supply were acknowledged by Soviet authorities, it would be
clear that the accumulation of unmet claims was largely a monetary phenomena, the result of nominal wage increases un-
matched by increased supplies of goods. But the Soviet government steadfastly refuses to admit that the wage increases granted
during the last decade have not brought about the anticipated
productivity gains. This excerpt from an editorial published in
Soviet Life encapsulates the problem, no doubt unwittingly:

> The price index will help us see things in their true light. Over the
> past 20 years the Soviet price index has risen by 10 points, much
> less than in any market economy. At the same time average wages
> have increased by 100 percent, and the free social services and
> allowances citizens are entitled to by 200 percent. This means that
> our real per capita income has doubled, compared with 20 years
> ago, largely thanks to the over all stability of prices.[4]

This assessment suggests that it is somehow possible to double
workers' wages and to triple the level of social services provided
cost-free by the government without materially affecting the relationship between the value of wages received and the available
pool of consumer goods and services. The magazine's writer implicitly assumes that the marginal value of labor has increased at
a herculean rate, that the manufacturing sector has succeeded in
producing sufficient goods and revenues not only to absorb the
increased purchasing power allotted to workers but also to underwrite the increase in free social services.

The hitch in the Soviet approach is the claim that "real per
capita income has doubled" because the government has imposed fixed prices. Herein lies the fundamental difference in the
way inflation is manifested in the Soviet Union as compared
with free market economies: An increase in the volume of money
and credit relative to available goods results in *shortages*, rather
than higher prices, because prices are fixed. If prices were flexible in the Soviet Union, they would increase in proportion to the
nominal wage increases paid to workers. In terms of real per
capita income, there would be no effects on consumption levels.
That is, assuming production output remained relatively stable,

a doubling in the amount of wages paid to workers could be accommodated by a doubling in the aggregate price of all consumer goods, and there would be no unmet claims in the consumption sector and no change in the standard of living.

Conceivably, if the real per capita earnings of a Soviet worker have doubled, he should be able to buy twice as many goods as before. But because the increased wages reflect nominal, not real, gains, what has actually happened is that there is now twice as much money in circulation relative to the same amount of goods. The implicit price of goods *has* doubled. But since prices are not allowed to rise, there is simply twice as much demand as before for the same items. At the fixed prices before the Soviet money supply was expanded, certain consumer goods were beyond the financial means of average Soviet workers. But with higher earnings, the same luxury goods now appear to be a bargain, if only they could be found and purchased.

This is the frustrating dilemma that now confronts Soviet citizens. Having accepted the premise that higher wages would translate into a better life, enriched with more consumer goods, they now find that pervasive shortages mean that few can take possession of the promised goods. Consumer demand swamps the available supply of goods at their old fixed prices; when products are suddenly made available in retail outlets, they sell out immediately. The ability to purchase a desired item thus has little to do with being able to afford it. In general, Soviet citizens do not complain about not having enough money. The problem is not having anything to spend it on.

In a sense, the situation in the consumption sector is worse than if production had remained stagnant and wages had been left unchanged. There would have been no increase in the Soviet standard of living, but neither would expectations have been unduly raised and confronted with inevitable disappointment. As it stands, the sense of deprivation among newly enriched Soviet workers comes from the feeling that they deserve the goods they can now afford to buy. If, as the government tells them, inflation is not a factor in the Soviet economy, they are left to wonder how it is that all the long-desired goods seem to have disappeared from the shelves. The shortages, reflecting the suppressed inflation, seem even greater somehow than the actual shortages caused by declining productivity and reduced output.

Shortages are the cause of the waiting lines, the endless queuing that has come to typify the plight of the Soviet consumer. At first, it was mostly the luxury items that were in short supply—cars and video cassette recorders. To buy them, Soviet citizens accepted the idea that they must wait years. But the shortages have now spread to more basic items. Just being able to buy a good pair of children's shoes does not strike most Soviet workers as an unreasonable luxury. Yet it is becoming increasingly difficult and time-consuming to procure such necessities as shoes, clothing, or household goods.

Even the availability of foodstuffs, the sacred cow of socialism, is now subject to pervasive shortages and exhausting waiting lines. Fresh vegetables, except for the ever present cabbage and onions, are a rarity. Fresh fruit is considered such a luxury that it is regularly diverted to Intourist hotels to impress foreigners. Vodka, once readily available to Soviet citizens, is now sold only in limited quantities as part of the crackdown against alcoholism. The lines for vodka start forming hours before it can be legally sold. Sugar, which also used to be in plentiful supply, is now hard to come by because it is being purchased in massive quantities to distill homemade liquor.

Bread remains the symbol of the compassion of socialism. It is available in great quantities and is so cheap that farmers feed it to their livestock, and, according to Gorbachev, children use it as a ball to play with.[5] The price of bread reflects the Soviet government's commitment to subsidizing the necessities of life to make them available to all citizens, regardless of means. That same commitment to the welfare of less fortunate members of Soviet society once also extended to meat, fish, dairy, and confectionary products, but the level of the subsidy has now made the policy prohibitively expensive for the Soviet government. The demand for them is virtually unlimited, given the distortion between Soviet wages and the cost of production. So, rather than make up the price difference, the Soviet government has chosen quietly to withdraw a wide variety of foodstuffs from store outlets.

The act of purchasing goods in the Soviet Union has become a ritual of waiting in line or perhaps suddenly happening onto a situation where new supplies have just come in; it has little to do with making a personal budgeting decision in advance to go out and purchase a specific item. As one former Moscow resident describes it:

> Soviet citizens never "buy" anything in lines, for example; they "scrounge" things, or "rip them off." Similarly, a Soviet person

joining a queue never asks what is being "sold," but "What are they giving out?" or "What are they throwing out?"[6]

Since so many people can afford to buy and so few can actually do so, there is no real link between money and purchasing power in the traditional sense. The act of exchanging rubles for goods has become a mere formality for procurement. In effect, the shortages have turned the ruble into an unconvertible currency within the Soviet Union itself, because the money cannot be readily converted into goods.

Corruption and the Black Market

Inflation cannot be permanently staunched by imposing fixed prices. When demand swamps supply so overwhelmingly that people are routinely forced to endure the torment of queues, some will look for other ways to get what they need or want. Until rubles lose their value completely, the most obvious way is to offer the storekeeper more than the official fixed price. That, of course, is dangerous because it is illegal. But the frustrated Soviet consumer has grown more and more inclined to resort to the black market.

A popular Soviet comedian, recently deceased, used to tell a story about the naïve shopper who finds only empty stores and yet keeps meeting people on the street with full shopping bags. A sympathetic passer-by finally advises the luckless shopper to "enter from the back, take from below, and pay high above."[7] To translate: The shopper must go in through the back door of the shop, get the goods from the special supply in the cellar, and be willing to pay more than the official price. Many Soviet consumers know that having a friend in a position to hold a private stock of goods on one's behalf is a valuable asset. So, too, is knowing people willing to deal on the side (nalyevo), to do business at prices higher than those determined by the State Committee for Prices.

Now that the shortages have begun to affect the basic necessities, many Soviets are finding that dealing "on the left" is a condition of survival. The fact that it is illegal arouses feelings of resentment, not pangs of conscience. Those who continue to abide by the old rules, the ones willing to wait in endless lines, cannot help but resent other consumers who are willing to pay more to get what they want. And while shopkeepers may be condemned for taking prices higher than what they must remit to the government, they too are caught in the bind between unofficial inflation and fixed prices.

What happens is that every time someone *does* consummate a sale at a price higher than the fixed price, the implicit price for that item is raised. Even though the sale was illegal—and the gain must be discounted for the associated risk—the seller has been given a new standard for evaluating the item at his disposal, and he makes a revised assessment of how much it is worth. If the black market price far exceeds the fixed price, the shopkeeper is even less inclined to make his inventory available to buyers at the official fixed price; as a reward for honesty, he loses the difference between the fixed price and what people are willing to pay.

Those who resist illegal activities thus become the victims of inflation as the supply-and-demand forces in the black market take their toll on the legitimate consumption sector. The supplies of goods that make their way to official retail outlets have usually been depleted already by those in a position to sell off a few items for personal gain. There are thus even fewer goods available at the fixed price, and the shortages in the legitimate consumption sector become even more pronounced.

Corruption affects not just the consumption sector but the productive and manufacturing sector of the Soviet economy as well. Enterprises have to compete with each other to procure supplies of materials and equipment, which are ravaged in transit by handlers and distributors who manage to divert them into the black market for untold profits. Inventories are subject to considerable shrinkage if not monitored carefully. Even so, an inordinate number of products are written off as losses because they have supposedly fallen off trucks or have been otherwise damaged. Meanwhile, restaurant workers commonly raid kitchen pantries for food supplies and carry them home for their own use or to exchange for other goods and services.

So widespread is the practice of conducting transactions at the price the market will bear—in a word, corruption—that the official price index set by the Soviet government is being pushed upward by the shadow value of goods established in the black market. Since the government can hardly afford to absorb the increasing price difference on the goods subsidized, officials are caught between having to withdraw certain items or raise the official price. An increase is not feasible for the most fundamental necessities. But even for goods not in that category, it is better not to manifest the price hike overtly. Instead, the government permits manufacturing enterprises to make some trivial change in the appearance of a consumer product; the so-called improvement then justifies a new higher price for the item.

With the official price index rising to accommodate overall excess purchasing power in the Soviet economy, a certain segment of the population is being financially squeezed. Despite the general wage increases introduced to elicit greater labor productivity at state-run enterprises and organizations, not all Soviet citizens are eligible to receive increased compensation. Workers in certain service industries have been left behind by the trend toward higher salaries, as have laborers occupying low-level jobs at factories. Meanwhile, pensioners on fixed incomes have no way of adapting to increases in the cost of living. These people are hit especially hard by the black market because, inclination aside, they do not have the means to participate in it.

In May 1987, Soviet newspapers began reporting for the first time what poorer members of Soviet society have been aware of for some time: Inflation is greatly affecting their quality of life.[8] For the millions of Soviets operating on the black market or offering semilegal consumer services, the main problem remains shortages. But with government-sanctioned increases in the fixed price index have come hard times for Soviet citizens unable to adjust to the higher cost of living. For those people, personal expenses are running ahead of their salaries and pensions. Food uses up more than half their income, even while it has become virtually impossible to purchase certain food items, such as lemons or tomatoes, without paying the free-market prices demanded by farmers.

When a journalist for the Soviet weekly *Literaturnaya Gazeta* asked readers to write in about the rising cost of living, he received hundreds of letters from people complaining that consumer prices were going up all out of proportion to their wages. The consensus among low-paid workers was that life was getting much more difficult. Even the government newspaper *Izvestiya* was compelled to admit that for a large proportion of the Soviet population, making ends meet has become a struggle. As summed up by Anatoli Rubinov of *Lituraturnaya Gazeta:* "Everyone knows about this and everyone constantly talks about it. Everyone, it seems, except the U.S.S.R. Central Statistical Administration."[9]

In many ways, the Soviet government would be better off if it could legalize the activities in the black market and allow prices in the consumption sector to rise significantly. As it stands, the overhang of stored-up purchasing power in the Soviet economy is a burden for the manufacturing sector, because more and more resources must be allocated toward the satisfaction of consumer needs if the government is to pacify a frustrated public.

The shortages are a constant reminder that central planners have failed to match monetary resources with production output. Besides being a symbol of budgetary mismanagement, the lines also represent a waste of manpower as people stand idly for hours, waiting for the chance to carry out transactions that should take only minutes. Soviet sociologists have estimated that, in Moscow, the waste of time amounts to 15 percent of total work time.[10]

It would embarrass the Soviet government, and perhaps irreparably damage the doctrine of socialism, to allow prices to adjust to equilibrium levels based on the total outstanding amounts of currency in the consumption sector. But that course would give the Soviet government a way to soak up the unused purchasing power that now distorts the fixed price allocation system. The winners would be the workers who are overpaid for their contribution to the output of state-run enterprises. The losers would obviously be the low-income workers, the pensioners, and, not so obviously, the black market racketeers, who would no longer be in an exclusive position to extract unearned profits by exploiting the natural forces of supply and demand.

Excess Savings

Because of the potential for black market transactions, the Soviet government has traditionally been suspicious of people who allow their cash balances to build up; hoarding is strongly discouraged with the insinuation that it is a precursor to illegal activity. Accordingly, after making their primary consumption purchases, citizens are expected to put the unused cash into their local savings bank. In that way, the government attempts to limit the amount of cash in actual circulation and discourage its potential use in circumventing the fixed price system. Only the state is deemed sufficiently responsible to hold idle cash balances.

The savings banks that exist throughout the Soviet Union have long been the only financial institutions available to Soviet citizens. People can use their cash to buy goods or they can put it into the savings banks, period. There are no marketable securities or other financial instruments available to individuals, for that would violate socialist doctrine prohibiting private ownership of the means of production. Citizens are allowed to purchase through the savings banks a 3 percent lottery bond issued by the Soviet government, but the bulk of unused cash goes into regular term savings accounts paying 2 to 3 percent interest or into pass-book accounts, which allow citizens to withdraw cash as needed.

The idea here is that excess funds are turned over to the state to fund capital investment within the socialist economy. Rather than have individuals make their own decisions about where to invest their money, everything is handled through the Soviet government on their behalf. The savings banks are little more than a network of collection points; they do not make loans, and they perform virtually no other financial services.

Incorporated into Gosbank in 1963, the savings banks thus function as the local branches for gathering up deposits from the population to provide a base for the credit resources extended by Gosbank. Under Soviet financial theory, the deposits of the population are used to support extensions of credit to enterprises and organizations in the socialist economy. Since Gosbank is responsible for granting the credits to Soviet firms, it is likewise deemed appropriate that Gosbank should exercise authority over the gathering of the deposits from the population. Presumably, the greater the pool of deposits from the savings of the population, the greater the level of credits that can justifiably be granted through Gosbank.

In stable monetary conditions, the theory makes perfect sense. The savings held by the population *do* constitute surplus funds that are available to finance capital investment. They reflect a collective decision to forgo current consumption in favor of investing the unused funds—seed money—in projects that will make it possible to enjoy higher levels of consumption in the future. Savings from the population are employed appropriately in the economy when they are used to take advantage of profitable investment–production opportunities.

Except for the voluntary aspect in making the actual investment decision, we can again make a comparison here with the United States. When people put their idle money balances into savings accounts at commercial banks, they are expanding the base of the lending operations of the banks. The deposits are channeled into loans, which, if they turn out to be good loans, generate positive returns and increase the output of the economy. As long as the bank maintains a portfolio of solidly performing loans, the only dangerous prospect is that all depositors will want to withdraw their funds at the same time, in which case we have a liquidity, not an insolvency, problem.

The problem in the Soviet Union, though, is that the logic behind using deposit holdings to justify extensions of credit from Gosbank to enterprises and organizations is dependent on the assumption of monetary stability. To the extent that the money supply in the Soviet Union has been expanded through unjustified wage increases, the aggregate consumption-versus-spending decision that would normally be reflected in the level of the savings accounts held by the population has been completely distorted.

What do Soviet citizens do with their increased earnings when the goods they wish to buy are unavailable? They put them in the savings banks. The pervasive shortages in the Soviet Union have thus created a higher level of savings, because people have few opportunities to spend their money. The savings accounts are merely registering the level of excess funds in the system stemming from too many rubles chasing too few goods. In other words, they do not represent the deliberate decisions of individuals to forgo current consumption, but indicate only the degree of forced savings to accommodate the overflow of rubles that cannot be spent in the consumption sector of the economy. It is, one might say, personal savings by default.

Table 2.2 shows the total level of savings deposits held by the Soviet population and the year-to-year increases since 1970. We can see that there has been a tremendous overall increase in the level of savings, a fact that ties in with our earlier observation about the rise in short-term credits granted by Gosbank and Stroibank. During the period from 1970 to 1986, the savings of the Soviet population increased by more than five times, growing from 46.6 billion rubles to 242.8 billion rubles.

Since the Soviet working population did not expand much in numbers during this period, and since revenues from the Soviet economy grew at little more than half the pace during the same interval, conventional Soviet banking theory cannot explain the dramatic growth in total deposits. In other words, it is hard to accept that the sudden increase in the level of deposits reflects a profound and spontaneous change in the voluntary savings be-

TABLE 2.2. Soviet Deposits in Savings Banks
(in billions of rubles)

	Level of Deposits	Increase Over Prior Year	
		Amount	%
Year	1	2	3
1970	46.6	—	—
1971	53.2	6.6	12.4
1972	60.7	7.5	12.4
1973	68.7	8.0	11.6
1974	78.9	10.2	12.9
1975	91.0	12.1	13.3
1976	103.0	12.0	11.7
1977	116.7	13.7	11.7
1978	131.1	14.4	11.0
1979	146.2	15.1	10.3
1980	156.5	10.3	6.6
1981	165.7	9.2	5.6
1982	174.3	8.6	4.9
1983	186.9	12.6	6.7
1984	202.1	15.2	7.5
1985	220.8	18.7	8.5
1986	242.8	22.0	9.1

SOURCES: Column 1:
  1970, 1980, 1985, 1986—Narodnoye Khozyaistvo za 70 let: Yu-bileinyy Statisticheskiy Yezhegodnik, p. 448.
  1971, 1972, 1973, 1974—Narodnoye Khozyaistvo v 1975 g.:Statisticheskiy Yezhegodnik, p. 597.
  1975, 1981, 1982, 1983, 1984—Narodnoye Khozyaistvo v 1984 g.:Statisticheskiy Yezhegodnik, p. 462.
  1976, 1977, 1978—Narodnoye Khozyaistvo v 1978 g.:Statisticheskiy Yezhegodnik, p. 415.
  1979—Narodnoye Khozyaistvo v 1980 g.:Statisticheskiy Yezhegodnik, p. 408.
Column 2: Increase in Column 1 over previous year
Column 3: Column 2 divided by Column 1

havior of the Soviet population or to believe that Soviet citizens have collectively decided to sacrifice consumption welfare today in favor of investing in the future. If that were the case, Gosbank officials could tap the unused financial resources in good conscience, investing them in the operations of state enterprises and operations to increase the productive output of the Soviet economy.

But instead there is a fundamental misconception inherent in the Soviet claim that increased deposits justify increased loans to the economy. It is a chicken-or-the-egg question: Does the higher level of deposits constitute an expanded pool of capital for supporting additional loans to the socialist economy? Or do the swollen savings reflect the excess money that has already been infused into the system as the result of prior unwarranted credits granted by Gosbank to nonproductive enterprises? The declining productivity of the Soviet economy, the deficit in the Soviet internal budget, the increased wages, and the resulting shortages in the consumption sector all testify to inflationary pressures that have severely distorted the meaning of traditional monetary signals. Gosbank is forced to recycle the unwarranted credits into the budget to accommodate the expenditures of the Soviet government.

In short, excess savings by the population are yet another symptom of the desperate straits into which the Soviet economy has fallen. Correctly interpreted, they measure the level to which unmet claims against the output of Soviet firms have been accumulated by members of the Soviet population. They are thus a burden to the Soviet government, not a resource.

Growing Distrust

The growth rate of savings deposits, as high as it is, does not reflect the full degree of the increase of currency in the consumption sector, because, as the Soviet government has long feared, some citizens are hoarding their cash. Black market activities require huge sums of cash, far beyond the levels that would be required for business at fixed prices; besides, there is, of course, a certain unpredictability about the black market for which participants must be prepared. Even for honest Soviet citizens who operate in the legitimate consumption sector, the irregularity in the availability of goods requires that ample cash be always at hand.

Working against the holding of cash, though, is the growing fear among Soviet citizens that the government may be getting ready to impose a form of currency reform that will penalize people who maintain large caches of currency. It has happened before. To combat inflationary pressures after World War II, the Soviet government suddenly announced that a new type of currency would be introduced. During the next two weeks, old rubles could be exchanged for new rubles; thereafter the old rubles would become worthless. People who turned in cash received one new ruble for every ten old rubles and effectively lost 90 percent of the nominal value of their holdings. People who kept their money in savings banks were less heavily penalized. The first 3,000 rubles in a savings account could be traded in at a one-to-one ration (no loss); from 3,001 to 10,000 rubles in savings the trade-in ratio was three to two (33 percent loss), and for deposited amounts in excess of 10,000 rubles the trade-in ratio was two to one (50 percent loss).[11]

If and when the Soviet government imposes monetary reform, the goal will be ostensibly to move to some more "efficient" money system. This was the stated purpose behind yet another ten-to-one reverse split effected in 1961. But the real objective is to reduce purchasing power and force hidden currency caches into the open. Anybody who has accumulated huge savings beyond some level deemed acceptable by the Soviet government will be penalized, the assumption being that an honest person could not possibly have become so wealthy relative to his fellow workers. Therefore, anyone who is hoarding large sums of cash or who has managed to deposit more than a certain amount of money in his savings account is presumed to be involved in black market activities.

The Soviet government is thus the all-powerful entity that regulates the value of the currency and determines the financial well-being of Soviet workers. It gives and it takes away. While some citizens have been the beneficiaries of the unwarranted wage increases approved by the government and implemented through Gosbank, others have been made relatively worse off by the resulting inflation. Everyone is negatively affected by the shortages in the consumption sector—everyone except those fortunate high-level party officials and bureaucrats, the nomenklatura, who enjoy access to special stores.

The vast majority of the Soviet population must fend for themselves in tracking down scarce resources in the consumption sector of the Soviet economy. Those who cannot resist the temptation of the black market become criminals in the process of obtaining goods at free market prices. Others, who accumulate earnings in savings banks, risk losing them as the result of an arbitrary currency reform imposed without warning. The most defenseless victims of the inflation, the people who receive low wages or who must survive on fixed incomes, find their predicament made even worse by a rising cost of living that is sanctioned by the government through insidious adjustments to the fixed price index.

The single most damaging aspect of the massive deficit in the Soviet internal budget may be the social divisiveness that is promoted as members of the Soviet population find themselves pitted against one another. Discernible signs of bitterness already exist toward those who are able to benefit from the inflation. Farmers who are able to sell their goods at free market prices, people who are in a position to divert goods to their own use, black market profiteers who skim off supplies of desirable items—all do so at the expense of people who cannot themselves escape from the tyranny of fixed prices in an inflationary environment.

The varying effects of inflation have thus created distinct classes in the Soviet Union: those who profit from it, those who are hurt by it, and those who are able to rise above it by having access to special outlets. Class resentment is spilling out, not just between the various segments of the Soviet population, but between ordinary Soviet workers and the leadership in Moscow. Citizens hardest hit by the inflation have even dared to question the managerial competence of government officials. In May 1987, public protest reached such a fervent pitch that Soviet financial officials were forced to respond.

Speaking at a news conference, Nikolai Belov, first deputy chairman of the Central Statistical Administration, responded by denouncing those who were "not competent to draw conclusions" about inflation. He proceeded to refute the insinuation that the standard of living had gone down for Soviet citizens, explaining that retail prices had risen by only 8 percent from 1970 to 1986, while average monthly wages had gone up 60 percent during the same period. Thus he insisted, "There can be no question of inflation or a drop in living standards in the Soviet Union."[12]

Belov's analysis itself begs the question, not only because it invokes the Soviet government's unbending assertion that it is possible to increase wages without introducing inflationary pressures into the economy, but because it suggests that this approach will be perpetuated in the face of painful evidence to the contrary. Soviet workers, in the meantime, clearly no longer accept the notion that their real per capita income is increasing. Nor are they willing to work harder for increased wages or bonuses. As Birman and Clarke have observed:

During the last two decades [the state] has pursued the "confidence trick" policy of trying to stimulate productivity by higher money

wages without raising the supply of consumer goods by nearly
sufficient to translate the increase in money wages into increased
real incomes. By now this has become ineffective—additional
unspendable money is no longer an incentive to work harder or
more productively.[13]

How can the Soviet people continue to trust a government that
has attempted to lure them into working harder with promises
of more prosperity—and then has left them to fight it out with
each other? The government effectively oversold the available
goods in the consumption sector by printing too many claims to
them. Soviet workers will not fall for the "confidence trick"
again. Responding in kind, they increasingly abide by the cynical
expression: "They pretend to pay us, and we pretend to work."
Cynicism and resentment do not meld well with the loftier notions of socialist doctrine. The personal sense of fulfillment supposedly felt by the lowliest worker who carries out his duties in
contributing to the welfare of society—and who accepts that the
state will provide for his basic needs—depends crucially on a fundamental belief in the system, not just philosophically, but as a
practical matter. The Soviet worker must believe that he is an
important cog in a functioning economic machine that produces
goods efficiently and distributes them equitably. To the extent
that the economic fallout from running a budget deficit destroys
that belief, the foundation of Soviet society is undermined.
As conditions grow more severe, disenchanted citizens begin
to ascribe bad faith to their government. Why are the workers
forced to stand in line for hours to purchase goods when party
officials are not? Why are the best goods reserved for the nomenklatura? The message is that the work of party officials is more
important than that of average workers, that a big shot's time is
more valuable. This is not good socialism. In fact, the society
begins to resemble officers and soldiers, masters and slaves. One
Soviet emigré posited:

> Perhaps the waiting line is the Soviet Union's civilian equivalent of
> military service—a clever way of nipping any kind of protest in the
> bud by means of mass exhaustion of the people in the course of a
> day, a week, a year, an entire life, and reducing the ideals and goals
> of individuals and of the people to the level of day-to-day
> requirements.[14]

It is truly ironic that socialism, which is aimed at appealing to
humanity's highest intellectual ideals, is now represented by an

economic system that can barely satisfy the most basic physical needs. Even if the rest of the world has come to discount communist theory, the Soviet people are expected to continue to have faith that their world is not about to come crashing down. They have seen the integrity of the Soviet internal financial system compromised beyond repair, the economy utterly mismanaged by party officials. Soviet money itself can no longer be trusted. The question is, how much longer can the people trust their government?

3

Perestroika to the Rescue

> Problems snowballed faster than they were resolved. On the whole, society was becoming increasingly unmanageable. We only thought that we were in the saddle, while the actual situation that was arising was one that Lenin warned against: the automobile was not going where the one at the steering wheel thought it was going.[1]

With this, from his book *Perestroika*, Gorbachev confirms our suspicions that social divisiveness and resentment are becoming manifest in the Soviet Union, that society is growing increasingly "unmanageable." That does not necessarily mean outright rebellion against the government or rioting in the streets. The manifestations are generally more subtle: lackadaisical attitudes toward work, skepticism about promised prosperity, and undue—in socialist terms—preoccupation with improving one's personal welfare at the expense of others. Society is becoming unmanageable in that it can no longer be persuaded to carry out the economic dictates of the state without question.

Gorbachev's book also identifies the critical problem as the attitude of party officials who continue to behave as if the complaints of the public and the slow strangulation of the Soviet economy can somehow be ignored. They refuse to acknowledge that production has declined, that revenues to the state are insufficient to cover government expenditures, that shortages are everywhere, and that consumer lines are getting longer and longer, as if that kind of denial could ensure that the good life will go on as before for high-level Soviet bureaucrats.

But the growing gulf between the classes, the workers and their rulers, has intensified the problems caused by economic dysfunctions. We only thought we were in the saddle, Gorbachev admits on behalf of his fellow party members, when the truth was (to mix metaphors) that the automobile was not going where its driver thought it was going. The Soviet Union was not moving toward its destiny—more and more power, greater and greater wealth—as imagined by its leaders at the top. Instead, the society was coming apart at the bottom

That is the situation Gorbachev is forced to confront. The need is critical and the time is short. In his words: "Any delay in beginning perestroika could have led to an exacerbated internal situation in the near future, which, to put it bluntly, would have been fraught with serious social, economic and political crises."[2] What is interesting about the way Gorbachev refers in his book to Soviet economic pressures and social tensions is his use of the past tense in describing them; these are the potential problems that the Soviet Union *might* have been forced to contend with if it had not chosen to implement his program for economic restructuring, perestroika.

Implicit in Gorbachev's assessment of the situation is the notion that by acknowledging the cause of the troubles, he is well on his way to resolving them; that by citing the potential for social, economic, and political turmoil, he has somehow addressed the systemic problems and managed to avoid collapse. His commitment to perestroika is intensified by the difficulties of the past, inspired by his faith in the future. Gorbachev genuinely believes that the new reforms can cure Soviet internal economic ills and put the country back on track.

Having analyzed for ourselves the economic fallout from the Soviet internal budget crisis, we can only concur with Gorbachev that radical measures are needed. We can even admire Gorbachev's confident optimism. But we cannot share his belief that perestroika will prove the economic salvation of socialism. It is by no means clear that the internal forces now pushing the Soviet Union toward upheaval and subsequent crash can even be slowed, let alone reversed, by the new reforms.

Self-Financing: Easier Said Than Done

Gorbachev has probably analyzed the Soviet internal budget situation much the same as we have and concluded, as we have, that the basic problem stems from falling revenues due to mismanagement and unwarranted subsidization of the state-run enterprises and organizations. Declining output from operations is bad news. It shows that marginal gains are no longer being derived through increases in the productivity of either labor or capital.

But what has complicated and worsened the basic problem of declining productivity, Gorbachev has likewise observed, is the cozy relationship between the state enterprises and Gosbank. To accommodate its dual responsibilities as both supervisor and banker, Gosbank has been far too willing to compensate for inadequate production by supplying additional credit. To stop the practice, and its damaging consequences for the internal state budget, Gorbachev has made the decision to cut the umbilical cord. Where unprofitable firms could once count on being bailed out by the state-run banking system, he has decreed that they be forced to sink or swim.

The centerpiece of Gorbachev's program for economic reform is the exhortation that Soviet firms become self-financing. In June 1987, explaining the tenets of perestroika in a 111-page speech before the Central Committee of the Communist Party, Gorbachev called for

> . . . firstly, a drastic extension of the margins of independence for amalgamations and factories, their conversion to full-scale profit-and-loss accounting and self-financing, increased responsibility for achieving the highest end results, fulfillment of obligations to clients, a direct linkage of the collective's income level to its work performance and extensive use of the team contract in labor relations.[3]

What that means is a total upheaval in the administrative and financing apparatus that has so long governed the operation of Soviet plants and factories. Now, instead of exerting its authority to control the means of production, the state is proposing to back off and allow Soviet firms to operate with relative autonomy.

Full-scale accounting means that firms must supply their own working funds out of the revenues they generate. After receiving their allocations of initial capital, firms are expected to earn their own way and to manage their own financial affairs. They must match sources and uses of funds appropriately and coordinate the timing of financial inflows and outflows on their own behalf; they will no longer have recourse to automatic credits from the government granted through Gosbank. Moreover, expenditures for materials and wages must be justified by increased output, and capital expenditures must be financed out of retained earnings. One thing that won't change: The Soviet government will still be entitled to extract a firm's residual profits.

In short, individual enterprises are expected to operate autonomously, sharing the wealth with the state during good times, but left to their own devices during bad. Under the old rules, profitability was an irrelevant concept in practice. But with perestroika, profitability will provide the measure by which a firm gauges its success as a productive venture—it will be the ultimate test of its economic validity. Nikolai Shmelyov, a Soviet economist at the Institute for the U.S. and Canada in Moscow, explains:

> Our suspicious attitude toward profit is a historical misunderstanding, the result of the economic illiteracy of people who thought that socialism would eliminate profit and loss. In point of fact, the criterion of profit under socialism is in no way tainted. It simply tells whether you are working well or not.[4]

Starting on January 1, 1988, some 60 percent of the Soviet Union's 48,000 industrial enterprises have been switched to the new system of self-financing. In Russian, the system is called *khozraschiot,* or economic accountability. In theory, individual enterprise managers can now allocate their financial resources as they see fit. They can make decisions about where to buy materials and how much to pay workers to maximize the output of their firms. They are responsible, too, for the quality of what is produced. Since total firm revenues will now be based on how much of the firm's output is actually sold, enterprise managers will have to determine how to achieve the optimum combination of quantity and quality. This is all in keeping with Gorbachev's prescription that Soviet firms bear "increased responsibility for achieving the highest end results."

Changing the method of accounting, though, does not mean that firms will suddenly begin operating profitably and supplying more revenues to the state. The switch itself is more a matter of form than of substance. The only real difference under the new system is that the spigot regulating the flow of credit has been turned off. There is little reason to think that severing the relationship between enterprise managers and Gosbank officials will itself magically produce economic gains. Gosbank may have been responsible for covering up the failings of enterprises, but it can hardly be blamed for the operational decisions that led to declining productivity.

No, if the enterprises are to become profitable, it will not happen simply because the accounting methods have been changed, but rather because managers choose to make different, better decisions than they would have under the old system. It is not clear, however, why that should necessarily be the case. If the managers made bad decisions before out of incompetence, there is no reason to think they are now suddenly more competent because of an accounting change. If they once made bad decisions because they were dishonest, they are likely to be dishonest still; whether they will be subject to more scrutiny or less under the new system is difficult to tell. If firms were unprofitable before because of economic circumstances beyond the control of managers—such as lack of materials or too few customers—the switch to self-financing will only mean that no revenues will be remitted to the state, whereas before empty credits could be tapped to technically fulfill the requirement.

But the rationale behind khozraschiot is that enterprise managers will face a whole new world. For one thing, they will have the opportunity to procure materials outside of traditional channels. In the past, materials were requisitioned to enterprises through the giant state supply agency, Gossnab. Under perestroika, according to Soviet statements, a number of "manufacturers' chain stores" and "territorial supply-and-sales agencies" will be created. Those supply organizations will be independent, self-sustaining enterprises themselves, functioning to service producers and users. Within four years, the entire country will effect a transition to the "marketing of capital goods by way of wholesale trade."[5]

This vision of the future is a far cry from the current situation. So great a change is it that many enterprise managers can scarcely imagine how it will come about, or how it will affect their own ability to manage their firm profitably. The head of one textile factory said that he went out into the wholesale market to look for raw materials and came up 20 percent short. His assessment of the new system: "Under khozraschiot, it is going to be tough. We even calculated our future losses from the lack of raw materials: our profits will be down by 1 million rubles."[6] In 1987, 160 enterprises in Moscow were operated according to the self-financing system on an experimental basis. Results were mixed. According to figures cited in the Communist Party newspaper *Pravda*, enterprises working under khozraschiot turned in better performances, recording higher productivity and profits, than ones working under the old system. However, one-sixth of the self-financing firms failed to deliver on their contracts. For the failure, they were fined 30 million rubles.[7]

Besides granting new freedom to look for sources of supplies, perestroika also gives enterprises new latitude to expand their customer base and increase overall demand for their products. Previously, finished goods were sold to the state according to quotas and predetermined orders; now they can be sold directly to other enterprises or individuals or even, for some firms, exported to foreign purchasers. The idea is to introduce competition as an incentive to produce higher-quality goods. If buyers have a choice in deciding where to buy supplies, they will opt for the best goods and thereby reward the most conscientious firms.

However, many Soviet managers are worried that having to satisfy an array of demanding customers, as opposed to fulfilling a single state order, is more a burden than an advantage. For one thing, quality control, *gospriemka*, is a pervasive problem. When 15 percent of the tractors produced by the Zhdanov plant were rejected under the state inspection program in 1987, the plant missed its production quota for the year; as a result, some 16,000 workers and managers lost part of their bonuses. Previously, the U.S.S.R. Tractor Ministry would buy up the plant's entire annual output of 36,500, 30-horsepower tractors and make arrangements to distribute them domestically and internationally. Now the firm has its own foreign trade firm to market its goods directly to buyers abroad. (The tractors sell for about $5,000 in the United States.)[8]

Despite the talk about opening channels for making sales to other buyers, most firms will still be selling their goods to the Soviet government for at least the next few years. State orders are expected to cover 80 to 90 percent of industrial output during the three-year transitional period until 1991. Some firms, especially those involved in heavy industry, will continue to have their entire output purchased by the state. Thus many managers can safely continue their old practices knowing they have a captive customer who must not only supply total revenues by purchasing the goods produced but also guarantee the delivery of raw materials.

Another significant new area now left to the discretion of enterprise managers is how much to pay their employees and how to structure bonus programs. Instead of being entitled to receive the generally equalized compensation packages of the past, workers are to be paid directly on the basis of personal effort and achievement. If this smacks of capitalism, perhaps a clarification is in order. According to Gorbachev:

> Socialism cannot ensure conditions of life and consumption in accordance with the principle "From each according to his ability, to each according to his needs." This will be under communism. Socialism has a different criterion for distributing social benefits: "From each according to his ability, to each according to his work."[9]

Because individual managers, not the Soviet government, are in the best position to judge the value of their employees' work, they will now be determining how to set up incentive programs based on monetary inducements. They are advised, under perestroika, to make extensive use of the team contract in labor relations. That means setting up work brigades composed of ten or so employees who function as a team; depending on the quantity and quality of their unit's output, members of the team can earn bonuses that increase their regular monthly wages by up to 40 percent.

Good workers will probably welcome bonus programs based on individual effort rather than the performance of the enterprise as a whole. Nevertheless, the central problem from earlier efforts to increase productivity remains, namely the inordinately high wages paid to workers relative to output. To bring about overall improvements in productivity and firm profitability, the ratio of wage increases to the additional revenues created through incentive programs must be lowered.

Gorbachev has declared that labor costs have to be cut "decisively."[10] Enterprise managers are told to widen the pay differentials between high-quality work and low-quality work and to offer bonuses to motivate workers to produce more goods; at the same time, they are also being told to keep overall labor costs down.

Accordingly, one worker's bonus is now taken from part of another worker's wages. Gorbachev has said that total workers' pay has already been cut 20 to 30 percent at some plants, and he insists that this is being accepted without complaint because those affected are too proud to want to be paid for shoddy work.[11]

Maybe so, maybe not. In any case, it is not just the workers who are to become the masters of their own fate under perestroika. The reforms call for direct linkage between a firm's work performance and its income level. If an enterprise fails to justify its own existence by demonstrated profitability, it will not be allowed to survive; if it cannot produce enough revenues to cover its own expenditures, it will go bankrupt. So the days when financial life-preservers were tossed out by Gosbank as a matter of course have ended. During the transitional period between now and 1991, it has been announced that subsidized credits will be made available on a special case basis. After that, though, retribution for inefficiency will be swift and, in socialist terms, brutal. It may also prove to be widespread; according to Soviet estimates, some 13 percent of the state-run enterprises are currently operating unprofitably.[12]

Under the self-financing regimen imposed by the perestroika reforms, then, enterprises will be judged by the tenets of capitalism, while still bound by the patterns of socialism. They will be expected to operate efficiently even as they are asked to fill state orders subject to inadequate resources and overpaid workers. The crucial concept of profitability is held hostage most of all by a factor that remains beyond the control of individual firms: fixed prices. This in itself is the biggest hurdle for implementing full cost accounting at the level of the enterprise. How can firm managers relate production costs to revenues when prices are dictated from above? How can they gauge genuine demand for their products if prices are set artificially low? What kind of incentive do they have to be efficient if their earnings are used to subsidize the operations of less productive firms?

Gorbachev is fully aware of this conundrum. He too asks, "How can the economy advance if it creates preferential conditions for backward enterprises and penalizes the foremost ones?"[13] But for Gorbachev, the answer is perestroika. Changing the accounting system for state-run firms is the quickest way to sever the debilitating easy-credit relationship between enterprise managers and Gosbank officials and, according to Gorbachev's vision, the first step toward repairing the Soviet economy.

Less Interference from the Top

Another reform, which must be effected in tandem with self-financing, is to dismantle the bureaucratic mechanism of central planning that chokes off the development of individual initiative. In his June 1987 presentation before the Central Committee, Gorbachev followed up his proposal for granting economic independence to state enterprises with the statement that perestroika would require

> . . . secondly, radically transforming centralized economic management, raising its qualitative level and focusing it on the main issues determining the strategy, quality, pace and proportion of development of the national economy as a whole and its balance, while at the same time decisively relieving the center of interference in the day-to-day activities of subordinate economic bodies.[14]

The statement is both complimentary and insulting. Gorbachev is suggesting that the kind of judgment exercised by officials in charge of centralized economic management is too precious to be wasted on the day-to-day affairs of individual enterprises. It should be devoted instead exclusively to the broader issues of national economic strategy, to the pace and proportion of development in macro terms. Gorbachev then insinuates that advice from centralized planners at the level of individual firms will no longer be welcomed or tolerated.

The Soviet officials who make up the apparatus for centralized economic management have effectively been kicked upstairs, no longer having the authority to preside over the operations of enterprises. They have also been stripped of their power to influence the acquisition and distribution of goods, which, in a system plagued by shortages, constitutes a valuable privilege. Soviet bureaucrats are not apt to derive much satisfaction from being transformed from hands-on functionaries to hands-off visionaries. They have another problem to contend with as well: How many national strategists can the system absorb under perestroika? Some 18 million bureaucrats currently have a hand in running the economy.[15]

Gorbachev has made it clear he wants to cut the ranks of bureaucrats to improve efficiency at the planning level. In the past, he has accomplished this by merging several ministries into one large government agency, in the process eliminating a substantial number of the managerial positions. Gorbachev proudly describes how, in 1985, seven separate ministries and departments charged with managing agriculture and food processing were consolidated into a single central organ of state management. The resulting U.S.S.R. State Agro-Industrial Committee, or Gosagroprom, emerged with little more than half of the former managerial staff.[16]

Yet the paper-pushers have entrenched complexity working in their favor. Soviet officials have perfected the art of making endless administrative decisions and passing them on to subordinates. Marshall Goldman of Harvard's Russian Research Center estimates that Gosplan alone (the central planning committee) makes 83 million calculations a year concerning the management of the economy, mostly without the aid of computers, and handles 7 million documents.[17] Similar functions are carried out at the regional level by some 200,000 officials of the Communist Party, the *apparatchiki,* who execute the administrative responsibilities of the state agencies at the local level.

Gorbachev is convinced that there are too many bureaucrats doing too little. Although he claims that the changes in central planning set forth under the reforms of perestroika "will take place within the mainstream of socialist goals and principles of management," there can be no doubt that he opposes the traditional bureaucratic structure and intends to dismantle it, even in the face of opposition:

> It is now clear to everyone that given the present scale of the economy, no ministerial or departmental apparatus, however qualified, can take upon itself the solution of absolutely every question, nor can it replace the thought and initiative of work collectives. Redistribution of rights between the central departments and the enterprises is not proceeding smoothly. The apparatus of the ministries and the ministers themselves are unwilling to give up the habit of deciding minor matters themselves. They are used to that practice, which makes it so much easier for them. Any transfer of rights from the center to the localities is, in general, painful, although, I repeat, the necessity of this is obvious to all, to both ministers and staff. They realize that this action benefits the cause, but, nevertheless, narrow departmental and sometimes group interests are put above those of society and the people.[18]

To show that he will not back down in his efforts to remove stubborn bureaucrats, Gorbachev is enlisting *Pravda* to publicize stories of graft and bribery involving high-ranking officials. In late January 1988 a series of articles about political scandals in Armenia, massive corruption in Uzbekistan, and abuses of police power in the Ukraine appeared. The cases were presented not as isolated incidents but as evidence of an entire network of criminal activities carried out with the full knowledge and assistance of high-ranking apparatchiki. In one case it was hinted in *Pravda* that the corruption had spread to very high levels, involving the son-in-law of the late Soviet leader Leonid Brezhnev.[19]

The focus of the attacks seems to be the special privileges granted to party officials and how they exploit them. For Gorbachev, the press coverage serves two purposes. First, it puts regional officials on notice that if they fail to support the reforms of perestroika they risk being likewise publicly attacked. Second, it validates Gorbachev's contention that the overstaffed apparatus of central planning inflicts economic penalties on socialist society. Rather than increase productivity and output by helping to manage enterprises, the bureaucracy only throws up additional obstacles, in some cases with criminal intent. By exposing the abuses, Gorbachev wins support for his efforts to reduce the influence of central planning officials over the day-to-day activities of enterprises and organizations.

Nowhere is it more clear that Gorbachev prefers the relative efficiency of localized economic units over centralized bureaucracies than in his initiatives for entrepreneurship in the agricultural sector. In keeping with his background—he was in charge of Soviet agriculture from 1979 to 1983 and holds a degree in agricultural science—Gorbachev contends that farm workers and peasants are especially resourceful if left to their own devices. He is convinced that they yearn to reap the benefits of their own labor and will be the first to respond positively to less interference from the bureaucracy. Accordingly, he wants to turn large-scale collective farms into something resembling their former model under Lenin, where traditional peasant family farming was practiced through voluntary cooperation with others. The idea is to give farm workers greater incentive to increase productivity and yield and to improve the quality of agricultural commodities.[20]

The team contract idea, in which workers become members of brigades whose productivity is measured, will be applied extensively to agriculture under perestroika. The brigades may be composed of family members who rent plots of land on collective farms. Brigades can use machinery and fertilizer supplied by the collective and can contract with the collective to deliver a certain amount of output at a certain price. Any produce in excess of the amount can then be sold at bonus prices to the collective or at higher free market prices. Once they have fulfilled their commitments to the state, the collectives will be permitted to sell up to 30 percent of their planned production of fruit and vegetables directly to consumers.

Gorbachev has a lot riding on the performance of the agricultural collectives, but he may have placed a smart bet here. He knows that under the burdensome restrictions of central planning, farm workers had little incentive to produce and felt little responsibility for the quality of what they did produce. But with the chance to make money as a direct result of personal effort, the same farm workers become extremely conscientious and productive. More than 25 percent of the Soviet Union's food supplies is raised now on the less than 3 percent of the land that is farmed privately.[21] True, the private effort relies on tools and other resources supplied by the state, but there is no denying that the productivity of the land is greatly increased when it is put in the hands of people working largely for themselves.

The brigades can be as small as two people, man and wife, who manage—but don't own—a tract of cropland, some livestock, or some other capital asset under contract to the state. For example, at the Ilyich's Legacy collective farm outside Moscow, a man and his wife have contracted to raise 220 calves to milking age.[22] The collective owns the cows but pays the couple on the basis of the weight gained by the animals under their care. If a cow dies, the collective farm can sue the couple for damages. So far, however, the couple is doing well; the husband earns nearly twice the monthly income he received as a farm truck driver. The couple works as long as fifteen hours a day, hoping that they may one day be able to buy a car. Their overall assessment: "The work is harder, but more interesting."

The appeal to the entrepreneurial spirit under the reforms of perestroika already extends beyond agriculture. In Moscow, a number of restaurants have been formed under the new contractual rules allowing them to serve food at prices the market will bear and to retain a percentage of profits. The managers and cooks at those profit-oriented restaurants (called "collectives") are not restricted to using supplies provided by the local ministry. They can buy on free markets, create their own menus, and serve an array of expensive meats, vegetables, and fruits to their customers at prices they deem appropriate. As experimental operations, they are not yet allowed by the state to serve alcohol to patrons, but the cooperative restaurants are never-the-less extremely popular with customers tired of the unchanging fare and bad service typical of state-run operations.

Other consumer goods and services are also being offered through private initiative. In Tallinn, some five hundred private taxi drivers are now competing with a thousand state operators. The private drivers work in their spare time, after finishing their normal duties at state jobs; they also use their own automobiles. Other private services include hairdressing, the delivery of theater tickets, knife-sharpening, and a brokering service that arranges apartment swaps for interested parties and takes a cut from both sides.

But cooperatives only account for a tiny percentage of the nonagricultural goods and services provided to the population. By late 1987, only about nine thousand cooperatives employing about 90,000 Soviet citizens had been set up to provide goods and services outside of state-controlled channels; Gorbachev had hoped for ten times those figures by that time.[23] A major culprit behind the disappointment has been the state bureaucracy. Central planning officials feel threatened by would-be cooperatives providing parallel services. Local authorities make it hard for individuals to obtain necessary materials or facilities. Licenses are denied because cooperatives are accused of offering redundant rather than additional new services. As Gorbachev predicted, obstructionism is proving to be a powerful form of resistance to perestroika.

Mitigating Inflation

The idea behind private initiative, of course, is to increase production in the consumption sector the better to meet pent-up demand and to help alleviate shortages. Because foodstuffs are the most pressing need, it makes sense to encourage farm workers in particular to supply additional output, which is why Gorbachev has made economic reform in the agricultural sector a top priority. But to get farmers to work harder, the instrument of incentive is, once again, increased monetary compensation. Farmers now have the chance to reap greater cash rewards by selling their goods in the free markets.

In Moscow, citizens have the opportunity to purchase high-quality cuts of meat and attractive vegetables without having to wait in line. The free markets here offer aisles of open-air booths and refrigerated counters manned by individual proprietors who hawk their wares with the enthusiasm of capitalist zealots. Unlike the dreary state stores where patrons stolidly wait their turn to get what is being given out, the free markets have a carnival air about them. The array of fruits, vegetables, nuts, meats, and cheeses offered is staggering in comparison with what is available through official outlets. The proprietors coerce, flatter, and remonstrate potential purchasers as they stroll past their counters laden with foodstuffs. Buyers are urged, with winks and gestures, to sample the goods.

There is just one catch: The food is very expensive. In the free markets, for example, tomatoes sell for 10 rubles a kilo (at the official exchange rate, over $7 a pound), which is five times more than they cost in the state stores—assuming you can find them at all and are willing to wait in line for a long time. Because the state technically sells the same goods at a cheaper price, very few Soviet citizens are willing to pay the free market prices unless they want something very badly, perhaps for a special occasion. Even though the quality is generally much better and shopping itself much more pleasurable, the free markets are relatively uncrowded.

It is almost as if Soviet citizens have an aversion to buying foodstuffs at market-determined prices, as if doing so somehow makes them conspirators in a capitalist plot. It is not only the price that seems to put people off; there is also a sense that they are being personally exploited by profiteers. True, having to wait in line is a time-consuming nuisance, and there's no guarantee that one will actually be able to buy the desired goods before they run out. But for Soviet citizens, wages do not dictate the standard of living nearly to the extent they do in Western industrialized countries. Most Westerners shun lines because they don't want to waste the time; time, after all, is money. But because wages are low in the Soviet Union, with housing and other basic necessities supplied by the state, a person's time does not so readily translate into money. If the main difference between the expensive tomatoes and the cheap tomatoes is the time it takes to wait in line, most Soviets will opt for the cheap tomatoes.

Yet the trick is to get people to spend their money, to release some of the excess purchasing power without unleashing runaway inflationary pressures on the system. One benefit of the black market, as pointed out, is that it soaks up currency in the consumption sector. What Gorbachev needs is to create a legitimate black market, with flexible prices, to further absorb the accumulated currency and savings and reduce the level of unmet claims against the economy. Ideally, increased prices would lead directly to increased production. That way, inflationary pressures could be relieved on both the demand side and the supply side as prices rise on an expanding inventory of consumer goods.

The free markets that have already been established accord perfectly with this logic. They are very expensive, tempting people to spend large quantities of stored-up cash, which in turn results in greater productivity from farmers and fosters individual initiative among workers. Even though the producers receive more money, as long as the gains in productivity exceed the value of the additional money earned, it is a net economic gain for society. It would be even better for the Soviet government if it could be the direct beneficiary of market-determined prices. Then the money would not be subject to further turnover in the consumption sector but would effectively be taken out of circulation with a corresponding drop in inflationary pressures.

In short, the position the Soviet government wants to occupy is that of middleman between the productive sector and the consumption sector. For the defense sector, of course, it is both producer and consumer; the Soviet government is not yet ready to get out of the business of running certain segments of the economy. But instead of being forced to subsidize consumers by paying inflated prices to suppliers and then making the goods available at low fixed prices on the demand side, the government would like to reverse the relationship—to buy low and sell high. Buying low means reducing the costs of production while increasing the output, that is, lowering unit costs. The first two elements of perestroika are aimed precisely at this side of the equation. The imposition of self-financing, together with the decentralization of control, are meant to increase the efficiency of production.

But how to sell high? It is too late to go back to a pre-inflationary standard of value for compensating the factors of production. Productivity gains can only be hoped for from now on; except for some minor rollback in overall wages, existing costs must be taken as given. Therefore, if the role of middleman is to be a source of profit for the Soviet government, official prices in the consumption sector must be allowed to rise. In other words, the Soviet government must effectively take over the black market activities it has in the past so vigorously condemned. The economics of doing so are compelling: Criminal speculators are currently getting rich at the Soviet government's expense, taking the profit that would go directly to the government if prices were set at levels accounting for inflation in the system. Gorbachev's objective should not be to do away with the black market—which, after all, merely reflects increased costs in the productive sector—but rather to wrest it away from private individuals, absorb its functions as a matter of official policy, and turn its operations over to the government.

Price reform, however, represents a truly radical step for the Soviet government, a shocking refutation of its long-standing position that low fixed prices are one of the fundamental benefits of a socialist system. Even in recent years, as it has become more and more of a burden on the government to absorb the difference between the cost of production and the fixed selling price on basic consumer goods, one could discern a certain sense of martyrdom, but no hint that official fixed prices would be raised. A Soviet commentator has explained:

> The prices of milk, meat and butter in the store have not changed in more than 20 years, even though the state's expenditure for their production has grown markedly because of the increase in the prices paid to producers, in farmers' wages and the huge sums that are annually invested for the construction of livestock-breeding farms, storage facilities, stores, and so on. Today the state's expenses exceed its receipts from meat and dairy products. The difference, which amounted to 40 billion rubles last year, is subsidized from the State Budget. Last year these subsidies amounted to twice the budget expenditures for the prewar year of 1940. In the USSR we have chosen subsidies because by maintaining a relatively low and stable level of prices on basic consumer goods, the state puts them within the reach of all citizens irrespective of their income. This applies to meat and dairy products, other consumer goods, rent and many services.[24]

The key phrase is, "we have *chosen* subsidies" in the Soviet Union. It may be expensive for us, the Soviet government says, but we have consciously chosen the policy, basically for humanitarian reasons. The statement does not explain satisfactorily why production costs have gone up, why farmers' wages were arbi-

trarily increased, or why no economies of scale were realized by
increasing the number of livestock raised and the capacity of
grain storage facilities. All the commentator endeavors to get
across is that the state places a higher priority on the needs and
rights of the people than it does on financial considerations and
the exigencies of the budget.

Until now. In Gorbachev's June 1987 presentation before the
Central Committee, in which he laid out the key elements of perestroika—the self-financing of enterprises and the decentralization of economic control—he also made it clear that the Soviet
government would no longer feel obliged to demonstrate its devotion to the people by picking up the tab for massive subsidies.
The last time rents were raised was in 1928, while bread, sugar,
and eggs have remained at the same price since 1954. The price
of meat has not budged since 1962. According to Gorbachev, a
"radical reform of the pricing system is a most important part of
the economic overhaul. Without it, a complete transition to the
new mechanism is impossible."[25]

Clearly, Gorbachev is correct. All the notions of enhanced productivity and profitability so fundamental to the logic of perestroika, are thwarted under a system of fixed prices. Yet reforming
the pricing system will be one of the most sensitive and difficult
elements of Gorbachev's program. For one thing, "reform" can
only mean that prices will generally be raised, not a popular measure with Soviet workers. Still, the goal for the Soviet government is to eventually eliminate nearly all consumer subsidies,
which means bringing the official price of goods at least up to
the same price the government now pays to purchase them from
the producer.

The Soviet Union spent 75 billion rubles ($122 billion) on con-
sumer subsidies in 1986. Some 57 billion (about $93 billion) of
that went to support the fixed price on meat and dairy products.
Gorbachev's key economic adviser, Abel Aganbegyan, is advocat-
ing "drastic reductions" that would cut government subsidies by
more than 80 percent. He would like to slash the amount spent
on subsidies in the budget to a level between 10 and 15 billion
rubles, less than one-fifth of the present figure.[26] Aganbegyan
also calls the current system of fixed prices "irrational."[27] He
does not venture a guess about how much subsidies will actually
be reduced or how quickly the reductions will be phased in. But
he does insist that there is no question about whether prices will
be raised—it is only a matter of how much.

The fixed prices on foodstuffs are unquestionably low: two rubles a kilo for meat ($1.50 a pound), about 50 cents for a quart of milk, about 20 cents for a loaf of white bread. But Western observers must remember that the average Soviet wage-earner makes $312 a month. Food may be relatively cheap, but other basic consumer items are very expensive. A skirt costs $101, a blouse $93, an average coat $312, a full month's salary.[28]

As Gorbachev noted in a speech in Murmansk in October 1987, something is wrong when a pair of women's boots costs 122 rubles ($200), enough to buy one person's annual supply (136 pounds) of meat. But the Soviet citizens who will have to bear the brunt of price reform do not necessarily have the same perspective as their leader. Writing to *Izvestiya* in the spirit of *glasnost*, one Soviet consumer took exception to Gorbachev's example. "The problem isn't the price of meat. It's the price of boots."[29]

The problem in both cases is the underlying inflation that has distorted monetary values in the consumption sector. In the case of the meat, the Soviet government has so far opted to make up the increasing difference between the cost of production and the price to the consumer. In the case of the boots, it has allowed the fixed price to accommodate the wage increases and other rising costs of production. Gorbachev clearly intends to bring up food prices in line with boot prices, rather than vice versa. Moreover, to the extent that some goods, perceived as luxury items, are now being offered at inordinately expensive prices to cover the inordinately low prices of other goods, there may even be room to reduce the price on certain high-priced items as the prices on more general goods are raised, creating the impression that prices are being adjusted in both directions.

Overall, though, the direction will be up. And that is exactly how Gorbachev plans to fight inflation in the Soviet system: by raising prices. This is the mirror image of what occurs in a free market economy, when, worried about inflation, the government decides to impose wage and price controls to "freeze" further increases. Such an action affects only the chief symptom of inflation within a free market system: rising prices. Since the fundamental cause of inflation, the excess creation of credit and money relative to the supply of goods, is not cured by the freeze, the eventual result of wage and price controls in a free market system is to convert the inflation into shortages.

In the Soviet Union, where prices are permanently frozen by

the government, inflation is *automatically* manifested in the form of shortages. To relieve the symptom, then, the Soviet government must resort to raising prices. But that doesn't affect the underlying cause of inflation, which is still the excess creation of credit and money relative to the supply of goods. So the Soviet move is merely a stopgap measure to take some of the immediate pressure off while the government regroups and assesses the damage inflicted on the budget by the deficit. In other words, Gorbachev's call for raising prices to fight inflation is the socialist equivalent to Nixon's imposition of wage and price controls.

Pressure Points

We can now see Gorbachev's three-pronged game plan in its entirety. First, he is trying to increase total revenues to the government from the state enterprises and organizations. He wants to stop the practice of channeling empty Gosbank credits through to the government as "payments"; instead, he wants genuine revenues out of real profits. That means Soviet firms are going to have to become more productive, as measured under the new accounting rules, by cutting costs and taking in more sales revenues. The resulting profits, of course, will be shared with the Soviet government.

The second prong is to reduce the cost of government itself through decentralization. The savings will come from the firing of a substantial portion (perhaps up to half) of the bureaucrats. If what they were doing before was hurting, and not helping the economy, as Gorbachev asserts, there will be savings even if the fired bureaucrats are kept on the dole at their former salaries. It is more likely, though, that they will be shifted into less prestigious jobs at lower salaries that will result in a bottom-line plus for the economy.

The third prong, price reform, takes aim at the expenditure side of the Soviet budget by reducing government subsidies. If Aganbegyan has his way, prices will go up substantially and soon. The immediate effect of higher fixed prices will be cost savings that will be realized from higher revenues obtained on consumer goods sold through the official retail stores. Even a marginal increase in prices will dampen some demand—from the poorest members of the Soviet population—and reduce total sales. And a reduction of the demand for subsidized goods will save the government money.

All three measures are aimed at reducing the Soviet internal budget deficit, the first by increasing the level of revenues, the third by reducing government expenditures, and the second by doing a bit of both—enhancing productivity by removing bureaucratic interference and reducing the cost of economic administration. Gorbachev quite obviously understands the essence of the budgetary problem. It is important to understand, however, that perestroika recommends virtually nothing in the way of reducing expenditures for defense or fixed capital investment. The reforms are almost wholly directed at getting more out of workers and reducing government spending on consumption, which means that the bottom-line objective of the reforms is to put pressure on the ratio of output to wages. Workers will be forced to work harder for less money, and the money will not go nearly as far in view of the rising prices. In short, perestroika is a financial squeeze for the average Soviet consumer.

In choosing to balance the Soviet budget on the backs of the workers, Gorbachev is taking a path that historically has proven dangerous. The combination of lower wages and higher prices has led to socially explosive results in Poland. Two communist leaders, Wladyslaw Gomulka and Eduard Gierek, were ousted when workers rebelled against price increases; in 1980, meat price hikes prompted the strikes that led to the birth of the Solidarity movement. Already there are similar signs of growing unrest in the Soviet Union. Although the word "strike" is not used in Soviet newspapers, there have been an increasing number of articles about temporary stoppages.

In September 1987, bus drivers walked off the job in the town of Chekhov, 40 miles south of Moscow, to protest a new pay system under which their wages were docked if they did not keep to their schedules. Drivers complained that it was not fair to hold them responsible, because they were forced to drive buses that were aging, decrepit, and subject to breakdown. The following month another seven hundred workers put down their tools and refused to work at a bus factory in the town of Likino, near the Ural mountains. They too resented having their compensation held hostage to the equipment they were required to use. As one worker told Moscow News, inadequate and aging tools kept the factory from reaching its targets and left workers unable to earn their bonuses.[30]

In the protests, the basic complaint is the unfairness of a system that penalizes workers for factors beyond their control. The
team contract system promoted by Gorbachev under perestroika
may establish tighter links between performance and compensation, but without a smooth transition throughout the whole economy to the new economic methods, imbalances and disruptions
are bound to occur, with punishing effects for the most conscientious workers. A brigade leader at one Soviet plant told journalists how his crew was penalized because a factory in another
town did not produce its share of work in time. His lament: "We
worked normally, so why should we pay out of our own pockets
for the miscalculations of others?"[31]

If docked pay is enough to bring out verbal protests and sullen
resentment, one wonders what will happen if Soviet enterprises
and organizations are indeed allowed to go bankrupt and workers find themselves unemployed. The threat of bankruptcy is
held out as a real possibility for firms that continue to produce
losses and look to the state for handouts. Although officials insist
they only need to let a few firms actually go bankrupt, just
enough to set an example, the new law contains explicit procedures for determining when to cut the cord on a losing enterprise. During the transitional period, the government will en-
deavor to assist by paying generous purchase prices on state
orders, but only up to a certain point. "We will give them a
chance," according to a senior Soviet economist at the Institute
for Economy. "How they will use that chance I cannot say."[32]

If firms do go bankrupt, or if enterprise managers feel compelled to fire some of their employees to cut costs, Gorbachev
insists that the workers will not be left unemployed; unemployment, after all, was officially abolished in the Soviet Union in the
1930s. While it may seem little more than a matter of semantics,
Gorbachev is careful to make a distinction:

> Problems of employment under socialism acquire a new
> dimension. The release of workers in conditions of the socialist
> economy will not bring about unemployment, with the specter of
> which both our own opponents of restructuring and Western
> "sovietologists" are trying to scare us.[33]

Instead, the released workers will get help, according to the government, through a nationwide network of job placement centers
financed by the enterprises. Workers have been assured that they
will continue to receive their salaries for three months after be-

ing laid off, although it's not clear what happens after that. In all, based on indications in *Pravda*, some 20 million jobs are likely to be eliminated.[34]

The primary task of the job placement centers will be to retrain temporarily displaced workers and find them new employment. There is no shortage of jobs in the Soviet Union; Western analysts estimate that there are currently more than 13 million job vacancies in the service sector and more than a million jobs in construction. The problem is, the vacancies are in the remote areas of the country: the northern regions, Siberia, and Central Asia.[35] Persuading displaced city workers, especially headquarter bureaucrats from Moscow and other metropolitan areas, to move to the back country may require considerable coercion.

Perhaps they will need to be reminded that the interests of society must be placed above their own petty personal desires. There is no turning back from perestroika. According to Gorbachev, perestroika is no less than a revolution:

> One of the signs of a revolutionary period is a more or less pronounced discrepancy between vital interests of society whose front ranks are ready for major changes, and the immediate, day-to-day interests of people. Perestroika hits hardest those who are used to working in the old way. We have no political opposition, but this does not mean there is no confrontation with those who, for various reasons, do not accept perestroika. Everyone will probably have to make sacrifices at the first stage of perestroika, but some will have to give up for good the privileges and prerogatives which they do not deserve and which they have acquired illegitimately, and the rights which have impeded our progress.[36]

The Soviet people are well known for their capacity to make sacrifices. Their dedication to the socialist cause has carried them through other periods of restructuring, through Khrushchev's reforms in the 1950s and through Kosygin's in the 1960s. They have been asked, again and again, to undergo wrenching personal adjustments for the sake of improving the society at large. The need for reform is inevitably invoked, not as any refutation of socialist policies, but in the spirit of perfecting the socialist system and putting the country back on the road to the dreamed-of communist utopia.

But mass unemployment and rising food prices are not part of that dream. Gorbachev may find that resistance goes beyond the mere stubbornness of people accustomed to working in the old way. One Soviet journalist wrote in *Literaturnaya Gazeta:* "I am afraid that in the event of a price hike on foodstuffs, people could turn away from perestroika, as they would from a con game. And then the real opponents of perestroika will raise their heads."[37]

Perestroika certainly has plenty of real opponents. When Gorbachev finished laying out his proposals before the Central Committee in June 1987, the debate that followed was described by Aganbegyan as "sharp," with "quite a lot of emotional speeches." Unless Gorbachev can persuade the Soviet people at all levels—from the humblest factory workers to the highest-ranking members of the Politburo—to support perestroika, his plans for economic rejuvenation may go the way of earlier attempts to reform the socialist system, all sound and fury signifying nothing. And the Soviet economy, after a few spasmodic lurches to the right and to the left, will finally end up in the ditch.

4

How the West Fits In

Gorbachev's chances to make it all work are marginal at best. If that assessment seems unduly pessimistic, or perhaps a reflection of Western prejudice, consider the seriousness of the Soviet Union's situation and the bitterness of the medicine it must now swallow. The working population is under pressure to produce more with less, while also being asked to accept lower living standards. The entire economy is being squeezed to yield additional fixed investment capital, the benefits of which may not be felt for years. Subsidies are being withdrawn as prices are allowed to rise. The future promises factory closings and widespread unemployment, perhaps even forced relocation by the government. All the while, socialist principles are being suspended to allow the selfish practices of capitalism to rescue the Soviet economy.

As difficult as the problems of the domestic economy are, there are additional concerns. Externally, the Soviet government finds itself having to support such increasingly burdensome wards as Cuba and North Vietnam. It has been drained, economically and politically, by a war in Afghanistan. It faces the distinct possibility of having to spend more money on sophisticated military technology to confront SDI at a time when defense expenditures are already consuming too great a share of GNP. In reconciling internal and external objectives with economic realities, Gorbachev must contend with rebellious bureaucrats, sullen military officials, resentful enterprise managers, antagonized workers, and outraged consumers.

Many Westerners, compared with uncooperative, potentially treacherous detractors within the Soviet Union, seem rather charitably disposed toward Gorbachev. The objectives of perestroika, after all, flatter those who believe in free market principles, even as they threaten advocates of central planning. Moreover, Gorbachev's willingness to take on the Soviet bureaucracy strikes a sympathetic chord among people in Western countries, especially in the United States. To many Americans, Gorbachev is seen as someone with the guts to fight city hall.

Indeed, Gorbachev may be destined to be more popular abroad than at home. He probably even wishes he could import a few freewheeling American business types, not just for their political support but to demonstrate what a little entrepreneurship can accomplish. The maverick spirit of American drive is precisely what is lacking in the Soviet population at large. What finally undermines perestroika could turn out to be the general passivity of the Soviet people, their tendency to hesitate and avoid all risk, which has come from decades of being asked to suppress individual initiative in the name of social progress.

Already it is clear that the socialist mentality does not easily accept the logic of differential wages and varying standards of living among comrades. Numerous complaints have been lodged against the private cooperatives and the high prices they ask. Co-op participants are criticized for becoming too rich, and there is talk of sharply raising the taxes on their profits. Drivers for the state-owned taxi organization have gone so far as to puncture the tires of private cabbies. When asked what is wrong with private taxi service, one state driver replied: "Nothing, except that I don't have my own car."[1]

The Soviet people have perhaps been indoctrinated too well in the values of socialism to embrace now the new thinking of perestroika. That seems to be the case, certainly, in the short run. Maybe, as they begin to realize that individuals are able to create a better life for themselves by taking risks and working hard, the resentment and envy will give way to emulation and competition. It can hardly happen soon enough for Gorbachev. During the transition, while so many Soviets are prudently standing back to see what happens, mulling over the impact of perestroika on their lives in only the most abstract terms, Gorbachev is under tremendous pressure to provide concrete evidence of success.

Timing is critical. As one West German official put it: "Gorbachev is playing for broke—he's giving himself two years."[2] That period could be extended with a few booster shots of encouraging economic news or perceived foreign policy victories. Social tolerance of perestroika could last perhaps as long as three to five years, up to the point when various government subsidies are withdrawn and the full impact of the wage–price squeeze is felt. How much time Gorbachev has probably depends most on when the specific consumer reforms are implemented.

Gorbachev seems to think the entire Soviet economy will have made the switch before the beginning of the thirteenth five-year plan in 1991. In the meantime, he is looking for support wherever he can find it, including from friends in the West. The task, as Gorbachev defines it, is formidable indeed: Bring Soviet economic performance up to world-class standards. To that end, he will need all the friends he can get.

The Internal Dilemma

Even if the Soviet people eventually swallow the notion that perestroika represents a perfecting of socialism, the capacity of the Soviet economy to embrace Gorbachev's reforms is a matter less of ideological conflict than of physical impossibility. The Soviet spirit may be willing, but the flesh is weak. After decades of phenomenal growth, the Soviet economic machine began to run out of steam during the mid-1970s. It was as if Russia itself, forcibly transformed into an industrial power by Lenin and Stalin, had finally grown fatigued, exhausted. No longer was there an inner desire to keep pushing; the effort, after all, seemed never to translate into a better life. The people and the system reached the point of burnout.

The economic facts may be less dramatic than that analogy, but they are in some ways even more compelling. The Soviet Union's adjusted gross national product, based on CIA estimates, is equal to about 50 percent of the United States'. In other words, the 280 million people of the Soviet Union today produce about half as much as the 240 million people of the United States. Meanwhile, the CIA estimates that 17 percent of Soviet production goes for defense—some Western experts think the actual figure could be over 25 percent[3]—as against about 8 percent in the United States. Finally, agriculture takes up over a quarter of the Soviet economy, while it is only about 5 percent of the American economy.

According to CIA estimates, the Soviet GNP since the mid-1970s has averaged about 2 percent growth annually. Henry S. Rowen, former chairman of the National Intelligence Council and former president of the RAND Corporation, suggests the actual rate of growth might have been much less, "perhaps close to zero."[4] Gorbachev himself concedes:

> At some stage—this became particularly clear in the latter half of the seventies—something happened that was at first sight inexplicable. The country began to lose momentum. Economic failures became more frequent. Difficulties began to accumulate and deteriorate, and unresolved problems to multiply. Elements of what we call stagnation and other phenomena alien to socialism began to appear in the life of society. A kind of "braking mechanism" affecting social and economic development formed.[5]

The problem is, it is not enough now simply to get rid of the braking mechanism. What is absolutely essential is a jumpstart from an external source if Gorbachev is to move the economy out of its old patterns of performance. In short, he desperately needs to raise the productivity of the Soviet economy and there are only two ways, based on classic economic theory, to get that done: (1) by improving the productivity of labor or (2) by improving the productivity of capital. But Gorbachev finds that financial distortions caused by budget mismanagement continue to aggravate underlying difficulties in the domestic economy.

Improving the productivity of labor is clearly a leading objective of perestroika. All the new approaches linking compensation to performance rely on self-interest as an inducement to get people to work harder and longer. Asked to share her view of perestroika, one worker at a tractor plant replied: "Dengee, dengee, dengee" (money, money, money).[6] For most factory and plant workers, then, creativity and initiative are not genuinely relevant. Workers are expected to perform, over and over again, the specific work routines of mass production assembly lines. So being more productive means performing the same thing more often within the same amount of time, or doing the same thing at the same speed for a longer time.

Workers who face the dismal prospect of having to increase

output deserve to know, at least, that the additional effort will be rewarded. To the extent that money translates into a higher standard of living, it is perhaps worthwhile to work harder for more money. But here is where the internal conundrum between financial effects and economic effects confounds the objectives of perestroika. Until fixed prices on consumer goods are substantially raised—and the question of when to do it is, we know, the trickiest part of perestroika—the problem of severe shortages will persist. In the face of shortages, money means very little. If money means very little, how do you entice workers to be more productive?

Moreover, it has been estimated that if the Soviet people were to quit working entirely, their collective savings would sustain them at current levels of consumption for seven months or longer.[7] So additional pay is clearly not the key to immediate survival. In short, more money is no inspiration to work harder *unless* a worker can purchase desirable goods with the money. Therefore Gorbachev must put more goods—high-quality, expensive goods—before consumers *now* to induce workers to work. Without something appealing to buy, Soviet laborers have little incentive to work more efficiently.

The answer, in terms of jumpstarting the economy, is to import consumer goods from outside the Soviet system. Imports from the West are highly sought after in the Soviet Union; they are also extremely expensive, not only compared with domestically produced Soviet goods (which, other than basic foodstuffs, are quite dear) but also compared with the prices at which they sell outside the Soviet Union. To the extent that Gorbachev can bring in consumer goods from the West and make them available to workers at prices high enough to soak up savings but low enough to be affordable to a critical mass within the labor force, he can capture the interest of average Soviet workers. It is not the Rolex watches and the Gucci luggage that ignite worker incentive so much as the high-quality household appliances, video cassette recorders, and personal items like clothing and cosmetics.

What is important from Moscow's perspective is that imported goods do not use up Soviet resources or drain Soviet productive capacity. Imports are an exogenous source of help that can both relieve internal pressure and stimulate adjustment to perestroika. Ultimately, the Soviet Union's goal is to produce its own high-quality consumer goods in sufficient quantity to keep workers hard at their labors. But until that day arrives, importing Western consumer goods is one way Gorbachev can get past the obstacles caused by financial failings in the Soviet internal economy. Let the West provide the carrot for Soviet workers to get perestroika rolling.

For improving the productivity of capital, the Soviet Union has even more to gain by looking outside its own borders. The productivity of capital is improved by applying new technology, and the West has more of it for use in manufacturing than the Soviet Union could hope to develop on its own in the next decade. Lacking the physical infrastructure and the organizational flexibility to support high-tech advances domestically, the Soviet Union would do well to harvest the benefits of existing Western product and process technology.

While the Soviet Union's inability now to motivate labor stems from unearned wage increases in the past, its failure to foster technological progress in the manufacturing sector comes from past decisions not to fund research and development. Gorbachev acknowledges:

> Analysis of industry's performance has shown mistakes in the investment policy. For many years our policy had been to build more and more enterprises. The construction of workshops and administrative buildings absorbed vast sums. The existing enterprises, meanwhile, remained at the same technological level. Of course, if good use is made of everything available in two or three shifts, the targets of the Twelfth Five-Year Plan can be met using the existing equipment. But obsolescent equipment would in one way or another drag us backward, since old machinery must be given up. This is why we are so drastically changing our structural and investment policies.[8]

To raise the level of Soviet technology to modern standards, Gorbachev has sought to redress the investment misallocations of the past. Under the current five-year plan, he is devoting twice as much money than in the previous plan to fixed capital investment to spur scientific and technological progress and to effect a radical modernization in mechanical engineering. He has assigned leading Soviet scientists to upgrade manufacturing processes by redesigning factories to accommodate new equipment and production techniques. The emphasis, in particular, will be on machine-tool-building, instrument-making, electronics, and electrical engineering. There are also ambitious plans to modernize Soviet iron-and-steel and chemical facilities.

But during a period of overall budgetary austerity—and because of political pressure to rack up productivity gains as
quickly as possible—Gorbachev can hardly afford to wait for domestic efforts aimed at technological innovation to bear fruit. In
the first place, there is no guarantee that scientific advancement
will be achieved in a timely fashion; creative technological advances cannot be dictated from the top down. In the second
place, Gorbachev knows that the very technology that would
make such a tremendous contribution to Soviet productive output today *already exists.* Why incur the expense, the delay, and
the uncertainty of domestic research efforts when the required
technology has already been developed in the West?

For the Soviet Union simply to procure Western technology
outright, rather than taking the pains to develop it internally, the
benefits are so obvious that Gorbachev feels compelled to com-
ment:

> We have found ourselves in this situation technologically because
> we underestimated our scientific potential and placed too great a
> reliance on external ties. As I see it, we accepted the policy of
> détente with too radiant hopes; I would say, too trustingly. Many
> thought it would be irreversible and open up unbounded
> possibilities, in particular for expanding trade and economic
> relations with the West. We even discontinued some of our
> research and technological developments, hoping for the
> international division of labor, and thinking that some machines
> would be more advantageous to buy than to manufacture at home.
> But what happened in reality? We were severely punished for our
> naïveté.[9]

Gorbachev thus acknowledges the dangers of becoming overly
dependent on politically fickle Western partners, who, with relative suddenness, can cut off supplies of high-tech goods through
trade sanctions and embargoes. Indeed, he displays righteous indignation over what he sees as a trap set by the West to get the
Soviet Union to abandon its own research efforts—as if the Soviet Union would be much further advanced technologically had
it not been for an earlier decision, prompted by fiscal considerations, to buy from abroad. He vows never again to allow the
Soviet Union to be a victim of the West's technological arro-
gance.

But, indignation aside, this does not mean he doesn't want to
tap Western-produced technology in the meantime, while the So-

viet Union endeavors to develop the necessary infrastructure, experience, and talent to support its own high-tech industry. Just as Gorbachev ultimately seeks to provide more consumer goods as the result of increased Soviet productivity in the future, he also hopes to eventually attain world technological standards.

Again, it is a matter of timing. The longer-term objectives of perestroika are to create a Soviet Union that is self-sufficient, a country that can motivate its own workers with an array of high-quality, domestically produced goods and that can maximize the productivity of capital with increasingly sophisticated technology, developed internally. When it comes to capturing productivity gains in the short run, however, expediency is more important than domestic pride. Gorbachev knows he needs outside help during the period of transition if perestroika is to survive long enough to produce economic results.

Nothing to Sell

If it makes eminent sense for the Soviet Union to import Western consumer goods and technology to get perestroika going, the question then becomes how to pay for them. The only way the Soviet Union can earn the needed hard currency outright is by selling its own products to Western consumers. Yet little is produced in the Soviet Union for which much market demand exists in the West, especially in the way of finished consumer goods.

Ideally, Gorbachev would like to expand the list of Soviet products that carry appeal for Western buyers. That is one motive behind the push to bring Soviet manufacturing up to world-class standards. But demand for Soviet manufactured goods in the West is unlikely to increase anytime soon. So for the immediate future, to generate the hard currency needed to pay for Western imports, Gorbachev must rely heavily on the Soviet Union's more traditional offerings: energy, gold, and weapons.

The Soviet Union's preeminence in selling energy-related commodities reflects its status as the world's largest producer of oil, some 12 million barrels a day. The country also sells large quantities of natural gas. The two products alone account for about 60 percent of Soviet total hard currency earnings. The Soviet Union could conceivably expand production and increase the volume of sales to the West, but, just when Gorbachev needs to earn all the hard currency he can, the Soviet oil industry has run into problems.

In 1984, for the first time since World War II, annual Soviet oil production declined, followed by another decline in 1985. There was a slight upturn in 1986, but according to a report by the energy expert Jonathan Stern, this was an aberration in the general trend. Stern predicts that Soviet oil production will decline slowly in the early 1990s and that it will fall steeply by the end of the decade. Oil exports to the West, which have averaged about 70 million tons a year during the 1980s, are likely to drop to around 40 million tons sometime in the mid-1990s and down to just 25 million tons by the year 2000, Stern says.[10]

The problem is that it is becoming more and more expensive to produce the oil. The oil fields close to the industrialized areas of the Soviet Union are being rapidly depleted. Thus, Soviet oil must come increasingly from the desolate areas of Siberia and elsewhere, where the costs of extraction are much higher. Poorly built roads make it difficult to transport equipment and personnel to outlying regions; it is also harder to get the oil to refineries for processing. There is a lack of skilled labor in those areas as well, hence it must be brought in at additional expense. Finally, poor planning decisions out of Moscow and inefficient management in general have not helped.

Reduced production and sales to the West could be more than offset if the price of oil were to go up. Selling less oil at a higher price would be very nice indeed. But during Gorbachev's tenure, just the opposite has happened. Starting in 1985, there was a steady decline in the world price of oil, and in 1986 a dramatic collapse occurred. During a period of four months, the price fell from about $30 a barrel (in November 1985) to less than $15 a barrel (in March 1986). The price of oil began to move up some in 1987, but in May 1988 it was back to about $16 a barrel, scarcely more than half of what it was in November 1985.

That was a severe blow to the Soviet Union. The exchange rate also worked against Moscow. Oil, as a world commodity, is priced in U.S. dollars. As the price of oil dropped, the U.S. dollar was similarly depreciating against the currencies of Western Europe and Japan. Except for grain purchases, the Soviet Union does most of its shopping in West Germany, Japan, France, and Italy, so the dollar's decline further dampened the purchasing power of Soviet oil in the West.

The Soviet Union is accustomed to running a surplus in its foreign trade dealings, selling more to the West than it buys. In the early 1980s the Soviet Union maintained an annual hard currency trade surplus of more than $4 billion, according to CIA statistics.[11] But as Soviet oil exports declined, the surplus shrank to $534 million in 1985. When the price of oil dropped precipitously the following year, Moscow moved quickly to salvage its trade account. In 1986, by canceling orders and slashing imports, the Soviet Union pushed its trade surplus back over $2 billion.

But cutting back imports from the West is just the opposite of what Gorbachev now wants to do. To counteract the lower price of oil, the Soviets could increase the volume of exports to the West. With the rising domestic cost of producing oil, however, this is not an attractive option. Another way to sell more to the West would be to use energy more prudently in the Soviet Union; much is simply wasted through inefficient domestic consumption. In fact, as a proportion of GNP, the Soviet Union's use of energy is about 2.5 times higher than the average for European Community countries.

Increased energy efficiency is required, and Gorbachev makes clear to his fellow countrymen that supplies of oil and gas are no longer so plentiful and easily accessible. In 1985, he explained, the cost of extracting Soviet oil had risen by 70 percent in ten years.[12] But reducing waste and conserving domestic energy supplies are long-term projects involving fundamental changes in attitudes and industrial design. They offer no near-term way for Gorbachev to earn hard currency by selling more energy to the West.

Another option, one that would produce quicker results, is to cut back on the oil supplied by the Soviet Union to its allies in Eastern Europe. Moscow has already made it more expensive for them to pay for Soviet energy; the price charged is based on a five-year running average, which means that as the world price drops, a premium is paid to Moscow. Obviously, though, there are substantial political risks in pressing Eastern Europe too hard. Drastic economic austerity spawns political resentment and social protest.

The bottom-line conclusion for the Soviet Union is that unless the price of oil increases substantially on world markets, Moscow will have to deal with reduced hard currency earnings from its primary export to the West. Therefore, if the level of Western imports is to be raised without building up a trade deficit, Moscow will have to sell other products in higher quantities to make up for the difference in lost oil revenues and to expand total Soviet purchasing power in the West.

The most obvious alternative, rarely mentioned in Moscow, is to sell gold. The Soviets seem to attribute near-mythical qualities to their gold holdings, and selling it to the West is viewed as akin to having to part with the family jewels. Yet after oil earnings began to decline in 1985, Moscow did resort to selling increased quantities of gold to hard currency purchasers. Gold sales, which averaged less than 100 tons a year from 1982 to 1984, doubled to 200 tons in 1985 and tripled to 300 tons in 1986.[13] Not that the Soviet Union was in any danger of exhausting its domestic supply. Though Moscow remains secretive about the value of its gold hoard, it is estimated by the CIA to be worth nearly $34 billion at $450 per ounce.[14]

Even with its vast holdings and production capacity, the Soviet Union is still only the world's second largest producer of gold. South Africa remains the leader, mining about 600 tons a year. If Moscow had hoped to obtain the maximum amount of hard currency from its gold reserves, its plans were thwarted by South Africa's own compelling need to sell gold on world markets. Besieged with political turmoil and economic disruption, South Africa has been forced to attempt to replace the capital being withdrawn by West European and U.S. companies with additional sources of revenue, and gold is the one most easily transformed into cash.

The Soviets are astute commodity traders in international markets, fully understanding the relationship between supply and demand when it affects world prices for Soviet exports. With occasional exceptions prompted by necessity, they avoid dumping practices that end up being financially self-defeating. During a six-month period in 1984, the Soviets sold twice their normal amount of cut and polished gem diamonds. That prompted outcries from dealers in Antwerp, who accused the Soviets of flooding the market, upsetting the normal equilibrium, and launching a depression in the price of diamonds. Shortly afterward, the Soviets eased their sales.[15]

Besides selling oil and gold, both of which are subject to fluctuating world supplies and prices, the Soviets have one other major export to offer to outside buyers: weapons. Indeed, military-related products are virtually the only manufactured goods from the Soviet Union for which much global demand exists. The problem, however, is that the best clients for Soviet weaponry are countries that have also been hit by the declining price of oil, such as Iraq and Syria, and thus have fewer revenues themselves for purchasing luxury military goods.

Because Soviet clients in the Middle East are scrambling to obtain sufficient dollars to cover their own purchases from the West, they do not have extra cash to pay for Soviet weapons. In the past, Moscow has been willing to sell weapons to Third World clients on credit. Iraq, for example, had long been a dependable customer, always paying with cash derived from oil revenues. But as its war with Iran has dragged on, it has gone further into debt to the Soviet Union. According to CIA analysts, Iraq has received at least $1.5 billion in credits from the Soviet Union in recent years.[16]

Providing credits to deficit-ridden sovereign borrowers is hardly something the Soviet Union wants to do these days. With economic and financial pressures threatening to overwhelm the fledgling reforms of perestroika, the objective is to draw in financial capital, not dispense it. The big question for Moscow—the one that commands Gorbachev's full attention—is how much the Soviet Union itself can borrow.

Going into Debt

The fall in the price of oil and the reduced demand for weapons from oil-producing Third World countries could not have come at a worse time for Gorbachev. Even as Konstantin Chernenko was going through the motions of leading the country, Gorbachev was probably already concentrating on the problems of the internal budget and developing his basic ideas for perestroika. He seems to have been the first high-ranking Soviet official to pierce the veil on the budget statistics submitted by the Central Statistical Administration. He was also the first, apparently, to demand an explanation about the phantom revenues. And then, on learning that a significant portion of the funds flowing back to the Soviet government were merely paper entries extended by Gosbank, he quickly realized that much of the country was running on empty.

Gorbachev intends, of course, to change that. The next few years, however, are critical, and there is no substitute for high-quality consumer goods and state-of-the-art technology. Access to both can make the difference in perestroika's outcome. In other words, Gorbachev knows what he wants and where to get it. *How* to get it is the more complicated question.

Western producers generally insist on being paid for what they sell. It pains the Soviet Union to give up finite national resources at bargain-basement prices, but these are desperate times, and the Soviet economy is engaged in a make-or-break struggle. Gorbachev will go ahead with maximum sales of oil and gold, subject to the prudent judgment of his market traders, to increase the amount of hard currency available to the Soviet Union. But that will not be enough. The only way Gorbachev can get the money to pay for the needed imports is *to borrow it from the West.*

Borrowing is not a happy option for Gorbachev, merely an expedient one. The Soviet Union's history is fraught with images of Lenin and his followers fighting to release the nation from the grip of outside investors. Foreign outside bankers were always portrayed as partners of the Tsar, sharing a mutual evil intent to exploit mankind for imperialistic purposes. Never is there mention of the role of outsiders in financing such projects as the Trans-Siberian railroad in the 1890s or in providing the resources to supply Russian troops in their battle against the Japanese a decade later. True, the foreigners did have a vested interest in the continued reign of the Tsar; it was his government that was supplying the guarantees behind the billions in loans that were being funded by outsiders. But there was no denying that much of the money was being used to expand the economic capacity of Russia itself.

The activists of the Bolshevik movement never saw it that way. To them, anything that helped the Tsar—including the investment decision by a foreigner to buy Russian bonds—was an act of aggression against the people. The day after Lenin came to power in 1917, he sent a contingent of armed revolutionaries to occupy the tsarist state bank in Petrograd. Not long after, the shares of foreign investors in Russian banks were simply canceled. Commercial banks were then merged into the existing state bank, and the resulting mammoth organization was christened *Narodny Bank* (People's Bank). Within four years, the Peoples' Bank would be liquidated, only to reemerge under its earlier name, Gosbank (state bank), and made an arm of the new Soviet government.

In the meantime, the takeover by Lenin and the subsequent expropriation of foreign financial interests devastated investors in Western Europe. France was especially hard hit; more than one-quarter of total French foreign investment had been sunk into Russia.[17] But it was not just the private investors who were victimized. While Lenin was calculating how to wrest control away from the provisional government, the rest of Russia, as well as England, France and the United States, was engaged in a war with Germany. Western governments were supplying Russia not only with manpower but with loans to purchase armaments and supplies to fight Germany.

For Lenin, World War I was merely the backdrop for the more important task of establishing a Soviet government. In some ways, the confusion fostered by the war helped, having created the circumstances that gave Lenin his opportunity to seize power. But once he had established himself as the new leader of the country, he had little use for outside support. Foreign loans to finance the war were then dismissed as easily as the claims of private investors. Lenin seemed to feel that he could burn Russia's bridges with outside investors and never give a thought to what it might mean to the Soviet Union in the future.

But did the Bolshevik accession to power mean that the old country no longer existed? Did the birth of the Soviet Union symbolize the death of Russia? To this day the Soviets have yet to fully make peace with their Russian heritage by paying off tsarist debts. If many private investors in the West jeer at the thought of granting loans to the Soviet government, it is perhaps because it has not been that long since Lenin denounced foreign financial claims as contrary to socialist doctrine and thus invalid. So like confederate money, Russian bonds became novelty items. For the many private investors who bought them in good faith, the Soviets blatantly violated the rules of international finance.

Foreign governments were likewise burned for assuming the inviolability of sovereign obligation. Over the course of any country's development, the structure of government may change. New ideas, new social movements, new leaders and administrations come and go. This is to be expected. But the country itself continues to exist. So when a new government replaces the existing government, it must be prepared to take on the sovereign debts incurred under prior regimes. International law is clear on this point, stipulating in absolute terms that, whether a change in government springs from internal revolution or from invasion by an outside conqueror, the new government is legally responsible for the country's outstanding debts. Like the rules of war, the rules of sovereign borrowing are unaffectedly civilized.

Fifteen years after the Soviet coup, Britain, the United States, and several other Western countries were still wondering when the Soviet Union would get around to acknowledging Russia's financial obligations to private foreign investors as well as governments. For the international financial community, the Soviet Union was in default. Britain went so far as to apply liens against Russian assets in London, which the Soviets would claim legally belonged to them. Again, the indefensible Soviet position: It was the rightful heir to all the wealth formerly belonging to Russia and the Tsar, but had no responsibility to compensate other legitimate claimants to that wealth.

If spurned creditors could not recover, they could at least make sure that the debtor nation would never again be in a position to renege on financial obligations to Western lenders. A number of countries, including the United States, established laws during the 1930s that made it illegal for private citizens to lend money to governments already in default on past loans. Because of its outstanding obligations to the U.S. government from World War I, the Soviet Union was barred under the Johnson Debt Default Act from selling sovereign bonds to U.S. citizens.

That did not prevent the U.S. government itself from extending loans to the Soviet Union a decade later under the Lend-Lease program during World War II. But it did not help Moscow's image as a borrower when it decided not to pay back those loans either, this time on the grounds that the United States and the Soviet Union had been fighting the same enemy. The Soviet Union contended that the suffering it endured at the hands of the Germans should mitigate its financial obligations to the United States.

After the war, the temporary alliance that had sprung up between the two countries gave way to mutual suspicion and distrust. In the mid-1940s, as representatives from all over the world worked together to structure the postwar international monetary system and establish a new foundation for expanded trade relationships, the Soviets turned their back on an invitation to be a major global financial player. Stalin had put in a request for yet another loan from the U.S. government. When it was turned down, the Soviets reacted by walking away from IMF and World Bank membership in a huff.

If the Soviet Union did not want to participate in a global financial system, the United States was happy to exclude it. Indeed, some U.S. politicians wanted to curtail what limited trade there was between the two countries, especially the sale of technologically advanced equipment. During the 1950s the Soviet Union became so concerned that the United States might freeze Soviet hard currency deposits that it kept all its U.S. dollars outside U.S. borders, reputedly giving birth to the Eurodollar market. The message was clear: Direct financial dealings between the two global rivals would be kept to a minimum. The Cold War was in full swing.

Things began to shift quietly the other way sometime during the 1960s. After the Cuban missile crisis, a few private efforts were made to establish economic and financial relations. In 1964 David Rockefeller, head of Chase Manhattan Bank, traveled to the Soviet Union to meet with Khrushchev; soon after, Chase Manhattan opened a representative office in Moscow. If U.S. businessmen and bankers were willing to forget the bad experiences of the past, the U.S. government might be willing to do the same. By 1971 President Richard Nixon himself would be extolling the benefits of détente.

Official encouragement seemed to be all Western bankers and businessmen were waiting for, because the Soviet Union, indeed, all of Eastern Europe, was being portrayed as one vast market opportunity. Bankers moved en masse to supply the Soviet bloc with the resources to carry out its hard currency transactions with the West. Entire factories were designed by Western engineers, constructed with Western-supplied materials and equipment, and financed by Western banks for sale to the Soviet Union and Eastern Europe. During the early 1970s, the total debt of the Soviet bloc grew rapidly. Bankers seemed to find mutual reinforcement in the fact that so many of them were involved in East European lending. There was a general belief, too, that the Soviet Union would ultimately cover the debts of any of its allies in Eastern Europe—a presumption Moscow did nothing to discourage.

The frenzy to make loans and do business with the Soviet bloc began to dissipate sometime after the mid-1970s. North Korea's default served to remind lenders that capitalist countries could run into problems when they tried to collect from communist ones. Poland was getting into financial trouble, too, with no hint of a bailout from Moscow: The "umbrella theory" turned sour among bankers. Meanwhile, the political climate was changing back home and Western bankers began pulling out of the area. By the end of the decade, relations had deteriorated to the point where détente was being decried as a scam to dupe the West into giving away technology and credits to Moscow. The Soviet invasion of Afghanistan in 1979 was the clincher.

The Soviets, for their part, were equally dismayed at the turn of events that had led to a broadening of economic and financial relations with the West, only to be followed by rapid withdrawal. Conservative voices in the Politburo issued I-told-you-so advice about relying on outside assistance. Anticipating a rebuff in the international credit markets, the Soviet Union saved face by staying away from them as much as possible. Western bankers had turned their attention to Latin America, in the meantime, and were already preoccupied with a new set of worries. For the five years following the Afghanistan invasion, the Soviet Union chose to sit on the sidelines, observing the interplay of high politics and high finance around the world.

If a more conservative leader had come to power in the Soviet Union, someone who was content to tolerate the decline in the internal economy, the U.S.S.R. might still be sitting on the credit sidelines. If the value of Soviet oil had gone up rather than down on world markets, Moscow might have been able to continue on its preferred path of shunning outside foreign investment. But with the requirements of perestroika coming up hard against internal economic limitations and financial dysfunction, and with the hard currency value of Soviet exports caught in the throes of unforeseen market forces, Gorbachev is too much of a pragmatist to resist borrowing Western capital.

In a speech on economic progress and planning delivered in June 1985, the newly installed Soviet leader made the obligatory remarks about avoiding economic reliance on the West:

> . . . [T]he need to accelerate our development is dictated by the need to ensure the Soviet state's complete economic independence of the capitalist countries. . . . [W]e cannot permit our country to depend upon deliveries from the West.[18]

But even as he was warning against the evils of Western economic and financial assistance, Gorbachev was directing a stepped-up campaign to obtain record levels of commercial loans through Soviet solicitations in Western financial markets.

Global Staging

Gorbachev must, in effect, pacify his critics on both the internal and external fronts. Periodic references to the mistakes of détente help to stave off potential interference from fellow party members. But we must remember that one of the fundamental goals of perestroika is to bring in foreign capital and technology. That even means allowing outside investors to exploit Soviet resources and manpower through joint ventures, which is not exactly in keeping with socialist doctrine and long-held Soviet preferences. This aspect of perestroika has been promoted as delicately as the concepts of bankruptcy and unemployment. Gorbachev's problems at home clearly require careful handling, but so far his proposals for joint ventures have met with grudging approval.

The larger task of convincing the outside world that it should invest in the Soviet Union requires even more elaborate and comprehensive efforts. After deciding to accelerate Soviet borrowing from Western commercial banks, Gorbachev's first problem was how to move fast enough to procure loans before the creditworthiness of the Soviet Union was called into question by the falling value of its main source of collateral: oil. That proved to be relatively easy. Having notoriously short memories, bankers exhibit a tendency to converge on a region, flood it with credits until it becomes saturated, attempt to wring some liquidity out of it, and then withdraw to a new area. When the Soviet Union suddenly began applying for syndicated commercial bank loans in late 1984, bankers saw it as a new opportunity, a fresh address in the international credit markets. Soviet requests for funds were oversubscribed by a horde of enthusiastic Western bankers.

However, shortly after the Soviet Union began to be ranked in the international country risk guides used by bankers to evaluate sovereign creditworthiness, the rating began to slip. The more risky the loan, the higher the interest rate charged. The Soviet Union has always worried about paying too high an interest rate on its loans from the West, lest it be perceived as being in the same category as Third World borrowers. So for the sake of pride and preserving appearances, the Soviets have been willing to pay up-front fees and points in exchange for a lower rate of interest. As a result, the total return on the loan is unaffected, and bankers are generally only too happy to pick up fees in advance. The important thing for the Soviets is that the published rate of interest on the loan suggests that their country belongs within the elite group of low-risk borrowers.

Gorbachev knew that the Soviet Union could not continue to obtain credits indefinitely through syndicated bank loans with-

out being subjected to higher and higher borrowing costs. It was
therefore important to move on other fronts as well, to expand
the array of borrowing opportunities available. The most logical
course was to pursue the perfect complement to private banking:
government-granted credits. Western governments were already
providing billions in subsidized loans to the Soviet Union for the
stated purpose of promoting domestic exports. The unstated reason was to stay on the good side of Moscow. Gorbachev was
ready to exploit either motive.

He quickly moved to arrange high-level meetings with officials
from those countries that had the most to offer the Soviet Union
in the way of consumer goods and technology, and who could
likewise be coerced to provide the credits to pay for Soviet purchases. Gorbachev met personally with a number of West European heads of state. He sent his deputy, Shevardnadze, to meet
with the Japanese foreign minister and to hint that long-sought-
after political concessions might be possible to arrange. Since the
end of World War II, the Soviets have held four Japanese islands,
part of the southern Kuriles, which the Japanese insist rightfully
belong to them. For the Soviets, the islands have geographic and
military significance. For the Japanese, the attachment is more
emotional, because Japanese soldiers are buried there.

Herein lie the makings of an extremely satisfying deal between
Japan and the Soviet Union, if Gorbachev plays his hand skill-
fully. The Soviet Union has vast undeveloped resources and is
desperately in need of financial capital and technical know-how.
And this is precisely what the Japanese have in abundance. Indeed, all Japan lacks are natural resources and land. The economic and financial fit between the two countries is perfect and
holds out synergistic benefits for both sides—if only the political
resentments can be cooled. Gorbachev is clearly thinking along
those lines himself; he has made it known that he might follow
up Shevardnadze's trip with a personal visit to Tokyo.

But even as Gorbachev attempts to forge closer ties with individual Western countries, he knows that nothing significant can
change in the fundamental nature of the relationship between
East and West unless the United States implicitly grants its approval. Individual countries may be willing to suffer U.S. disapproval from time to time for issuing excessive amounts of credits
or for being lax about sales of restricted technology to the Soviets, but they do not want to risk full-scale alienation from
Washington just for the sake of transacting a little business with

Moscow. Witness the furor over Toshiba's transgression in allowing sensitive submarine technology to fall into Soviet hands, and Japan's subsequent pleas for absolution.

To keep the imports flowing from the West—indeed, to lay the groundwork for a much higher level of assistance—what Gorbachev needs to do is enlist the United States directly in the cause of bailing out the Soviet economy. Reducing the level of perceived military tensions is a prerequisite for fostering the kind of political atmosphere needed to persuade U.S. businessmen and bankers to furnish vast quantities of consumer goods and technology to Moscow on credit. Ideally, Gorbachev would like to induce the U.S. government itself to grant most-favored-nation trade status to the Soviet Union, and make it eligible for loans from the U.S. Export-Import Bank. At the very least, Gorbachev hopes to dissuade U.S. officials from imposing restrictions on financial institutions that would make bankers leery about lending to the Soviet Union.

The trick is to avoid publicizing the fungibility aspect of capital. Gorbachev wants to promote the idea that the Soviet Union is merely trying to preserve the stability of its economy for the benefit of its people. There are veiled hints that if perestroika does not succeed, the United States may find itself forced to deal with a more sinister, less visionary Soviet leader who might well revert to old patterns of hostility toward the West. Gorbachev well understands that the United States must regard a positive response to requests to help salvage the Soviet economy as being in its own interests. Given the capitalistic flavor of perestroika, the prospect of helping Gorbachev is not necessarily distasteful to Americans. If loans are packaged more or less as humanitarian aid to help raise the Soviet standard of living, they can be made downright palatable.

Of course, capital is fungible. Funds can be used to produce washing machines, run prison camps, or build nuclear warheads. In other words, when goods are manufactured outside the Soviet Union, paid for with Western credits, and then imported for use in the internal Soviet economy, they permit scarce Soviet resources to be deployed elsewhere. It makes little difference what the specific imported goods are, so long as they meet some aspect of Soviet internal economic needs as defined by preset plans for budgetary outlays. The goal is to ration Soviet domestic expenditures as carefully as possible. Imports from the West, financed by the suppliers, constitute a direct savings to the Soviet government.

For that matter, joint ventures with Western firms to produce high-quality consumer goods in the Soviet Union are the culmination of what Gorbachev seeks to achieve with the West: access to the technology and the goods themselves without having to go into debt to obtain the hard currency to pay for them—without having to give up Soviet oil or gold. Even in the event of a subsequent deterioration in East–West political relations, there is little risk; the joint ventures are effectively held captive in the Soviet Union. Gorbachev has ensured, through Soviet laws governing joint ventures, that Moscow will always be the majority shareholder.

In all respects, Gorbachev is proving to be a competent stage manager. He still needs to convince the West that, in seeking consumer goods and technology, Soviet intentions are strictly honorable, and he must obscure the fact that strengthening the Soviet economy means fortifying its military might. In general he must continue to win over the American people and their political leaders to the objectives of perestroika and must enlist their cooperation in helping the Soviet Union through its difficult period of transition. While working on Western political sentiment, he must also keep moving his country toward a more flexible borrowing position by entering new markets and knocking down long-established barriers against Soviet participation in the world of high finance.

Most of all, Gorbachev needs to make people forget. They must forget about what happened to foreign investors after Lenin seized power, about the Soviet government's welshing on wartime loans, and about the time the Soviets walked out on the IMF and the World Bank to set up a rival group. He needs to make them forget that governments sometimes default on their loans. He needs to make them forget also that the Soviet Union is picking up bills for Nicaragua and Cuba. And finally, he needs to make them forget where Soviet missiles are aimed.

How Moscow Acquires
Outside Financing

5

The Role of Banks

"**I**f a representative from the Soviet Union asked to borrow
$200 million on behalf of his government, would you lend him
the money?" That question was posed to a number of U.S. banks
in late 1984, and the range of answers given helps us understand
the complicated connection between high finance and high politics. The responses, which were published in the *Wall Street Journal*, ranged from pure profit motive to consideration of social
implications.[1] One executive vice president answered candidly
that, if a loan to the Soviet Union could satisfy the bank's 1-
percent-after-taxes test for profitability, "we might very well be
interested in making it." Another banker offered the more
guarded observation that, if the purpose of the loan were con-
structive and if it suited the bank's portfolio mix and its level of
exposure in that area, "we might look at it." A third banker vo-
lunteered that his institution had recently adopted the policy of
refusing loans to South Africa because apartheid was practiced
there. What about loans to the Soviet Union? The bank's spokesman couldn't answer that question. "It depends on a lot," he
said.

One thing it does not depend on is permission from the U.S.
government. There are no automatic restrictions against extend-

ing loans to the Soviet Union, no sanctions that prohibit U.S. banks from trading with the enemy, so to speak, in the sense of making capital available. Member banks of the Federal Reserve system are subject to regulatory guidelines that limit the percentage of a bank's equity that can be loaned to any one customer. In other words, they cannot exceed the "10 percent rule." Nor can they provide loans explicitly to finance the sale of restricted goods such as high-technology equipment or sophisticated weaponry, but this is not so much a financial restriction as a COCOM (technology transfer) rule. U.S. banks are permitted to furnish untied credits not connected with a particular trade transaction, the funds from which may be used for whatever purpose needed by the Soviets, as long as it is done through a foreign branch. Banks are prohibited by the foreign assets control division of the U.S. Treasury Department from making loans to certain countries, but the Soviet Union is not one of them. (They are South Africa, Panama, Iran, Libya, Nicaragua, Cuba, Vietnam, North Korea, and Cambodia.)

When the Soviet Union suddenly began to borrow heavily through Western financial markets, U.S. banks were at first hesitant to participate. One U.S. banker in Europe was quoted in the financial press as stating that "no self-respecting chairman of an American bank wants to be labeled pinko."[2] It was also true that early Soviet loans were not especially profitable, because Soviet officials were successful in obtaining low rates of interest in keeping with their own perceptions about the inherent credit-worthiness of a global superpower. Oil prices were strong. U.S. banks expressed interest in a $250-million borrowing organized by Dresdner Bank International, co-managed by Lloyds Bank International of London and Credit Agricole of Paris, which was being syndicated to thirty other Western banks in May 1984. Ultimately, though, they decided not to take part.[3]

In early 1985 the U.S.S.R. Bank for Foreign Trade, Vneshtorgbank, was paying about 1/2 percent over the international prime rate (London Interbank Offered Rate, or LIBOR) on medium-term loans granted mostly by banks in West Germany, Luxembourg, Britain, France, and Japan. Including management fees and up-front charges, and relative to other lending opportunities, the Soviet loans were seen as rather lucrative ventures for commercial banks. U.S. banks began to get edgy about waiting on the sidelines while their counterparts in Western Europe and Japan made profitable deals on Soviet credits. By mid-year, they were leaping into the fray and contributing to the competitive pressures that were driving down interest rates on Soviet loans. At the end of June 1985, the level of credits to the Soviet Union from U.S. banks stood at $257 million, an 80 percent increase over six months earlier.

U.S. banks had managed to overcome their initial hesitation. Still, First National Bank of Chicago made what was considered a rather bold move in July 1985 when it announced it would be a lead manager on a $200 million loan to the Soviet Union. That was the first time a U.S. bank had publicly managed a syndicated loan on behalf of the Soviets since 1979. The purpose of the loan was unspecific, simply an eight-year credit for general Soviet trade financing. A few months later, First Chicago participated in a second syndication led by the Royal Bank of Canada, for a $200-million credit line to finance Soviet purchases of U.S. and Canadian grain. Three New York banks—Bankers Trust, Morgan Guaranty, and Irving Trust—also took part in the loan. If there were any worries about being labeled "pinko," they were apparently offset by the prospect of making collectible loans. American bankers were reportedly eager to do business with the Kremlin because, unlike Latin American borrowers, the Soviets had a reputation for making debt payments promptly.[4]

A Business Decision

It is not surprising that bankers focus on profitability and credit risk when assessing loans to the Soviets. Indeed, it is a bit disconcerting to hear a bank official say that, by making credit available to the Soviet Union, his bank is somehow contributing to positive superpower relations or supporting the U.S. economy. Yet that is precisely the rationale offered by First Chicago after it put together a syndicate for the Soviet Union: By helping the Soviets, the bank was ultimately helping American farmers and tractor manufacturers, because the Soviet Union might decide to use some of the money to buy U.S. goods. Testifying before the Senate Banking Committee in September 1985, the chief financial officer of First Chicago, William McDonough, went so far as to suggest that legislation aimed at curtailing Soviet loans "might undermine the efforts of the President to enhance our security by expanding peaceful trade with the U.S.S.R."[5]

Bankers would seem to be on more solid ground when they

justify Soviet loans using financial ratios and credit rankings. The criteria used to analyze how reliable foreign borrowers are involves making predictions about the political future of various governments and the likelihood of external conflict or internal revolution. The stability of a government counts for a lot in determining overall creditworthiness. So does a country's past performance in paying back its debts. It is difficult, of course, to attach a precise measurement to matters such as the level of corruption within a government or its tendency to expropriate private investments. But bankers are in the business of quantifying risk, of gauging creditworthiness on the basis of the borrower's "character," as well as financial resources. By assigning numbers to various factors affecting a borrowing country's ability and inclination to repay, by calculating its credit ranking on the basis of some composite measure of risk, it is possible to come up with a quantitative guide for evaluating and ranking sovereign borrowers on a purely numerical basis.

One such guide for bankers is published by International Reports, Inc., a subsidiary of the prestigious *Financial Times* newspaper organization in London. Monthly issues of the International Country Risk Guide (ICRG) include a statistical section wherein some 130 countries are ranked in descending order as borrowers. In September 1986, for example, the country borrower with which the least risk was associated was Switzerland. The country with the highest risk, the least attractive borrower among the 130 countries ranked, was Nicaragua. The use of the term "attractive" does not mean that lenders would necessarily choose to make loans only to countries near the top of the list. The real criterion for making a profitable loan is the optimal risk/return ratio; the point is to receive the highest possible interest rate at an acceptable risk level. If a bank offered credit only to countries ranked as low risk, it might not get a sufficient interest rate spread to justify its existence. The point of using a country risk guide is to measure the potential return from a loan relative to the risk inherent in that loan. The guide evaluates sovereign risk and makes a quantitative assessment about the creditworthiness of individual country borrowers; it is then up to the banker to decide if the rate of interest he can charge that country is worth the risk.

For the armchair observer of world events, it perhaps seems odd to attach a number to sovereign risk. How can one quantify risk, for example, as a function of "Organized Religion in Politics" or "Quality of the Bureaucracy"? But under the ICRG rating system, those two and eleven other factors contribute to an overall score for political risk. There are also separate scores to define a country's economic risk (based on six factors) and its financial risk (based on five factors). Combining political, economic, and financial risk produces an overall score, called composite risk, which determines where a country ranks on the global scoreboard of borrowers.

The Soviet Union ranked no. 31 in composite risk among the 130 countries listed by the ICRG in the September 1986 edition. For comparison's sake, the United States ranked no. 6, and Japan, no. 2. Flanking the Soviet Union on either side were Gabon and the People's Republic of China. To understand how the overall Soviet score was derived by risk analysts, let's look at the separate calculations made for political, economic, and financial risk. Under the first, the Soviet Union scored fairly high in its capacity to avoid "External Conflict Risk" and its ability to control "Organized Religion in Politics." It also scored very well for not being subject to "Political Terrorism" or "Civil War Risks." It did not do so well in "Economic Expectations versus Reality" and "Economic Planning Failures." Out of a total possible score of 100 points (which would mean the least risky) the Soviet Union received 65 points for political risk, which tied it with Botswana and Costa Rica.

Under economic risk, the Soviet Union scored very well on "Current Account as Percent of Exports of Goods and Services" and about average on "Foreign Debt Service as Percent of Exports of Goods and Services." It got zero points for having a "Parallel Foreign Exchange Market Indicator," presumably because the ruble is not convertible. Where scores were meant to measure "Inflation" and "International Liquidity" for the Soviet Union, the entries were simply marked "not available." In all, a total score of 31.5 out of 50 was awarded for economic risk. We must note, however, that the Soviet score for economic risk was averaged with two out of six factors shown as not available. The Soviets incurred no apparent penalty in their score for refusing to furnish the information to creditors.

Finally, under financial risk, the Soviet Union scored extremely well on "Expropriation," basically because outside investment was not allowed at the time and foreign private interests thus were not subject to that hazard. The Soviets received lower scores for "Delayed Payment of Suppliers' Credits" and for "Repudiation of Contracts by Governments." The overall financial risk score was 36 out of a possible 50.

By the numbers, then, bankers had as much justification in September 1986 for extending credits to the Soviet Union as to many other sovereign debtors rated by the same scale. More so, in some cases. Mexico, Brazil, and Venezuela were ranked much further down than the Soviet Union for total risk. Yet commercial banks in the United States, Western Europe, and Japan were being exhorted by U.S. Treasury Secretary James Baker to continue lending to Latin American debtors to comply with the "Baker Plan" introduced a year earlier at the annual IMF/World Bank meetings in Seoul. Under the plan, substantial new credits were to flow to the fifteen most troubled debtors between 1986 and 1988; most of the money was to come from the World Bank and private commercial banks. But profit-minded bankers were inclined to do just the opposite, to refuse new credits to troubled debtors and look for markets elsewhere. The last thing their portfolios needed, from a business point of view, was more loans to risky borrowers at low rates. No wonder commercial Western banks clamored to participate in loans to the Soviet Union, a fresh face on the international credit markets in 1985 and 1986.

In March 1987 First Chicago took a lead position once again on a $200 million syndicated loan to the Soviet Union. The loan was obtained by the U.S.S.R. Bank for Foreign Trade (now called the Bank for Foreign Economic Affairs) and priced at a mere 1/8 percent above LIBOR. With the interest rate set so low, banking sources speculated that it would be hard for banks to make any profit on the loan. But First Chicago reportedly received a substantial fee for acting as agent on the loan; according to a Chicago securities firm analyst, the bank picked up as much as $1 million in accordance with the standard fee of 0.2 percent to 0.5 percent for such services.[6] A spokesman for First Chicago explained that the purpose of the loan was "fostering civil exports," but he admitted that the funds could theoretically be used for anything, because the loan was not tied to a specific purpose.[7] A few months earlier, two French banks had put together syndicated loans to the Soviet Union carrying similar terms. The Banque Nationale de Paris set up a $300 million loan to the Soviets for eight years at the same low 1/8 over LIBOR rate, and Credit Lyonnais arranged for a $100 million loan to Moscow.[8]

The willingness of other banks in Western Europe and Japan to make loans to the Soviet Union is often cited by U.S. bankers as reason enough to allow American banks to extend credits without restrictions. An executive vice president of Citibank, George Clark, suggested in September 1985 that legislative attempts to control the activities of U.S. banks would be offset by the activities of foreign banks:

> In my judgment, restraints on the U.S. banks alone, in view of their relatively small share of the marketplace, will not significantly affect either the volume of hard currency available to the U.S.S.R. or the pricing of credits available to them.[9]

The point being made here is that total U.S. bank lending to the Soviet Union is so small as to be insignificant. Judged by the amounts recorded in the Country Exposure Lending Survey administered through the Federal Reserve, U.S. bank loans to the Soviet Union are quite small relative to total Soviet indebtedness to Western commercial banks, less than 2 percent. But this figure underrepresents the role of U.S. banks in making capital available to the Soviets. For one thing, the Fed statistics reflect the practice of selling off syndicated loans to other Western banks outside the United States. Thus, for example, even though First Chicago served as a lead manager on its July 1985 loan to the Soviet Union, more than twenty-seven banks from Finland, France, Japan, Jordan, and West Germany participated in the syndication. At the final signing, First Chicago held just 7 percent of the total loan, and this entire amount was raised in international markets, according to First Chicago's chief financial officer, with domestic American funds playing no role in the transaction.[10]

There is the fact, too, that loans from U.S. banks to Soviet-owned banks operating in the West are not counted as loans to the Soviet Union. Under the rules governing how banks fill out their quarterly Country Exposure Report to the Federal Reserve, risk exposure is based on the borrower's physical residence—that is, the country where it is located—unless the borrower is a branch of a banking organization headquartered in another country or unless there is an explicit guarantee coming from another country. Thus, loans from U.S. banks to Moscow Narodny Bank in London are reported, not as risk exposure to the Soviet Union, but as risk exposure to the United Kingdom. Likewise, loans from U.S. banks to the Soviet-owned bank in Paris, Banque Commerciale pour l'Europe du Nord, are counted as French exposure, and so on for Soviet-owned banks operating in

Frankfurt, Vienna, and Luxembourg. In every case, the banks are owned entirely by Soviet state interests but are incorporated as limited liability companies in the resident Western country.

The same rules apply to interbank deposits as well. Interbank deposits are the temporarily idle funds banks keep on deposit with one another to earn interest. According to Roger W. Robinson, Jr., former senior director for international economic affairs (1982–1985) at the National Security Council, "The Soviet Union and its network of wholly-owned subsidiary banks in the West have been major players in the interbank market for many years."[11] Robinson argues that Western interbank deposits serve as a sort of reserve checking account for the Soviets. He recommends that American and other Western commercial banks be requested to aggregate their interbank exposure to all Soviet-owned banking entities and periodically to report these aggregate exposures to their respective government regulatory agencies.[12]

That there exists some confusion over the reporting of interbank deposits is evident in the following exchange that took place in September 1985 when the then chairman of the Senate Banking Committee, Jake Garn (R—Utah), was questioning George Clark, Citibank's executive vice president, and William McDonough, First Chicago's executive vice president and chief financial officer:

> *Garn:* Mr. Clark, your bank operates branches and offices all over the world. Loans can be made from these—any of these branches, I assume. Trying to understand the extent of U.S. exposure in Soviet Bloc countries, aggregate figures are available for long-term and medium-term loans. Do those aggregates also adequately represent short-term loan exposures, such as trade credits and bankers acceptances?

> *Clark:* I don't know what data you have there, Senator Garn, but we do report to the U.S. Government our total exposure in all of these countries, including short-term. I notice the Polish Ambassador said that short-term was not in there. Our short-term is in there. And I don't know what your data has.

> *Garn:* Well, there's another form of exposure as well, and I'm referring to deposits of Western banks and Soviet-owned banks in the West, which are located in London and Paris and Vienna, Zurich and elsewhere. Examples are the Moscow Narodny Bank in

London, the Singapore Eurobank, and so on, various countries.
What is the extent of Citibank's current worldwide exposure in the
form of deposits in Soviet-owned banks?

Clark: Well, it happens to be zero. We don't have any. If we did
have placements with Moscow Narodny in London, it would
appear as part of our Soviet exposure, and we don't have any.

McDonough: We have the same methodology, Mr. Chairman, and
the number, i.e., zero.

Garn: But in any event, if you did, you are saying it would be
reported in the aggregate.

Clark: Yes, as Soviet exposure.[13]

The bank officers are perhaps referring to internal systems for
recording total Soviet exposure within their own banks since
U.S. bank claims on Soviet-owned banks operating in the West
are *not* reported to the Federal Reserve as Soviet exposure. It
may well be true that First Chicago and Citibank do not keep any
interbank deposits with Moscow Narodny. If they did, however,
it would not show up on the Country Exposure Lending Survey.
Interesting, though not necessarily damning, certainly, is the fact
that Moscow Narodny in recent years has listed the following
banks as its correspondents: BankAmerica International, New
York; Bankers Trust Company, New York; Chase Manhattan
Bank, N.A., New York; Chemical Bank, New York; Citibank,
N.A., New York; Irving Trust Company, New York; Manufac-
turers Hanover Trust Company, New York; Morgan Guaranty
Trust Company, New York; Banca Comerciale Italiana, New
York; and Mellon Bank International, New York.

For bankers, in short, extending loans to the Soviet Union
makes sense for several reasons. First and foremost, the Soviet
Union ranks as a better credit risk on a quantitative basis than
many other sovereign borrowers, particularly when compared
with Third World debtor nations. Second, the Soviets are willing
to pay generous up-front fees to banks that manage syndicates
on their behalf at low publicized interest rates. There is, of
course, the occasional legislative hearing and the potential for
bad publicity. But U.S. banks with foreign branches can make
the claim that the money raised was derived from foreign sources
and that exposure to the Soviet Union for U.S. banks is extremely
low.

Lessons from History

From the outside nothing looks unusual about the Moscow Narodny Bank in London. Indeed, the premises at 81 King William Street epitomize the image of traditional British banking: the solid stone walls and heavy glass doors in keeping with the appearance of the numerous other banks fronting the street. Just inside the door of Moscow Narodny, however, one encounters a guard sitting behind a console of closed-circuit television screens displaying various scenes of the interior and exterior of the bank. A request to see the bank's balance sheet—the sort of information that is routinely published in brochures and left lying on lobby counters in U.S. banks—prompts a phone call from the guard to one of the bank's officers, who in turn wants to know why an outsider is interested. A journalist's curiosity is the answer, and the request is granted. A dark-suited bank officer hand-delivers a copy of the bank's 1985 annual report in a manila envelope and quickly disappears.

The building at 81 King William Street has only recently become the headquarters for Moscow Narodny. After careful planning and renovation, the bank staff moved its operations to the address in August 1985 to fulfill management's desire to conduct sophisticated financial transactions in the most traditional of settings. According to an annual report, that has happened. "The building has come up to our full expectations in that it combines a modern interior behind a classical facade."[14] The location may be new, but the bank itself has existed since October 1919, when it was incorporated in London as a British registered company. Earlier it was an agency of the Moscow People's Bank, which was the central bank of the Russian cooperative movement. The banking cooperatives, set up before World War I, serviced thousands of farmers who maintained shareholder interests. The functions of the cooperatives were compatible with Bolshevik objectives, but they were controlled by rival socialist parties. When Lenin took over the tsarist banking system, he at first spared Moscow Narodny Bank from the nationalization to which all other commercial banks were forced to yield. But after attempting unsuccessfully for a year to wrest away leadership of the cooperative banking network, Lenin proceeded to merge Moscow Narodny into the new Soviet state-controlled bank.

Lenin had, of course, once dismissed global banks as parasites, the vehicles by which "a handful of exceptionally rich and power-

ful states plunder the whole world simply by clipping cou-
pons."[15] But he also appreciated that he could use the same power
over finance capital to advance his own causes. The new role he
envisioned for banking under socialism was not limited to the Soviet Union alone. Because communism was expected to become a
worldwide social movement and because the Soviets hoped
Western investors would support the legitimacy of the new government, there was an effort to extend the Soviet banking pres-
ence to other parts of the world. Moscow Narodny Bank opened
a branch in Paris in 1925, a branch in New York in 1926, and a
branch in Berlin in 1928. Following the Depression, however, the
Soviet government was forced to close them down. The Moscow
Narodny in London survived, we know, as did another bank in
Paris that was purchased separately by the Soviet government
in 1925. In fact, the Banque Commerciale pour l'Europe du Nord,
first organized by a group of Russian anticommunist emigres,
has now grown to become the largest of the Soviet-owned banks
operating in the West. Its cable address, "Eurobank," gives cre-
dence to the theory that this very bank started the Eurodollar
market in the 1950s by enabling communist governments to accumulate dollar deposits outside the supervision of U.S. banking
authorities.

During the 1960s and the 1970s the Soviets chartered additional banks in the West in Zürich (1966), Frankfurt (1971), Vienna (1974), and Luxembourg (1974) to carry out commercial
transactions with Western firms on behalf of the Soviet government. The Moscow Narodny Bank in London also maintains a
branch in Singapore opened in 1971. The Zürich bank was closed
in 1985 after the Soviets discovered they had suffered huge losses
due to unauthorized trades by the bank's chief gold dealer, a
Swiss national. The bank has subsequently been reopened as a
branch of the Soviet Bank for Foreign Economic Affairs. In general, all of the Soviet-owned banks in the West function on behalf
of the state-controlled banking system. According to O. Kuschpeta:

> By way of summary we can qualify the Soviet foreign banks as
> legally independent entities which are, in fact, instruments of the
> Soviet banking system destined to promote and develop trade with
> the modern capitalistic nations on the one hand and with the
> developing countries on the other. Besides trade they also operate
> on the world's currency and gold markets. By adapting the foreign

banking establishments to the national law of the host country, the U.S.S.R. has created the optimum conditions for its gold and currency transactions. On the other hand, these banks can act as scouts in international trade.[16]

Soviet eagerness in the 1960s and 1970s to expand the banking network beyond domestic borders coincided, of course, with détente and a new ideological flexibility on the part of Western businessmen and bankers. Rockefeller felt that communist clients were in some ways more reliable and consistent than many capitalist democracies. In terms of credit risk, they could point to a better record of continuity of government. Chase Manhattan's representative office in Moscow—the first to be opened by an American bank—was located at 1 Karl Marx Square.[17]

Rockefeller was not the only banker who saw potential in the communist bloc. Spurred by visions of extending credits to support sales by Western suppliers, who in turn bought into the vision of the Soviet bloc as an untapped market, Western banks began pouring money into Eastern Europe after 1970. The industrialized countries of Western Europe were experiencing slow growth following the first oil shock in 1973. So even though credit statistics on East European borrowers were in many cases nonexistent or blatantly false, the communist countries somehow held more appeal for bankers than the lackluster numbers produced by free world sovereign borrowers. Western bankers were especially enthusiastic about extending credits to Poland without even determining whether or not the country could actually afford to purchase all those expensive imports, including entire factories, from the West. An editorial in the *Wall Street Journal* observed:

> The banks asked Poland precious little about its economic health or how it expected to pay all the money back. Frugal middle-class Americans would have had to give more information to their friendly neighborhood banker to get a car loan than Poland gave to develop a country.[18]

Perhaps the reason bankers were not worried was that they felt the real debtor was not Poland but the Soviet Union. There was a matter of image involved. Bank analysts were quite sure that the Soviet Union would never permit anything that might hurt its reputation as a borrower, a sophisticated participant in world economic affairs. And it was assumed that same aversion to bad publicity would apply to subjugated Poland, as well as to all the other East European nations under the political and economic hegemony of the Soviet Union. The umbrella theory provided the underlying justification for the tremendous surge in loans to Eastern Europe during the 1970s. The net hard-currency debt (gross debt offset by deposits held in Western banks) of the Soviet Union and its six East European allies went from 7.0 billion in 1970 to 62.9 billion in 1980, which represented a ninefold increase in indebtedness to the West (see Table 5.1). Gross debt, the total amount borrowed by the Soviet Union and Eastern Europe, stood at $84 billion in 1980.[19] By comparison, Mexico's foreign debt in 1980 was $53 billion and Brazil's, $65 billion.[20]

By the late 1970s, Western bankers were beginning to realize that they had gone too far in making loans to Eastern Europe. The Soviet invasion of Afghanistan caused American banks to curtail their lending to Soviet bloc countries sharply, and West European bankers likewise started to slow down. Poland's debt suddenly began to loom as a potential financial disaster. Without new loans from the West, Poland could no longer make payments on its old loans. The brutal suppression of Polish Solidarity and the imposition of martial law by the Soviets in 1981 finally laid to bitter rest the umbrella theory that had sustained Western bankers for so many years. As Dale Delamaide observes in *Debt Shock*:

Once the Polish crisis broke, it was apparent to everyone that the short-term financial resources even of the Soviet Union were

TABLE 5.1. Net Hard-Currency Debt of the Soviet Union and Eastern Europe, 1970–80 (*in billions of U.S. dollars*)

	1970	1975	1980
Soviet Union	1.0	7.8	8.7
Eastern Europe			
Bulgaria	.7	2.1	2.5
Czechoslovakia	.6	1.2	3.4
East Germany	1.4	4.8	11.2
Hungary	.6	2.3	5.8
Poland	1.1	7.7	22.0
Romania	1.6	3.1	9.3
Total	7.0	29.0	62.9

SOURCE: Wharton Econometrics, *Centrally Planned Economies Outlook*, March 1983 and April 1985, cited in Benjamin J. Cohen, *In Whose Interest* (New Haven and London: Yale University Press, 1986), p. 181.

nowhere near equal to coping with the swollen payments requirements of Poland alone, let alone the entire bloc. In the past, the Soviet Union and its charges had been punctilious in all financial dealings with the West. Financial correctness was part of the credibility Moscow wanted to have vis-à-vis the West. What surprised Western bankers was the Kremlin's careful calculation that the banks' need for credibility would require action sooner than Moscow's.[21]

Political Ramifications

With Polish loans in trouble, bankers started to point fingers. Hadn't the U.S. government encouraged this sort of lending as part of its overall diplomatic strategy toward the Soviet bloc? Didn't détente mean the traffic light had been switched from red to green? Indeed, the Nixon–Brezhnev summit of 1972 had resulted in a joint U.S.–Soviet call for strengthening economic ties, and increased lending from American and other Western banks was surely an implicit part of the deal. Didn't that mean the U.S. government was under some obligation to help commercial banks, now that they found themselves in an untenable financial situation?

The government had not exactly twisted bankers' arms to get funds flowing to Eastern Europe. No specific directive was issued to U.S. banks to do what they did; they took the initiative themselves. Still, the lending did carry strong political overtones, especially the lending to Poland. Washington had earlier wanted to reward Polish efforts to promote political liberalization. There was a feeling that Poland could be weaned away from the Soviet Union through enhanced economic contacts with the West. After the events of 1981 and the installation of General Jaruzelski, however, the goal turned into the tricky task of punishing the governing regime without jeopardizing the fledgling Polish labor movement, and meanwhile trying to cajole nervous bankers anxious to mitigate anticipated losses. One observer has noted:

> Washington found its strategic interaction with the Polish authorities to be inescapably linked to a strategic interaction with its own financial institutions. Once again, officials had to find some way to balance the legitimate interests of both the banking community and U.S. foreign policy.[22]

While U.S. government officials tried to persuade bankers not to abandon Poland, they could not ask banks to compromise their business decisions. The U.S. government could, however, show good faith. So in 1982 our government paid off commercial banks on loans to Poland that had been guaranteed through the Commodity Credit Corporation of the Department of Agriculture. Normally commercial banks have to file a formal notification of default in order to collect on government-guaranteed loans, but the Reagan administration had quietly moved to waive the requirement to avoid triggering "cross-default" clauses on other loans to Poland.[23] In the end, commercial banks were bailed out by Western governments. Poland was never forced to acknowledge publicly that it had welshed on its debts, and the Soviets reimposed political control upon Poland without taking on its financial obligations.

That brings us to the question of the relationship between banking and government. Should the president of the United States be able to utilize private banks as instruments for carrying out foreign policy goals? Turning the question around, should U.S. banks be subject to restrictions and penalties for engaging in lending activities that are inconsistent with the stated diplomatic and strategic objectives of the administration or the perceived interests of the American citizenry? If a relationship does exist between the activities of bankers and the foreign policy interests of the U.S. government, how formal should that relationship be, and how should it be structured? To address the questions, Benjamin J. Cohen has said:

> With the growing internationalization and politicization of banking activity, financial decisions have come more and more to encroach on the traditional terrain of policymakers. When Americans were taken hostage in Iran in 1979, banking relationships turned out to be one of the key elements in their eventual release. When Poland suppressed the Solidarity trade union movement in 1981, Polish debt to Western banks seriously compromised U.S. efforts to retaliate with economic sanctions. And when bank loans in Latin America started to go bad in 1982, the U.S. government had to step in to keep the financial crisis from getting out of control. Today, high finance is much of what international diplomacy is all about.[24]

The idea that actions taken by private commercial banks can compromise or thwart the interests of the U.S. government is not, of course, new. In 1934 the U.S. Congress made it unlawful within the United States for any person to purchase or sell the bonds, securities, or other obligations of a foreign government, or to make any loan to a foreign government while that government "is in default in the payment of its obligations, or any part thereof, to the Government of the United States." Any person caught violating the provisions of the act remains subject to a $10,000 fine and/or imprisonment for up to five years. Called the Johnson Debt Default Act, or the Johnson Act, the legislation was aimed at preventing American investors from purchasing sovereign bonds issued by foreign governments that had yet to make good on their borrowings from the U.S. government. The Soviet Union was one of the many foreign governments in that category. Between March 1917 and July 1918, $192.6 million was loaned to Russia by the U.S. government to help finance World War I. Insisting that the debt was incurred by the tsarist regime and not the Soviet government, Moscow asserted that it did not owe the money to the United States.

The Johnson Act was amended in 1948 to exclude the governments of those countries that chose to become members of the newly formed International Monetary Fund and the International Bank for Reconstruction and Development (later known as the World Bank). The exemption did not alter the act's application to the Soviet Union, however. Soviet representatives had attended the meetings leading up to the agreement at Bretton Woods, and it appeared that the Soviet Union would be joining the post–World War II international monetary system. Indeed, the Soviet Union was slated to have the third largest quota (and voting bloc) after the United States and the United Kingdom. But when a Soviet request for a $10-billion loan from the United States was turned down, the Soviets withdrew from IMF discussions in 1946 to start their own multilateral economic organization, the Council for Mutual Economic Assistance (CMEA).

The Soviet government, then, remains officially in default to the U.S. government. Moreover, the Soviet Union is not exempted from the restrictions of the Johnson Act, because it is not a member of the IMF and the World Bank. The question then becomes: How are U.S. banks able to make loans to the Soviet Union without violating the Johnson Act?

Tracing the legislative history of the act is very tricky. It requires painstaking definitions of such concepts as "within the United States" and determining whether bank deposits represent claims on loans to foreign governments. An opinion from the

Attorney General in 1939 established that branches of banks in-corporated in foreign countries were not subject to the provi-sions of the Johnson Act. A 1963 opinion issued by Attorney Gen-eral Robert F. Kennedy ruled that credit sales of agricultural commodities to nations in default of their obligations to the United States were not loans prohibited by the Johnson Act if the credit extended was within the range of that commonly encoun-tered in export sales of such commodities, that is, if the loan was specifically tied to a particular transaction involving the sale of agricultural goods. In 1967, Attorney General Ramsey Clark ex-panded the exemption to include export sales of goods and ser-vices in general, provided that the financing was tied to a partic-ular transaction. At the same time, Clark reinforced the opinion that the Johnson Act prohibits general purpose loans to default-ing foreign governments made with monies obtained through the sale of their instruments of indebtedness to the American public.

U.S. banks have leaned toward the position that loans to the Soviet Union have been backed by monies obtained through for-eign branches, so the money did not come from American depos-its. While First Chicago has admitted that its loans have been general purpose loans, untied to any specific project or transac-tion, its chief financial officer has taken pains to point out that the money was "sourced from the Eurodollar market."[25] Thus it seems that by arranging general purpose loans to the Soviet Union through foreign branches, U.S. banks are able to get around the Johnson Act. Meanwhile, commodity-specific loans can be extended by U.S. banks to the Soviet Union as long as they are tied to a particular export transaction. But general purpose lending to the Soviet Union is not allowed in the United States under the Johnson Act, and the marketing of Soviet government obligations to the American public is likewise prohibited.

Recent Developments

Whereas the Johnson Act was originally adopted to prevent American investors from being defrauded and to ensure finan-cial prudence among sovereign borrowers, more recent attempts to legislate U.S. bank loans to the Soviet Union are prompted by strategic and foreign policy considerations. In 1985 Senator Jake Garn (R—Utah), who then served as chairman of the Senate Banking Committee, co-sponsored a bill to control U.S. loans to the Soviet Union and its allies. If passed, Senate Bill 812, (later reintroduced as S.786) would amend the Export Administration Act of 1979 to give the president discretionary authority to prohibit, curtail, monitor, or otherwise regulate the transfer of money or other financial assets to communist countries, excluding Yugoslavia but including China.

Senator Garn's concern about unrestricted transfers of Western capital to the Eastern bloc was directly related to his efforts to restrict the export of strategic technology to the Soviets. Citing a Defense Department report claiming that the Soviet Union invests more than $1.5 billion a year to acquire U.S. technology, Garn noted at a Senate hearing on the proposed bill that the convicted spy "John Walker wasn't paid in rubles; he was paid in U.S. dollars which the Soviets had to get somehow."[26]

Testifying on behalf of the Reagan administration, Assistant Treasury Secretary David Mulford stated that legislation to control the flow of capital to Soviet bloc countries would send a message "directly counter to the message from Geneva" and would have a chilling effect on President Reagan's efforts to encourage mutually beneficial nonstrategic trade. Furthermore, he said, U.S. allies would resist any attempt to persuade them to cooperate in restricting credit to the Soviet Union. Thus, enactment of the bill could have the perverse effect of weakening the Western alliance, not the Soviet bloc.[27]

Reagan had apparently held a joint meeting of the National Security Council and the Economic Policy Council just before the hearing to determine the administration's position. The Cabinet was deeply divided over the issue. The Secretary of Defense, the Attorney General, the National Security Adviser, and the CIA Director all supported the legislation, while the Secretaries of State, Commerce, and the Treasury opposed it. Reagan decided to oppose the bill.[28]

In August 1987 another bill was introduced, this time by Representative Jack Kemp (R—New York), aimed at restricting untied loans from U.S. banks to the Soviet Union. Entitled the "International Financial Security Act of 1987," the measure would not affect loans that had already been made but would apply only to new Soviet loans not specifically dedicated to a project or product. Explaining the need for the proposed legislation, Kemp said:

> The Soviet bloc now receives low interest rate loans for non-specific projects or trade transactions at a rate lower than a small

businessman in America would pay. These loans can be used for any purpose, including financing military aggression abroad and oppression at home.[29]

Specifically, the bill would require U.S. banks to report to the president any loan made to a "controlled" country, most notably the Soviet Union and other members of the CMEA. In addition, the bill would give the president the right to regulate such loans in keeping with matters of U.S. security, foreign policy, and human rights considerations. U.S. banks would also be required under the bill to disclose Soviet loans to their shareholders. Finally, the bill would prohibit the Soviet Union from acquiring any U.S. bank.

This last point stems from the disclosure in 1986 that the Soviet Union was seeking surreptitiously to acquire three banks in Northern California and to purchase an interest in a fourth. A Singapore businessman, acting as an intermediary on behalf of the Soviets, informed U.S. federal investigators about pending transactions in Northern California. The CIA managed to block the attempt, for which financing was being provided by Moscow Narodny Bank, and thus prevented the Soviets from acquiring the target banks located in Silicon Valley. The banks had supplied financing for high-technology firms that manufactured restricted goods that could not be exported legally to the Soviet Union. There was speculation that the Kremlin's objective was to gain access to sensitive American technology through a banking connection.[30]

Saying that it had taken "fine investigative work and some luck" to foil the Soviet banking scheme, Senator Daniel Patrick Moynihan (D—New York) subsequently introduced a bill that would require disclosure of a bank purchaser's nationality. Failure to provide such information would be subject to a $100,000 fine and imprisonment of ten years. Control of a U.S. bank by the Soviet Union would be prohibited outright.[31]

Clearly there is grave concern among a number of U.S. lawmakers about the transfer of Western capital to the Soviet Union. Thus far U.S. banks have been on the receiving end of most of the criticism; banks are, after all, the most visible source of loans. But if commercial bankers in the United States are feeling any pressure from Congress, they have so far been able to count on the support of the White House. Beginning with the decision about Poland, there has been less and less inclination to heighten presidential authority over loans to ideologically hostile nations. According to Kemp, the State Department reacted in a "totally disdainful manner" to his proposal to restrict untied lending to the Soviet Union.[32]

The latest chapter in the story on Polish indebtedness has to do with statements made by Vice President George Bush in September 1987 during a trip to Warsaw. After a meeting between Bush and Jaruzelski, it was announced that the United States had agreed to help Poland obtain economic assistance to lighten its foreign debt burden. As part of the agreement, Polish leaders had given "assurances" that they were committed to internal political and economic change. No timetables or guarantees were offered, however, for the liberalization. And Jaruzelski bluntly told Bush that he had no intention of changing his position on the outlawed Solidarity because it would be "suicidal" to do so.[33]

American assistance is slated to come in the form of encouragement aimed at the Paris Club, an informal group of Western financial officials. Only official debt, government-to-government lending, is directly subject to Paris Club actions, and the blessing of the United States is needed primarily to allow Poland more favorable repayment arrangements from Western governments. However, leniency on official debt is historically a precursor to receiving more accommodating terms from commercial bankers, who have become quite perceptive at picking up signals, positive and negative, from the U.S. government.

Sometimes the signals are mixed. When West Germany's largest commercial bank announced in May 1988 that it was arranging a 3.5 billion deutsche mark ($2.1 billion) credit line for the Soviet Union to purchase West German industrial equipment to manufacture consumer goods, U.S. Defense Secretary Frank Carlucci was quick to express his dismay. "We are unhappy about these kinds of loans," he said at a hearing of the Senate Defense Appropriations subcommittee. "It puts an extra burden on our defense forces."[34] But officials in Bonn responded coolly to the U.S. criticism, which came just shortly before the Reagan-Gorbachev summit in Moscow, dismissing it as an overreaction and speculating that it was probably aimed for home consumption.[35]

Making loans to the Soviet Union and its allies in Eastern Europe may be a complicated legal and political affair, but one thing is clear: Bankers' actions are necessarily tied to what happens in Washington. And Washington has yet to commit itself one way or the other on the question of financing the Soviet bloc.

6

Government Lending

Estimates of total Soviet indebtedness to the West were roughly doubled overnight in May 1984. The new estimates had to be made after the Organization for Economic Cooperation and Development (OECD) had published information about the level of credits Western governments were extending to the Soviet Union. In earlier calculations of Soviet debt, only commercial bank loans had been measured; it had not occurred to analysts that considerable amounts of credits were being supplied to the Soviet Union by Western governments. Official trade credits, after all, are normally reserved for less developed countries unable to compete for financing in private markets. The Soviet Union hardly seemed to be a candidate for government-subsidized financing.

But the joint report issued by the OECD and the Bank for International Settlements (BIS) for loans outstanding as of the end of June 1983 showed that the Soviet Union ranked as the third largest hard-currency debtor in the world, excluding the sixteen industrial countries plus Liechtenstein who report to the OECD.[1] Only Brazil and Mexico owed more. That news startled observers. While the daily headlines featured the debt crises of Brazil and Mexico, little attention had been paid to the Soviet Union.

The most astonishing aspect of the report, though, was that the Soviet Union ranked *first* in the world in loans subsidized by Western governments. Just 10 percent of Mexico's total debt was made up of government credits, and less than 20 percent of Brazil's; but more than 60 percent of the Soviet debt to the West was in the form of Western government-sponsored loans. After the Soviet Union came Poland, with 38 percent of its Western debt backed by Western governments.[2]

Among the top ten borrowers from the West in the world, then, the Soviet Union and Poland were receiving the most generous shares of official trade credits from Western governments. This, prior to the May 1984 OECD report, had never before been publicly acknowledged by Western governments. It prompted the *Wall Street Journal* to ask: "When did taxpayers in the lending countries ever decide to subsidize communism?"[3]

In calculating levels of "official lending" from Western governments, the BIS/OECD report does not include loans from such multilateral institutions as the World Bank or the International Monetary Fund. Government loans refer to only two types of assistance: (1) export credits granted directly by governments or government agencies and (2) credits advanced through commercial banks that are officially guaranteed or insured by governments. In either case, the loans are essentially offered at subsidized rates. Official trade credits granted directly by governments are clearly an alternative to private financing; no rational importer would choose to finance a transaction with government-supplied credit if commercial credit could be obtained at a lower rate of interest. When governments give their own guarantee or agree to insure a commercial bank loan to a borrowing country, they supply their own reputation for creditworthiness in place of the borrowing country's. Assuming the commercial bank looks more favorably on loans to its own government than to foreign borrowers, the government guarantee constitutes an interest rate subsidy to the borrowing country.

The high level of subsidized loans to the Soviet Union does not reflect actions taken by the United States, but rather those taken by West European governments and Japan, who are inclined to provide favorable credit terms to the Soviet Union in spite of U.S. protests. Since 1975 the U.S. government has been prohibited from extending export credits or credit guarantees directly or indirectly to any nonmarket economy country that denies its citizens freedom of emigration. But even that legislation is not as restrictive as it sounds; Poland is exempt from its provisions and so, until recently, was Romania. So even while the U.S. government has sought to persuade its Western allies to curtail financial subsidies to the Soviet bloc, it has provided conflicting indications of its own intentions. For example, U.S. officials have hinted that the Soviet Union might receive most-favored-nation trade status in the future, and in September 1986 President Reagan approved an offer to sell grain to the Soviet Union at subsidized prices.

Perceived Benefits

Export credit programs are administered by Western governments as an instrument of trade policy. In general, they are used to promote exports for the presumed benefit of the domestic economy. Even when some governments—particularly the U.S. government—argue that the practice of providing subsidized credits conflicts with general principles of free trade, they continue to offer direct and indirect credit assistance, which they rationalize by asserting a need to stay competitive with the practices of other Western governments.

When export credits are granted to the Soviet Union and its allies, whether or not domestic benefits are achieved is subject to question. Western governments take the position that financial assistance to the Soviet Union brings about both economic benefits for domestic exporters and the furtherance of important foreign policy objectives. The economic welfare of the exporting country is believed to be enhanced by increased employment and production thanks to increased sales. Foreign policy is thought to be strengthened by providing the Soviet Union with a set of economic incentives to cooperate with the West: The Soviets will be less likely to initiate aggressive global behavior for fear of jeopardizing their preferential trade treatment. Such considerations have been characterized by the *Wall Street Journal* in less charitable terms:

> Two reasons can be offered for the Western generosity to the
> Soviets. As someone once noted, the Russians are like the
> Pentagon. They don't trade, they procure, and in huge amounts.
> Western businessmen and politicians simply can't resist those big
> deals. Since taxpayers aren't readily aware that they are providing

the subsidies, who worries? The second reason is that Western politicians mistakenly believe that credit generosity is a way of appeasing Soviet warlords.[4]

Whatever the reasons for granting official trade credits, the practice is widespread among Western governments. But the credits are issued through a variety of organizational structures ranging from official arrangements with private companies to semipublic agencies to full government departments. In West Germany, loans are guaranteed by a private insurance company, Hermes Kreditversicherungs AG, which acts as an agent for the German government. Because export financing is guaranteed through the Hermes insurance program rather than directly by the German government, the Germans argue that the loans are not government subsidies, a view disputed by U.S. authorities. In Britain, government insurance and guarantees are administered through the Export Credits Guarantee Department (ECGD), undisputedly recognized as part of the British government. In France, official export credit financing involves close cooperation between the commercial banks and two public institutions: the Banque Française du Commerce Extérieur (BFCE) and the Compagnie Française D'Assurance pour le Commerce Extérieur (COFACE), which is a semipublic joint stock company. COFACE covers short-term commercial risks on its own account, while operating a short- and medium-term credit insurance service on behalf of the French government. The BFCE likewise acts both on its own behalf as a bank and as a direct supplier of long-term credits to foreign countries on behalf of the government. In Japan, official export credit financing is extended through the Export–Import Bank of Japan, a government financial institution, in cooperation with commercial banks. Government-backed insurance is provided by the Export Insurance Division (EID) of the Ministry of International Trade and Industry, which is, of course, part of the Japanese government.

In the United States, official export credit financing is carried out through the Export–Import Bank of the United States (Eximbank), which was chartered in 1934 as an independent government agency. Eximbank coordinates its various programs with the Private Export Funding Corporation (PEFCO), a private corporation owned jointly by fifty-four commercial banks, seven industrial firms, and one investment banking firm. Eximbank also cooperates directly with private commercial banks in financing export transactions. The insurance program for the United States is likewise administered by Eximbank; providing government-backed insurance, Eximbank works with the Foreign Credit Insurance Association (FCIA), a group of the nation's leading private marine, property, and casualty insurance companies. Additional commercial guarantee programs, aimed at assisting U.S. exporters of agricultural commodities, are run by the Commodity Credit Corporation (CCC) of the Department of Agriculture.

Commenting on the existence of a variety of organizations, Stephen Salant of the Rand Corporation wryly observes: "Since export subsidies are theoretically proscribed by the General Agreement on Tariffs and Trade (GATT), exporting nations tend to be rather circumspect."[5] Nevertheless, Western governments have managed to be quite successful at making subsidized credits available to the Soviet Union and its East European allies. Out of some $14 billion in officially supported loans from OECD countries to communist countries in 1981, the value of direct and indirect subsidies was estimated at about $3 billion, slightly more than 20 percent of the total value of loans granted.[6]

Western governments would argue that the costs of the subsidies, borne by taxpayers, are more than offset by the benefits to the economy of the exporting country. However, Daniel Kohler argues, subsidies are more likely to *reduce* welfare in the exporting country than to increase it. He points out that the cost of subsidies must be covered somehow—either by increased taxes or by charging higher interest rates to domestic borrowers—and those costs to the economy are likely to lose more jobs than are gained in the exporting industry.[7] Credit subsidies clearly benefit particular individuals in the exporting industry who can tap into government financing programs to promote their products on world markets. But the subsidies are granted at the expense of consumers and taxpayers in the exporting country, who must bear the economic cost of government-supplied loans and guarantees. For the exporting country, then, the economic effects of providing official trade financing are mixed; Western export industries are beneficiaries, but their gains are more than offset by the losses in profits and employment in other industries and increased costs for Western consumers and taxpayers. For the importing country, the benefits are straightforward and take the form of loans at lower interest rates than could otherwise be obtained. As Kohler sums it up: "It follows that the only clearcut

winners under the current system are the Communist countries."[8]

Should we then use export credits as a tool of foreign policy?
The United States differs from its allies over the efficacy of promoting trade with the Soviet Union as a way to elicit responsible
global behavior from the Kremlin. The difference no doubt exists
because the governments of Western Europe and Japan are convinced that exporting to the Soviet Union provides substantive
benefits for their domestic economies. They are thus more inclined to claim that residual foreign policy benefits can be derived from expanded trade relations with the Soviets. Specifically, they assert that East–West trade is an integral part of
détente, a way of maintaining a continuing dialogue with Moscow. For West Germany, détente also offers a way to improve
relations with East Germany significantly. Soviet activities in regional conflicts may be seen as violations of an American-
defined code of conduct, but not necessarily a breach in the
Soviet Union's commitment to détente and preservation of the
status quo in European affairs.[9]

Constantine Menges argues that periods of détente, marked by
economic assistance and expanded trade relations, have not resulted in Soviet behavior consistent with Western objectives.
Menges has identified four distinct periods since the end of
World War II during which the West sought to establish a mood
of cooperation with the Soviet Union on the basis of increased
trade and financial relations. In every case, the détente era was
terminated by "a particularly ugly Soviet action":

> Détente I ended with the 1948 communist coup in Czechoslovakia
> and the Berlin blockade, Détente II with the Soviet invasion of
> Hungary in 1956, Détente III with the Berlin Wall in 1961, and
> Détente IV with the 1979 Afghanistan invasion.[10]

Joseph Finder likewise asserts that it is a mistake to believe doing
business with the Soviet Union can lead to improved political
relations. He disparages the "web of interlocking relations" theory, which holds that commerce commits nations to a mutual
dependency that can somehow keep peace in the world. According to Finder, the Soviets themselves do not entertain false
hopes about the political benefits of détente. "The expression
'business as usual' may signify international comity to capitalists," Finder explains, "but to the communists, who are less con-

vinced of the palliative effects of commerce, the phrase does not mean as much."[11]

Extent of Support

If official trade credits do not provide economic benefits to the exporting nation, and if their use as a foreign policy tool is measured by the dubious record of détente, it is hard to understand why Western governments persist in offering them to Soviet bloc nations. But it is clear from Table 6.1 that official credits—in the form of direct loans and government-supplied guarantees and insurance—are extensively used to channel credit to the Soviet Union and its allies. Some 30 percent of total debt to the West owed by the Soviet bloc, defined as the Soviet Union and six East European countries, is extended in the form of government-supported credits. As a percentage of total loans, Poland was, as of the end of June 1987, the largest recipient of credits with 50 percent of its total Western debt coming in the form of direct credits or government-guaranteed loans. In absolute amounts, however, the Soviet Union is still the West's largest beneficiary,

TABLE 6.1. Extent of Western Government-Supported Credits to Soviet Bloc Countries at End of June 1987 (in billions of U.S. dollars)

	Commercial Loans	%	Government-Supported	%	Total
Soviet Union	25.9	69	11.6	31	37.5
Eastern Europe					
Bulgaria	4.1	76	1.3	24	5.4
Czechoslovakia	3.2	73	1.2	27	4.4
East Germany[a]	11.0	77	3.3	23	14.3
Hungary	10.6	95	0.6	5	11.2
Poland	10.2	50	10.0	50	20.2
Romania	2.2	65	1.2	35	3.4
Soviet bloc	67.2	70	29.2	30	96.4
Yugoslavia	7.8	64	4.4	36	12.2

[a]Figures for East Germany do not include loans from West Germany; the West German government considers these "intra-German" transactions, not foreign loans.

NOTE: Loans shown do not include IMF/World Bank loans.

SOURCE: *Statistics on External Indebtedness: Bank and Trade-Related Non-Bank External Claims on Individual Borrowing Countries and Territories at End-June 1987,* BIS/OECD (Paris and Basel, January 1988).

even though government-supported credits have decreased as a percentage of total Soviet debt in recent years. Out of its total indebtedness to the West of $37.5 billion, the Soviet Union owes $11.6 billion (or 31 percent of its total loans) to Western governments, which is to say that if the Soviet Union were to default, the amounts under official guarantee would come out of the budgets of Western governments or the pockets of taxpayers, depending on your choice of terms.

The data in Table 6.1 are significant in a number of ways. They show that total Soviet bloc debt at the end of June 1987 stood at $96.4 billion. Based on the same BIS/OECD report, Brazil's debt at the end of June 1987 was $88.9 billion, and Mexico's $80.7 billion. The Soviet Union's debt, taken by itself at $37.5 billion, is certainly less than either Brazil's or Mexico's. No doubt for that reason some observers are not inclined to become alarmed over the amounts owed by the Soviet Union. However, if one believes that Moscow exerts considerable influence over the political and economic destinies of Bulgaria, Czechoslovakia, East Germany, Hungary, Poland, and Romania, it seems prudent to examine the total debt of the Soviet bloc if one wants to assess the potential credit risk in East European borrowing. Poland is committed, according to a former Polish official, to providing some $10 billion worth of credits to the Soviet Union over a fourteen-year period.[12] Other East European satellites have been pressured to repay their ruble debts to Moscow. They can pay off by supplying more exports to the Soviet Union, or they can sell their exports to hard-currency purchasers and furnish the Soviet Union with the receipts by an exchange-rate formula for transferring ruble debt in hard-currency amounts. It is also conceivable that a portion of the borrowings of East European satellites from Western sources are channeled directly to Moscow.

The point is that it makes sense to regard Soviet bloc debt as a single entity, rather than break it down by individual countries. At $96.4 billion, the Soviet bloc represents the most heavily indebted entity in the world based on individual country statistics compiled by the BIS and the OECD as of the end of June 1987. More alarming, perhaps, is the fact that Soviet bloc debt is increasing rapidly; from the end of June 1986 to the end of June 1987, Soviet bloc debt grew by $10.2 billion, from $86.2 billion to $96.4 billion, according to BIS/OECD statistics. During the same period, Brazil's debt increased by just $3.7 billion, going from

$85.2 billion to $88.9 billion. Mexico's debt increased by $2.6 billion, going from $78.1 billion to $80.7 billion.

The $96.4 billion total figure does not count Yugoslavia's debt to the West, which, if included, would push the level of debt owed by the Soviet bloc countries to the West up to $108.6 billion as of the end of June 1987. The statistics cited also exclude the amount of loans granted to East Germany from West Germany, not just for official trade credits but for commercial loans as well. The West German government does not divulge figures on money going to East Germany, which it considers not foreign but "intra-German" domestic loans. Loans from the IMF and the World Bank are excluded as well. If they were included, the amounts owed by Hungary, Romania, and Yugoslavia would be increased by some $1.5 billion, $2.2 billion, and $4.3 billion respectively. Meanwhile, Poland has been accepted into the IMF and is expected soon to borrow substantial amounts through the IMF and the World Bank.

So the figure of $96.4 billion for Soviet bloc debt to the West is extremely conservative. Moreover, the $10.2 billion increase in Soviet bloc debt from $86.2 billion at the end of June 1986 to $96.4 billion at the end of June 1987 constitutes a growth rate of nearly 12 percent in one year. If a 12 percent growth rate is sustained, the $86.2 billion figure will have roughly doubled by the middle of 1992, rising to some $170 billion (see Table 6.2) at just about the time the reforms of perestroika are expected to be in full swing. Of course, Soviet bloc borrowing may not continue to increase at that rate. But the growth in Soviet bloc indebtedness to the West is driven by the activities of the two largest borrowers, the Soviet Union and Poland. Because Gorbachev needs to import consumer goods and technology from the West, both fi-

TABLE 6.2. Projected Growth of Soviet Bloc Debt to West[a]
(in billions of U.S. dollars)

Actual		Estimated Based on 12% Growth				
End-June 1986	End-June 1987	End-June 1988	End-June 1989	End-June 1990	End-June 1991	End-June 1992
86.2	96.4	108	121	135	152	170

[a]Soviet bloc debt defined as debt of the Soviet Union, Bulgaria, Czechoslovakia, East Germany, Hungary, Poland, and Romania; not including loans from West Germany to East Germany and not including IMF/World Bank loans.

nanced with Western credits, we can assume that the Soviet Union will continue to borrow heavily from the West in the immediate future. The financial condition of Poland dictates that it too will apply for additional Western credits.

If Western governments continue to provide direct credits, guarantees, and insurance for Soviet bloc borrowers, not to speak of IMF and World Bank financing, they will be contributing in a substantial way to the total indebtedness of the Soviet Union and its allies in Eastern Europe. True, the bulk of the increase in the debt of the Soviet Union since the end of June 1983 has come in the form of commercial bank loans, not government-supported credits. As of the end of June 1987, government lending represented 31 percent of the Soviet Union's total debt to the West; as of the end of June 1983, 61 percent of the total. In absolute terms, the figure for government-supported loans declined by about $6.1 billion during the four-year period. The percentage amount changed so significantly because the total debt of the Soviet Union, fueled by borrowings from commercial banks, increased so dramatically.

"Gentlemen's Agreement"

Acknowledging that subsidized financing for exports was a beggar-thy-neighbor form of competition, six Western governments agreed among themselves in 1976 to reduce the level of the subsidies to CMEA members and other less developed countries. Talks had actually begun much earlier, in 1963, but governments were not prepared to do anything until interest rates climbed dramatically in the late 1970s. Export credits usually come in the form of long-term loans at low fixed-interest rates. So it was painfully obvious that the loans drained the budget when governments' borrowing costs on bonds escalated.[13] In April 1978, after much bickering about rules and sanctions, the "Arrangement on Guidelines for Officially Supported Export Credits" was formally signed by twenty Western governments.

Besides the United States, the participants include the European Economic Community (including Portugal and Spain), Australia, Austria, Canada, Finland, Japan, New Zealand, Norway, Sweden, and Switzerland. The signers pledged to charge certain minimum interest rates to foreign borrowers who purchase their exports; the objective was to move officially supported rates closer to market rates.

Countries are assigned to one of three categories: relatively rich countries to Category I, intermediate countries to Category II, and relatively poor countries to Category III. Richer borrowing countries have to pay a higher minimum interest rate than poor ones, and loans with shorter maturities must carry a higher rate than loans with longer ones. The Arrangement does not have the same status as the General Agreement on Tariffs and Trade (GATT), which is part of international law. Nor is there any supranational body with the authority to enforce the terms of the agreement or impose sanctions against violators. The Arrangement, which is facilitated by the OECD secretariat, is simply an institutional framework that has been accepted by its participants "to prevent an export credit race in which exporting countries compete on the basis of who grants the most favorable financing terms rather than on the basis of who provides the highest quality and the best service."[14]

The United States has supported the objectives of the Arrangement, not just out of devotion to free trade principles and opposition to government-subsidized financing, but expressly as a way to reduce the volume of Western credits made available to the Soviet Union and its allies. After the invasion of Afghanistan in 1979, the Carter administration asked its allies to reduce the amount of their official credits and guarantees to the Soviet Union by half; in addition, it asked that all such extensions of government-supported financing be furnished at the market rate of interest. The reaction of Western allies to the U.S. initiative was lukewarm at best. Most countries simply agreed that they would not offer long-term credits to the Soviet Union at rates lower than the consensus rates, those allowed under the Arrangement. The Italian and the Japanese governments temporarily delayed issuing new credits to the Soviets, and the British government decided not to renew a line of credit, but, as some observers pointed out at the time, the Soviet Union had not used up all of its existing line.[15]

The United States persisted in its efforts to raise the consensus rates, and in July 1980 the participants in the Agreement agreed to implement slight increases, which brought the highest consensus rate up to 8.75 percent—still far below what many governments were paying to borrow by issuing their own securities.

Nevertheless, a few months later the French government foiled efforts by the United States to bring official export rates still closer to market terms; instead, France persuaded other parties to the Agreement to limit changes in the consensus rates to very small increases. Those increases were derided by the United States as "grossly inadequate."[16]

At first, it appeared that the Reagan administration would have more success in persuading OECD members to limit the interest rate subsidies granted to the Soviet Union and its allies. Parties to the Arrangement agreed to raise the minimum interest rate to 10 percent in November 1981. Moreover, during the next few months, U.S. officials prevailed upon leaders of West European nations to relegate the Soviet Union to a separate category for all financial and economic relations; while the West Europeans did not honor that request, they did allow the issue to be put on the agenda for the Versailles economic summit in June 1982. A communiqué signed by the leaders of the Western world and issued at the conclusion of the summit contained the following declaration:

> . . . taking into account existing economic and financial considerations, we have agreed also to handle cautiously financial relations with the U.S.S.R. and other Eastern European countries in such a way as to ensure that they are conducted on a sound economic basis, including also the need for commercial prudence in limiting export credits.[17]

The concession to exercise "commercial prudence" was potentially meaningful, although it was certainly a watered-down version of what the United States had wanted. However, even this hint of allied cooperation was soon to be reversed. Less than two weeks after the 1982 summit, France's President Mitterrand declared publicly that France would not be bound by that part of the communiqué dealing with credit policies toward the Soviet Union. The French seemed to resent the United States for trying to impose an American agenda on Western Europe vis-à-vis the Soviet Union. U.S. officials had wanted to go much farther; they had sought to establish a mechanism for monitoring the efforts of Western governments to reduce subsidized credits and to declare a temporary moratorium against them. It was, perhaps, a delayed reaction to the pressure that prompted Mitterrand to make an overt showing of France's independence and, in so doing, to demonstrate the lack of a unified Western policy on financial and trade relations with the Soviet Union.

One positive result was effected by the U.S. initiative at Versailles. Participants in the OECD Arrangement agreed to push the Soviet Union (as well as East Germany and Czechoslovakia) from the intermediate to the relatively rich category. Accordingly, the OECD participants effectively increased the interest rate the Soviet Union would have to pay to finance its purchases of Western goods using government-supported credits. At the same time, minimum interest rates were raised for all but the poorest category. As can be seen in Table 6.3, the immediate effect of the changes implemented in July 1982 was to raise the minimum interest rate the Soviet Union was being charged from 10.5 percent to 12.15 percent on two- to five-year loans and from 11 percent to 12.4 percent on loans over five years up to eight and a half years. In July 1984 the rates for Category I borrowers were increased once again; about that time, the Soviet Union began to shift its reliance on official trade credits to greater use of commercial bank loans.

Did it make sense for the United States to risk alienating its allies to reduce credits going to the Soviet Union? According to Kohler, the value of the subsidies granted by OECD governments on loans to the Soviet bloc amounted to about $3 billion in 1981. Given the size of the Soviet economy and the resources of Eastern Europe, that amount might not seem to make much of a difference. However, Kohler notes:

TABLE 6.3. Changes in OECD Minimum Interest Rates Under Arrangement

Dates	Country Categories and Maturities (years)					
	I	I	II	II	III	III
	2–5	5–8.5	2–5	5–8.5	2–5	5–10
11/81–7/82	11.00	11.25	10.50	11.00	10.00	10.00
7/82–10/83	12.15	12.40	10.85	11.35	10.00	10.00
10/83–7/84	12.15	12.40	10.35	10.70	9.50	9.50
7/84–1/85	13.35	13.60	11.55	11.90	10.70	10.70
1/85–1/86	12.00	12.25	10.70	11.20	9.85	9.85
1/86–7/86	10.95	11.20	9.65	10.15	8.80	8.80
7/86	9.55	9.80	8.25	8.75	7.40	7.40

SOURCE: *The Export Credit Financing Systems in OECD Member Countries*, (Paris: OECD, 1987), p. 8.

This is of course no excuse for continuing the subsidies. We have
no reason for wanting to enable the Communist Bloc to expand
their military expenditure, and even small resource transfers ought
to be considered with suspicion. After all, $3 billion just about buys
an aircraft carrier. Under the current policy, we transfer the
equivalent of an aircraft carrier in resources to the Communist
world each year. If such transfers do not have substantial offsetting
benefits to us, as seems to be the case here, they should be
discontinued, regardless of their effect on the Soviet Union.[18]

The most recent efforts by the United States have brought
about an agreement among OECD countries—to be fully implemented by July 1988—to restrict the use of "tied aid" financing
whereby government credits are laced with foreign-aid grants to
promote export sales. The agreement is also aimed at eliminating
remaining interest rate subsidies on loans to the Soviet Union.
So after years of wrangling with its Western allies, the Reagan
administration seems finally to have elicited a critical level of
support for its position that Moscow doesn't need or deserve subsidies, that subsidies were intended originally to assist developing countries, not military superpowers. But if the most recent
agreement indicates that Western governments are philosophically committed to cutting off subsidized financing to the Soviet
Union, they are still under no enforceable sanctions to comply.
Deviations from the rules, referred to as "derogations," are permitted under the Arrangement. A Western government need
only notify all other parties to the Arrangement that it intends to
offer export credits involving some subsidy that might result in
a violation of the agreed-upon limits. At that point, other OECD
participants are free to match the derogation or even to underbid
it.

Jackson–Vanik Amendment

To a great extent, the arguments presented by the United States
at Versailles in 1982 had already been thoroughly debated in
Washington several years before and had resulted in an odd victory by Democratic "conservatives" over Republican "liberals."
President Nixon, working with Henry Kissinger, who was serving as his assistant for National Security Affairs, moved from
resisting détente to suddenly embracing it as administration pol-

icy in 1971. In so doing, the White House team joined such traditional liberal democrats as senators Edmund Muskie and Walter
Mondale, who insisted that trade restrictions were not hurting
communist economies so much as U.S. producers. They were
also postulating that increased trade restrictions with the West
might bring about a freer internal economy in the Soviet Union.[18]
However, while Nixon was in Moscow holding a summit meeting with Brezhnev in 1972, promising to bring about most-
favored-nation trade status for the U.S.S.R., forces led by Democratic Senator Henry "Scoop" Jackson (Washington) worked to
undermine administration strategy. As Nixon was pledging to
improve U.S.–Soviet relations based on principles of sovereignty,
equality, and noninterference in internal affairs, Jackson was attempting to make interference in Soviet internal affairs the key
criterion for doing business with the Soviet Union.

Jackson insisted that it was inappropriate for the United States
to consider ways to enhance U.S.–Soviet trade while Soviet leaders continued to suppress individual rights and liberties within
their country, particularly the right to emigrate. Jackson, with
Representative Charles Vanik (D.—Ohio), proposed an amendment to the Trade Act of 1974 to withhold most-favored-nation
status—and government-backed credits—from countries that did
not permit free migration of their citizens. About the same time,
Senator Adlai Stevenson III (D.—Ill.) proposed legislation to restrict the amount and types of credits made available from the
U.S. Export–Import Bank to finance U.S. exports to the Soviet
Union. The two measures, which reinforced each other effectively to deny the Soviet Union access to subsidized U.S. credits,
passed with strong congressional support.

The crux of the Trade Act of 1974 legislation, complete with
the Jackson–Vanik Amendment, is that the U.S. government is
prohibited from extending export credits, credit guarantees, or
investment guarantees directly or indirectly to any nonmarket
economy country that denies its citizens freedom of emigration.
The prohibition applies to all U.S. government programs, including those of the Export–Import Bank of the United States, the
Commodity Credit Corporation of the U.S. Department of Agriculture, and the Overseas Private Investment Corporation
(OPIC). Poland is exempt, because it had already enjoyed most-
favored-nation trade status at the time the Trade Act was enacted. A special waiver was given to Romania in April 1975 to
get around the freedom of emigration provisions, and Congress

approved in August 1975 the extension of most-favored-nation treatment to U.S. imports of Romanian goods. (In 1988, however, Romania chose to relinquish its most-favored-nation trade status rather than be subject to U.S. investigations on human rights and abuses.)

The credit restrictions imposed by the Stevenson Amendment put a $300-million ceiling on new Eximbank authorizations to finance U.S. exports to the Soviet Union. Of that amount, not more than $40 million may be used for the purchase, lease, or procurement of any product or service involving research and exploration of fossil fuel energy resources, and none of it can be used for actually producing, processing, or distributing fossil fuel energy resources. The ceiling may be raised by the president if he deems it in the national interest. Before the president's action can take effect, however, both houses of Congress must approve it by passage of a concurrent resolution.[19]

Enactment of the legislation offered by Jackson and Vanik put Congress at odds with the détente-minded Nixon. Under the trade agreement between the United States and the Soviet Union worked out after the first Nixon–Brezhnev summit, the two countries agreed to take specific actions to strengthen economic relations. Nixon was to ask Congress to grant most-favored-nation status to the Soviet Union. In return, the Soviet Union would resume making payments on its $722-million World War II lend-lease debt to the United States; with the resumption, the understanding was that the Soviet Union would become eligible for loans from Eximbank. Between October 1972 and July 1975, the Soviets made three token payments totaling $48 million.[20] It was becoming increasingly clear, however, that Nixon could not deliver on his part of the deal. Realizing that most-favored-nation status would not be forthcoming, the Soviets quit paying on their lend-lease debt. Oddly enough, U.S. officials still do not regard Soviet lend-lease loans to be in default; the principal amount due of $674 million remains in limbo because of the diplomatic misunderstanding involved.

In the meantime, the Jackson–Vanik Amendment has remained a sore point for the Soviet Union. In December 1985 Gorbachev singled out the Jackson–Vanik Amendment as the chief "political obstacle" holding back a significant increase in U.S.–Soviet trade.[21] Hosting a Kremlin dinner in honor of the U.S.–U.S.S.R. Trade Council, Gorbachev told some four hundred U.S. business executives and trade officials, including former U.S. Secretary of

Commerce Malcolm Baldrige, that "so long as those obstacles exist, there will be no normal development of Soviet–U.S. trade and other economic ties on a large scale."[22] He pointed out that a lifting of the barriers would give U.S. businesses the opportunity to compete for large long-term contracts in Soviet energy development, modernization of the machine industry, agribusiness, and other areas. Baldrige told reporters after the dinner that he doubted any attempt would be made soon to repeal the Jackson–Vanik Amendment, although "it's possible [most-favored-nation status] may develop in the future."[23]

As the world price for oil continued to drop over the next few months, Gorbachev's tone began to change. Instead of resisting the stipulations contained in Jackson–Vanik, he began to exhibit a willingness to accommodate them. If Americans were preoccupied with the matter of emigration, especially Jewish emigration, the Soviet Union would show its flexibility. In February 1986, Anatoly Shcharansky was allowed to leave the Soviet Union after nine years of confinement in labor camps as a political prisoner accused of spying for the United States. Yelena Bonner, wife of the well-known Soviet dissident Andrei Sakharov, received special permission to visit the United States for medical reasons. In May 1986 Moscow announced that it would allow 117 of its citizens to join relatives in the United States. The next month 127 more Soviet citizens received permission to emigrate to the United States. Commenting on the new Soviet attitude toward emigration, a spokesman for the U.S. State Department described the Kremlin initiative as "a positive step that will contribute to an improved atmosphere in our relations."[24]

Seeking a Waiver

Not only administration officials but Jewish leaders in the United States as well have responded favorably to signals from Moscow that the emigration issue can be satisfactorily resolved. Morris B. Abram, chairman of the National Conference on Soviet Jewry, and Edgar Bronfman, chairman of the World Jewish Congress, met with high-level Soviet officials in March 1987. Afterward, Abram stated that he believed the Soviets were ready to permit large-scale Jewish emigration and that nearly all the estimated 11,000 long-term "refuseniks," whose previous applications to leave had been rejected, would be free to go within the year.[25]

"The commitment made to the Soviets is that there would be a parallel response of an incremental nature," according to Jerry Goodman, executive director of the National Conference on Soviet Jewry. "If we see a substantial movement on emigration, starting with the core group, we would begin to consider either the Jackson–Vanik or the Stevenson amendment."[26] Bronfman went much farther. Unlike most Jewish leaders, who are willing to go only as far as supporting year-to-year waivers, Bronfman has called for the repeal of the Jackson–Vanik Amendment on the grounds that it has failed to open the door for emigrants.[27]

There is certainly a case to be made for this argument. The statistics in Table 6.4 suggest a close correlation between periods of U.S.–Soviet détente and the incidence of Jewish emigration. The number of emigrés allowed to leave the Soviet Union increased dramatically during the first few years of the 1970s. The figures leveled off after 1974 and the passage of the Jackson–Vanik and Stevenson amendments, which were enacted in January 1975. Jewish emigration began to rise once again in 1978 and reached an all-time high of 51,320 in 1979. With the dawning of the 1980s and the end of détente, the figure dwindled down to

TABLE 6.4. Jewish Emigration from the Soviet Union, October 1968–December 1987

Year	Number of Emigrés
Oct. 1968–1970	4,235
1971	13,022
1972	31,681
1973	34,733
1974	20,628
1975	13,221
1976	14,261
1977	16,736
1978	28,864
1979	51,320
1980	21,471
1981	9,447
1982	2,688
1983	1,314
1984	896
1985	1,140
1986	914
1987	8,155

SOURCE: National Conference on Soviet Jewry.

a mere trickle of a thousand or so emigrés per year. Then, in 1987, it increased by some nine-fold over the prior year.

The 1978–79 peak coincided with an unpublicized series of meetings and negotiations involving Soviet officials, leaders of the American Jewish community, Senator Henry Jackson, and members of the Carter administration. In essence, the Soviets wanted to know if, based on the high rates of emigration that had been permitted, the United States would be willing to waive the Jackson–Vanik Amendment, grant the Soviet Union most-favored-nation trade status, and allow it to become eligible for Eximbank credits. Jackson insisted that President Carter obtain explicit assurances from the Soviets, preferably in writing, that the high emigration rates would continue. The Jewish organizations supported Jackson's position, arguing that the Soviets might well cut off the flow of emigration after receiving the sought-after trade benefits. The Soviets stipulated that they would never provide formal assurances to foreign governments on matters of internal policy; the United States would have to decide whether or not the high emigration rates themselves warranted a waiver of the Jackson–Vanik Amendment. Anticipating a lack of public support, the Carter administration chose not to ask for a waiver.[28]

In hindsight, a number of American Jews believe they missed an opportunity; they should have called for an easing of the Jackson–Vanik Amendment in 1979, they thought, to encourage the Soviets further to permit high levels of emigration. But Shcharansky has taken the position that the Jackson–Vanik Amendment was a very correct approach and that it continues to exert economic and political pressure on the Soviet government. Asserting that some 400,000 Soviet Jews were still kept as prisoners of the Soviet Union, Shcharansky urged Congress in May 1986 to "maintain and reinforce" the Jackson–Vanik Amendment:

> No amount of bargaining, of give and take, of mutual concessions, can take the place of trust. Experience has taught the Jews of the Soviet Union, has taught me while I was in the camps struggling against the KGB, that lesser demands and fewer expectations lead to a situation where our aggressors feel that they should be rewarded for cosmetic concessions.[29]

In their eagerness to gain access to U.S. government-supported credits, the Soviets may be prepared to go far beyond cosmetic concessions on emigration. Vladimir Alkhimov, chair-

man of Gosbank, meeting with U.S. officials in Moscow in early
1985, made the less-than-subtle declaration that allowing the annual emigration of 50,000 Jews would be "no problem."[30] An un-
published interdepartmental report of a subsequent meeting in
Washington between the Soviet Deputy Foreign Trade Minister
and the U.S. Commerce Secretary states emphatically that the
Soviets "want credits as part of any economic deal that's
made."[31] For better or for worse, Gorbachev seems willing to use
what Moscow officials call "the Jewish question" to secure economic and financial concessions from the United States.

How far the Soviets will go to secure the rewards connected
with permitting higher emigration remains to be seen. At least
one prominent U.S. political figure has called for lifting the Jackson–Vanik trade and credit restrictions against the Soviet Union.
Speaking before the American Committee on East–West Accord
in April 1986, Senator Robert Dole (R.—Kans.) suggested that the
Jackson–Vanik Amendment be suspended for a year as an experi-
ment to see how the Soviets respond. Dole's remarks reportedly
caught Capitol Hill by surprise, and there was speculation that
his suggestion came at the behest of the White House.[32] But with
low prices and reduced sales plaguing the farm belt, Dole had
sufficient political reasons of his own to find ways to increase
U.S. grain exports.

Reagan administration attitudes toward the Jackson–Vanik
amendment were perhaps expressed more directly by C. William
Verity, Jr., who replaced Malcolm Baldrige in September 1987
as Commerce Secretary. At his confirmation hearing, Verity told
senators that he had "reservations" about the Jackson–Vanik restrictions. Acknowledging that "it is an important instrument for
the Jewish community to use as a lever," Verity stated that he
would support waiving the law if emigration levels could be
raised high enough. Asked if 50,000 emigrants per year would be
adequate, Verity replied that between 15,000 and 25,000 emigrants each year would probably be enough to consider granting
a waiver of the law.[31]

Should the U.S. government decide to lift the Jackson–Vanik
Amendment, it would be necessary for the president to inform
Congress that he had indeed received assurances from the Soviets that they would continue to permit high levels of emigration. A presidential waiver of Jackson–Vanik would give the
Soviets most-favored-nation status and preferential tariff treatment; to gain access to Eximbank credits would also require the

repeal of the Stevenson Amendment. Without the Jackson–Vanik and the Stevenson amendments, the U.S. government would be free to extend credits to the Soviet Union. Why? Because the Johnson Debt Default Act, which prohibits private individuals and commercial banks in the United States from making general purpose loans to the Soviet Union, specifically exempts public corporations created by special authorization of Congress, such as the Commodity Credit Corporation. Transactions in which the Eximbank participates are likewise exempt from the provisions of the Johnson Debt Default Act.

Once the U.S. government itself began granting credits to the Soviet Union, U.S. bankers and businessmen would take it as an unambiguous signal that stepped-up commercial relations with Moscow were in keeping with White House foreign policy objectives. For Gorbachev, of course, this would be a most gratifying outcome following a long campaign. He has had to endure the Jackson–Vanik Amendment for a number of years and is clearly eager to see it removed. "Why should the dead drag on the coattails of the living?" Gorbachev asked during the May 1988 summit in Moscow, according to an Associated Press story; in referring to the original sponsors of the legislation, he commented, "One is physically dead, the other is politically dead."[34]

7

Access to Private Capital

It looked like an ordinary edition of the *Wall Street Journal*, dated Monday, August 24, 1987. There on the front page, for example, was an article describing the inadequacies of the Soviet health system. But starting on page 5 and running through page 13, the prestigious financial newspaper included an insert that was a paean to the joys of doing business in the Soviet Union. It contained articles describing "new opportunities for cooperation" and "drastic changes to promote efficiency" in the Soviet economy. There was even a message from the Soviet Union's First Deputy Minister of Foreign Trade:

> I take this opportunity to convey my best wishes to the readers of The Wall Street Journal, one of the most influential newspapers in the U.S. business world. I hope that the publication of this special supplement will help Americans get a better understanding of the Soviet economy and of the untapped opportunities for expanding Soviet–U.S. trade.[1]

It was yet a further example of Gorbachev's style toward the West: If you can't beat them, join them. At least, join the ranks of business organizations and nations that advertise in the newspaper devoted to chronicling the daily achievements of capitalism. In general, the Kremlin wants to play down conflicting political ideologies and to play up mutual economic interests. The Gorbachev approach is not to confront or antagonize the West but to soothe it with talk of expanded trade and market opportunities. The nine-page *Wall Street Journal* special supplement cost the Soviets $300,000; it ran in 900,000 copies of the newspaper published in the Eastern United States, Europe, and Asia.[2]

In some ways, businessmen no doubt see themselves as being constrained less by the provincial business and trade practices of the Soviet Union than by their own governments. Business investment, planning, and management all thrive in an environment of stability and predictability. Businessmen, in general, are most comfortable when the rules—whatever they are—are firmly established, not subject to erratic change and political upheaval. It is thus relatively easy for Gorbachev to engage the sympathies of businessmen who, like him, may see themselves as victims of the political whims of Western governments. How is it possible to build plans around the increased availability of Western consumer goods or access to technology when the clear possibility exists that the White House may suddenly decide to impose an embargo, establish more restrictive export regulations, or strengthen efforts to link trade and financial relations with human rights? When Gorbachev explained to U.S. business executives in Moscow attending the annual meetings of the U.S.–U.S.S.R. Trade Council in December 1985 that the possibility of expanded trade could be realized only by removing the political obstacles that stood in the way, he was no doubt speaking to a receptive audience.

Not that Western businessmen are apolitical or insensitive to the larger issues of East–West relations. But, with a few notable exceptions, devising foreign policy is not what they are paid for. Instead, they would like to know what the rules are, whether the new détente can be expected to last, and whether business transactions with the Soviet Union can be carried out with the blessing of the White House. Gorbachev's efforts to reduce tensions with the United States are directed, at least in part, at eliciting a Washington political response that reassures Western corporate managers that they can expect stability if they begin to do business in earnest with the Soviet Union.

New Approach, New Set-up

One of the key elements of Gorbachev's perestroika is to reorganize the ministries responsible for carrying out foreign trade. The old organizational structure reflected the old attitudes: The Soviet economy was to be essentially self-sufficient, and foreign trade was grudgingly tolerated when technology had to be acquired. All aspects of foreign trade came under the supervision of central planning authorities, who selectively imported Western goods to fill gaps in Soviet production. That began to change somewhat in recent years as the Soviet standard of living and technological competence in consumer-oriented manufacturing fell behind world standards. The Soviet attitude of smug self-sufficiency gave way to taunts directed at the West's reluctance to develop expanded trade relations. American businessmen, in particular, were derided for missing opportunities and exhorted to accept the "realities" of future Soviet–American economic relations. As a director of the U.S.S.R. Ministry of Foreign Trade put it, "Otherwise, a situation might occur when the train leaving for the Soviet market would leave the U.S. firms watching its departure."[3]

That did not cause a rush of enthusiasm among American businessmen. U.S. firms no doubt liked the idea of expanding the markets for their products into a vast Soviet population, but it was not at all clear that doing business in the Soviet Union was a straightforward proposition or that Americans who refused to jump in with both feet were being naive or self-destructive. It wasn't until the Soviet pitch was modulated somewhat to include bottom-line advantages that U.S. businessmen began to show interest.

In early 1987 the Soviet organizational structure for foreign trade was completely revamped to become, according to Ivan Ivanov, Deputy Chairman of the State Foreign Economic Commission of the Council of Ministers, "less detailed, denominated in more value-oriented and less quantitative indicators."[4] The crux of the reorganization is to provide more flexibility and autonomy to individual Soviet ministries and enterprises. Some twenty-one ministries and sixty-seven enterprises received special permission to operate internationally and were empowered with direct access to the world market. This means, presumably, that those Soviet entities can negotiate and transact business with foreign partners without any intermediaries, without interference from the Ministry of Foreign Trade, which formerly held authority over all such business transactions. That ministry will continue to oversee trade involving food, raw materials, and other products deemed to have basic national importance. But the selected ministries and enterprises will transact business in their areas of industrial specialization. And a new Soviet governing body, the State Foreign Economic Commission, has been set up to coordinate national policy on foreign trade, to supervise planning, and to prepare relevant legislation to permit implementation of the new programs.

The ministries and enterprises designated are expected, of course, to embrace the main principles of Gorbachev's program for internal reform in terms of cost accounting and self-financing. Moreover, they must adhere to the principle of currency self-sufficiency; every enterprise is expected to cover its foreign currency payments with foreign currency proceeds. Clearly, the purpose of the reorganization is to increase the Soviet Union's net hard currency resources. In other words, the chosen ministries and enterprises will have to engage in transactions with foreign firms that result in increased sales of Soviet-made products to permit sufficient hard currency purchases of foreign-made goods. In general, to expand sales of Soviet exports to the West, the Soviet government is willing to tolerate greater autonomy and independence for the selected ministries and enterprises. In return, the Soviet entities must demonstrate that they can compete successfully on world markets.

Gorbachev is gambling as he reorganizes the previously highly centralized system for conducting foreign trade. In the past, only a very few elite Soviet officials were permitted direct contact with foreign businessmen, and the exposure of lower-level Soviet citizens to Western influence was very much discouraged. By expanding the number of people now able to work directly with foreigners and to take trips abroad, members of the former elite have had their privileges curtailed. No doubt many high-level bureaucrats in the Ministry of Foreign Trade are not happy. Nor are they entirely willing to concede that cost accounting, self-financing, and currency self-sufficiency will improve the productivity of the Soviet economy.

Anticipating inertia and quiet antagonism among veteran foreign trade officials, Gorbachev initiated the reforms by purging a number of them for being incompetent, corrupt, or both. More than two hundred foreign trade bureaucrats were fired, and several were sent to prison for taking bribes, not just from overseas suppliers but from Soviet enterprise managers who desperately needed to procure foreign equipment and materials to meet production quotas.[5] Among those punished were two highly placed foreign trade officials. In October 1985 Gorbachev sacked seventy-seven-year-old Nikolai Patolichev, who had been serving as the U.S.S.R. Minister of Foreign Trade since 1958; Patolichev had reportedly been opposed to a number of Gorbachev's proposals for reform. Three months later, Deputy Foreign Trade Minister Vladimir Sushkov was sent to jail on charges that he had accepted inappropriate favors and gifts, including a videotape recorder, from Japanese businessmen.[6] Sushkov had served as co-chairman of the U.S.–U.S.S.R. Trade and Economic Council for nine years. His co-chairman for part of that time had been C. William Verity, Jr., who would later become U.S. Secretary of Commerce under Reagan.

Even with the highly publicized purges, resistance to the Gorbachev proposals being implemented still exists. Of the sixty-seven enterprises in the Soviet Union that received foreign trade rights in January 1987, only five had penetrated the thick bureaucracy six months later to open their own independent bank accounts at Vneshtorgbank, the U.S.S.R. Bank for Foreign Trade. According to a private newsletter on Soviet business and trade matters, the officials at Vneshtorgbank "seem to be rather hesitant and timid in allowing these organizations free rein."[7] The lack of cooperation, of course, undermines the ability of the heads of newly commissioned Soviet enterprises to operate with flexibility and independence when negotiating with Western businessmen. For the new officials, it is embarrassing and ultimately fruitless to propound the competitive virtues of a new organizational structure that cannot stand apart from the stifling influences of the old system.

Joint Ventures

The most innovative and radical aspect of Gorbachev's new foreign trade initiative is a statute authorizing the creation of joint ventures with foreign participants within the Soviet Union. The Soviets proudly claim three objectives for the program: (1) They want to attract new technology and managerial experience from the West; (2) they want to stimulate import substitution; and (3) they want to expand Soviet exports. All three implicitly admit that Soviet goods are generally considered inferior to goods produced in the West. By improving the technology used to produce consumer and industrial goods and by using Western managerial expertise, Gorbachev hopes, the Soviet produced goods can become competitive on world markets. That would help the Soviet economy in two ways: by moving consumer tastes away from Western to domestically produced goods and by enhancing sales of Soviet exports abroad. Both would also help the Soviet hard currency situation; fewer consumer goods would have to be purchased from the West and paid for with hard currency, and the sale of Soviet manufactured exports to the West would generate additional revenue.

The key elements of the joint venture legislation include how ownership is structured, how much freedom and autonomy is granted to management, how operations are conducted with other Soviet enterprises, what kind of taxation treatment the joint ventures are given, how disputes are settled, and what kind of conditions govern employee compensation and benefits. There is also the matter of guarantees from the Soviet government to protect foreign investors from being expropriated. All the points here speak to concerns posed by Western businessmen. The fact that they have been incorporated into the joint venture legislation indicates a high degree of responsiveness from the Soviet government, which in turn indicates that joint ventures with Western firms are a high priority within the Gorbachev administration.

Specifically, the Soviet government has committed itself to allowing a foreign partner to hold up to 49 percent of the authorized capital of a joint venture. As for management, there are to be two echelons. One will function as a supervisory board responsible for making strategic decisions about the composition of the balance sheet and the distribution of profits; the other will be an executive body responsible for routine day-to-day management. Both levels will have representatives from both the foreign and the Soviet partners. However, the president and the executive director of the joint venture must, by legislative decree, be Soviet citizens. To U.S. businessmen who regard this as unfair, the Soviet response is: How many American managers are qualified to run an enterprise in the Soviet Union? "At least for a while, the only people who are qualified enough to do so are Soviets."[8]

Joint ventures will have the freedom to operate on foreign markets by license from the U.S.S.R. Ministry of Foreign Trade. Within the Soviet Union, joint ventures will be expected to deal with the appropriate foreign trade organizations, to sell to them and buy supplies from them at contractual prices to be paid in rubles. By "contractual" the Soviet government means that joint ventures can negotiate prices and choose their suppliers instead of having to pay official domestic wholesale and retail prices. That will put pressure on traditional Soviet enterprises not used to having to cater to customers or to compete against other suppliers—all part of the plan, according to the deputy chairman of the State Foreign Economic Commission: "We have already explained to our own managers that this competition has been introduced intentionally with the aim of pressing them to increase efficiency and quality of production."[9]

To attract Western firms to participate, the real sweetener offered by the Soviet government comes in the form of favorable tax treatment. For the first two years of operation, joint ventures will be favored with a tax "holiday" by the Soviet government, with no taxes on profits. There are also additional tax incentives after the first two years. A portion of joint venture profits can be sheltered tax-free in the form of reserves that may be retained up to a level of 25 percent of the authorized capital. A portion of profits can also be used for modernization and expansion and treated as reinvestment, also tax-free. The remaining profit is subject to a 30 percent tax. All after-tax profits are to be divided between the partners according to their shares of the authorized capital; the foreign partner presumably gets up to 49 percent. The profit coming to the foreign partner can be (1) put in a Soviet bank, (2) spent within the Soviet Union, or (3) transferred abroad in foreign currency. The last option is subject to a withholding fee, the exact rate of which depends on the tax agreements worked out between the Soviet Union and various Western countries. To induce other governments to support joint ventures and to grant Soviet enterprises reciprocal favorable tax treatment, the withholding fee is negotiable—ranging from zero to 20 percent.

In the event of a dispute, the joint venture legislation guarantees the foreign partner due process of law. Disputes may be settled either in the courts or through arbitration either in the Soviet Union or in a third country. The choice is up to the partners. Of course, since the partners are always represented in accordance with the capital structure, and the capital structure is always dominated by the 51 percent share owned by Soviet interests, one can assume that the choice of courts will tend to favor the Soviet side of the partnership. Thus, when the Soviet government guarantees that foreign property will be protected within the Soviet Union on the same basis as state property, that property cannot be confiscated or expropriated by administrative decision, and that actions pertaining to the property may be taken only through the court or arbitration, potential foreign investors should remember that what constitutes due process of law will be "up to the partners."

In general, working conditions and salaries for employees in joint ventures must comply with Soviet standards. Management will be allowed, however, to bring in foreign technicians, whose salaries will be determined by individual contracts. According to the joint venture legislation, the "residual" portion of a foreigner's salary may be transferred abroad in foreign currency subject to an income tax of 13 percent (the term "residual" suggesting that some portion of the salary will be automatically deducted on behalf of the government in keeping with Soviet practice). Some managements may wish, as stated in the legislation, to introduce additional personnel benefit plans "with the endorsement of the trade union."

Some other issues are also meant to reduce the concerns of foreign investors. The Soviet government guarantees remittance of profits in foreign currency—subject, of course, to the decisions reached by the partners about retained earnings and reinvestment. In case of liquidation, the foreign partner is entitled to transfer abroad his contribution to the authorized capital of the enterprise at its book value on the day of liquidation, part of the Soviet government's guarantee under due process of law.

In their pitch to potential Western investors, the Soviets stress particular advantages: abundant resources, skilled labor, and a huge market. Moreover, joint ventures have no state-imposed quotas or production plans to fulfill; management will be entirely free to determine the level of output. Joint ventures will also receive "favorable" treatment from Soviet transportation and communication services. Finally, they will be exempt from customs duties on machinery and equipment that represent contributions to the capital of the joint venture enterprise.

Western Reaction

The Soviets seem to have an exaggerated sense of how enticing their package is to Western businessmen. What began as a cautious willingness to tolerate foreign investment became an all-out selling effort, complete with inducements, to capture the imagination of multinational firms. Because no immediate enthusiastic response was forthcoming, the Soviets hastened to modify their pitch, adding more bottom-line financial incentives and reassuring Western firms that they will have some control over their capital investment. The biggest concession overall seems to be a Soviet willingness to be flexible. According to one American observer, "The Soviets suggest that the two sides to a negotiation simply sign a confidentiality agreement and start with two blank sheets of paper."[10]

Still, for the most part, Western businessmen remain skeptical about the Soviet system's capacity to do business by capitalist tenets. For example, many business executives are put off by the requirement that joint venture employees be covered by Soviet rules of employment. "It seems to take away the right of Western companies to hire and fire," one U.S. business executive said in Moscow. "That really undermines a Western businessman's means of exercising quality control."[11] It is a tricky matter. The architects of Gorbachev's new proposals are clearly reluctant to raise the ire of conservatives in the Communist Party who do not like the idea of giving foreign investors the right to hire and fire Soviet workers. The Soviet news service Tass was informed that the new legislation provides for joint authority in dealing with poor work and lack of discipline, but a worker can be discharged only if the trade union goes along.[12]

Another source of wariness is reliability of Soviet suppliers and access to them. For one thing, it is not clear that competitive bidding will provide joint enterprises with the market power they need to get things done in the Soviet system. For another, Western businessmen have expressed their reluctance to commit to large-scale projects that might be interrupted or interminably delayed down the line:

> They point out, for example, that while construction of housing is so slow and sloppy that buildings often begin to crumble before they are finished, the KGB headquarters on Dzerzhinsky Square is

now getting a huge second building, which is going up with astonishing speed and is using high-quality materials and workmanship. Businessmen have little faith in being able to compete for raw materials and labor with projects the state suddenly decides have a higher priority.[13]

The main objective of most businessmen, after all, is to make a profit. Accordingly, they criticize the Soviet legislation for being too vague about how profits from ruble transactions will be exchanged for hard currency and repatriated back home. Then, too, the amount of the withholding fee has yet to be determined, pending negotiations between the Soviet Union and Western countries about reciprocal tax arrangements. And at what exchange rate will rubles be converted into hard currencies? Professor Richard Ericson, a Columbia University economist, considers it "very unlikely" that the rules governing joint ventures will be structured to enable Western businessmen to take home ruble profits from domestic sales in the form of hard currency. "If the Soviets permit that at the official inflated exchange rate," he says, "they'll lose a lot of money."[14]

Underlying those difficult issues is the fact that Gorbachev is trying to reconcile conflicting objectives. For Western businessmen the primary attraction of a joint venture is access to the potentially massive Soviet market; what the Soviets have in mind is to increase their access to Western markets, to produce world-class goods that will be purchased by Western customers with hard currencies. So Western firms may find they are creating competition for themselves in their own domestic markets. And to the extent that the Soviets successfully develop import substitution, foreign participants in effect will be selling for rubles the same goods for which they once got hard currencies.

Despite the conflicts, resolved and otherwise, a number of Western firms, including several American companies, are moving ahead on joint ventures with the Soviet Union. Finland is one country that has traditionally shown great interest in the Soviet market. Shortly after the new legislation was announced, Finnair said that it planned to set up a joint venture with Intourist to restore and operate the Berlin Hotel in Moscow. Businessmen from West Germany also showed keen interest. Up to one hundred West German firms reportedly put out feelers, including Salamander, a shoe manufacturer; Liebherr (machinery); and Otto Wolff, a privately-owned steel and engineering group. The

Italian company Fata submitted to the Soviet authorities plans to build a factory outside Moscow for manufacturing $500 million worth of refrigerating equipment annually, 10 percent of it to be exported.[15] And PepsiCo, from the United States, made plans to build two Pizza Hut restaurants in Moscow.[16]

By October 1987, less than a year after the joint venture legislation was put into effect, the Soviets claimed they had received 250 joint venture proposals, including thirty from U.S. firms. Only eleven agreements had actually been signed by that time;[17] Soviet officials, stating that "We're not in a hurry," said they planned to sign up a limited number of firms and then monitor the results before inviting more proposals.[18] After reaching an agreement on a venture, the plans are submitted to various Soviet advisory, financial, and ministerial bodies, which decide whether the proposed joint venture meets Soviet foreign trade objectives. Five of the signed agreements were with West German companies, not surprising since that country is the Soviet Union's largest trade partner in the West. Other agreements signed the first year involved firms from Finland, Japan, Italy, India, and the United States.[19]

Combustion Engineering was the first American firm actually to commit, setting up a joint venture with the Soviet Ministry of Oil Refining and Petrochemical Industries. Several other major U.S. companies expressed interest in varying degrees. At least three—Monsanto, Occidental Petroleum, and SSMC (formerly part of Singer)—proceeded to sign letters of intent with Soviet foreign trade officials. Monsanto would help operate a herbicide plant in Kazakhstan; Occidental would cooperate in a secondary oil-extraction project in the Volga area; and SSMC would produce sewing machines in Byelorussia.[20] General Electric sent two U.S. managers to the Soviet Union to explore opportunities in gas turbines and industrial equipment. Archer-Daniels-Midland began exploring the possibility of an agribusiness venture with the Soviets, who want oilseed processing plants and grain storage systems.[21] Honeywell announced plans for a joint venture to modernize about 100 Soviet chemical fertilizer plants.[22] McDonald's, pursuing what it calls "hamburger diplomacy," had first started talking with the Soviets in 1976; in June 1987 a representative for the company told reporters, "We're going to do it."[23] In April 1988, McDonald's finally signed a joint venture agreement to begin opening restaurants in Moscow. The first one is slated to be located near the Kremlin on Gorky Street.[24]

Despite saying they were in no hurry to process applications for joint ventures, the Soviets moved extremely quickly to sign a joint agreement with the Banque de L'Union Européenne, a government-controlled French bank. In an announcement in March 1987, the French firm said it had agreed with two Soviet banks to set up a joint venture in the Soviet Union; the operating date was set for April 15. The French bank is to provide consulting services and to participate in the financing of joint ventures. According to the director of the bank's international affairs, "We were a bit surprised by the speed with which the Soviets moved, but our agreement reflects their seriousness to extend joint ventures to the banking sector."[25] Participating with the Banque de l'Union Européenne is another Paris-based commercial bank, the Banque Commerciale pour l'Europe du Nord. Although the latter bank is entirely owned and operated by the Soviets, it will be regarded as French in the joint venture, with the Soviet partners Gosbank and the U.S.S.R. Bank for Foreign Economic Affairs.[26]

In-house Transfers

Western bankers should not be surprised by how fast the Soviets are willing to move to secure financial partners. The whole purpose of the joint venture program, after all, is to expand Soviet financial resources and access to capital. Whether or not managerial expertise from the West can truly be utilized in conditions where the chief executive officer of every joint venture is by law a Soviet citizen is not certain. But gaining access to Western technology has long been a priority for the Soviet government, and the joint venture program makes it all much simpler than when high technology in particular had to be procured in the face of a maze of restrictions and paid for with scarce hard currency. Now the Soviets will have an in-house technical ally working with them.

For the Soviets, the real beauty of setting up joint ventures with Western firms is that the Western imports—consumer goods and technology—needed to reverse the trend of declining productivity in the Soviet economy will now be available *internally* in higher quantities than ever before. And it won't cost the Soviet Union one cent, pfennig, or centime in hard currency reserves. Previously, when oil prices declined on world markets and the demand for Soviet-made weapons dropped, the squeeze on hard currency resources inevitably forced the Soviet Union to cut back on Western imports. Under Gorbachev, there has been an expanded willingness to go into debt to Western banks rather than cut the imports, because they comprise too important an element of perestroika.

If the joint venture program takes hold, the Soviets will reduce their risks in the international oil and weapons markets and will benefit from a more diversified mix of products exported to the West. True, those exports will be shining examples not of Soviet creativity and workmanship but of West German, Finnish, Japanese, or Italian workmanship. Yet they will be Soviet-made products in that they will be physically produced within the Soviet Union. More important, they will generate hard currency revenues for the Soviet treasury. The key requirement for the operation of joint ventures is that they cover their foreign currency expenses with foreign currency proceeds, so in effect they will pay for themselves while providing the Soviets with all the benefits of foreign trade.

Essentially, when Western firms go into joint ventures with the Soviet Union, they are transferring capital to the Soviet economy. Given the customary distinction between debt and equity, it can be argued that putting up equity in a Soviet joint venture is not the same as making a loan to the Soviet government. But the difference is little more than a matter of defining precisely how the principal is to be repaid. On a loan, interest and principal are repaid out of earnings generated by Soviet exports, and there is no necessary and direct connection between the proceeds of the loan and the source of repayment. In a joint venture arrangement, Western investors do not expect to receive a predefined level of return on their capital. However, they do expect *some* return, presumably more than with a loan. For their equity investment, Western participants expect to share in the profits of the enterprise, which should be high enough to compensate them for the uncertainty as to exactly what the rate of return will be. In short, both debt and equity are claims on future revenues based on putting up capital.

Aside from the inconvenience and discomfort of having foreigners within its borders, joint ventures offer significant advantages over commercial and government-supported loans for the Soviet Union. It's a no-lose situation. If a particular joint venture fails to meet the goals imposed by the Soviet government, it can be liquidated by the Soviet Council of Ministers, because its activities "do not fall in line with the objectives and tasks envisaged" in the founding charter.[27] In the meantime, the Soviet economy gains from having had access to capital from outside the system, capital not monitored by the Bank for International Settlements or the Organization for Economic Cooperation and Development.

Western firms enjoy great privacy in their global investment activities and, except for the occasional outcry over the political ramifications of doing business with countries like South Africa, operate relatively free from government scrutiny or interference. Unless a firm chooses to use the services of a bank to carry out transactions directly with the Soviet Union or to take advantage of a government guarantee program, its exposure is not tallied under the global calculations based on commercial loans and official trade credits. A corporation may furnish its own financing to the Soviet Union, using suppliers' credits, or it may provide initial financing and then sell the bills of exchange or promissory notes issued by the Soviets in connection with the sale to a forfeiter, a financial organization that agrees to accept the notes at a certain price and to absorb the risk of collecting payment from the Soviets without recourse to the exporter. Such financing arrangements can be obtained through companies that are subsidiaries of bank holding companies, such as Finanz AG of Credit Suisse, and are not subject to the reporting requirements imposed on commercial banks.

In short, the activities of nonbank private firms are conducted outside any sphere of institutionalized scrutiny. Joint ventures with Western companies thus provide a potential conduit for channeling private capital to the Soviet Union. The benefits are so considerable that it is surprising that the terms for establishing joint ventures are not more generous. The Soviets can afford to provide additional inducements, given the lopsidedness of the arrangements as stipulated in the current joint venture legislation.

Consider the proposition of setting up a $100-million joint venture with the Soviets as an American firm might see it. At most, the U.S. partner will be allowed to own 49 percent of the initial capital, or $49 million. Assume the amount comes in the form of financial capital; meanwhile, the Soviets agree to provide $51 million worth of plant, property, licenses, and other capital assets. If the venture is typical of most start-up endeavors, it will not be profitable during the first two years of operation, and the much-vaunted "tax holiday" becomes irrelevant. Assume that in the third year the $100 million joint venture earns a 10 percent profit, or $10 million. According to the joint venture law, profits up to 25 percent of the enterprise's capital structure can be sheltered from taxes. The decision to do so will be made by representatives of the partners' interests, and since the Soviets will always maintain controlling interest, it is reasonable to assume that they will opt to keep the profits in the enterprise. The entire $10 million would thus be kept in retained earnings, making the value of the enterprise $110 million—$54 million of which will belong to the American partners and $56 million to the Soviet partners. Then assume that the enterprise again earns 10 percent in its fourth year, and the entire $11 million also is sheltered as retained earnings. So after four years in the Soviet Union, the American partner has not yet realized any take-home profits from an initial $49 million investment.

In the fifth year, assume that another 10 percent, or $12 million, is earned. To keep it simple, assume the 25 percent rule applies to the initial capital structure; thus only $4 million of the profits can be added to the total profits of the prior two years to be sheltered as retained earnings. The Soviet joint venture legislation refers to another means of sheltering profits, also to be used at the discretion of the partners, by "reinvesting" profits for modernization and expansion. The amount that can be put into expansion tax-free is not specified, but assume $4 million of the remaining $8 million in profits is assigned, leaving $4 million to be divided by the partners. That amount, however, is subject to the 30 percent tax imposed by the Soviet government. Thus, after-tax profits to the partners are $2.8 million, $1.37 million of which goes to the American investor.

The American partner now has three choices when it comes to taking out his return. He can put it in a Soviet bank, use it to buy Soviet goods, or convert it into hard currency and repatriate it back home. Shareholders can hardly get excited about a Soviet savings bank paying the standard 3 percent rate of interest. It is also unlikely that shareholders would want to purchase Soviet goods and take them back home. The most attractive option, of course, is to have the money in a usable form, in dollars. But if the U.S. partner wants to exchange ruble profits for dollars, the transaction is subject to a withholding fee, no doubt at the top rate of 20 percent.

So, for an initial investment of $49 million, the American partner after five years of operation receives total profits of $1.1 million. In the meantime, of course, the value of his holdings in the enterprise has grown. But the U.S. partner does not have a controlling interest in the venture and therefore has little to say about how profits are invested or disbursed. Nor can he be sure that the Soviet courts can be counted on to treat all parties fairly in the event of liquidation.

Still, American firms are showing creativity and proving very resourceful in structuring joint ventures with the Soviets that get around the problem of having to convert ruble profits into hard currency earnings. PepsiCo, for example, would set up one Pizza Hut restaurant open to the general public, dealing in rubles, while the other would be open only to tourists or those with hard currency. The local bills, including payroll and purchases of produce, would be paid out of earnings from the public restaurant; the hard currency restaurant would provide the funds to pay for necessary imported products and to compensate PepsiCo.[28]

Where there's a will, apparently, there's a way. In April 1988, it was announced at a Kremlin dinner in Moscow for more than 500 American businessmen that seven major U.S. corporations had formed a consortium to explore broader business contacts between the two countries through joint ventures.[29] The American Trade Consortium, made up of Archer-Daniels-Midland, Chevron, Eastman Kodak, Johnson and Johnson, Ford Motor Co., The Mercator Corp., and R.J.R. Nabisco, is intended to provide assistance to other U.S. companies to overcome the hurdles of the Soviet bureaucracy and to cope with financing difficulties. The consortium's president, James H. Giffen, pointed out that the American business initiative, in conjunction with the improved political atmosphere, could promote unprecedented new levels of commerce with the Soviet Union. He underscored the motivation for expanding U.S.–U.S.S.R. commercial contacts. "This is not aid, this is trade," Giffen said. "What we're after is profit."[30]

Issuing a Eurobond

The mark of prestige, the true measure of a nation's arrival in international financial markets, is its capacity to borrow by issuing sovereign bonds. Commercial loans and official trade credits are useful, of course, and carry a certain amount of weight by indicating how bankers and governments regard a nation's credit rating. An outside investor's willingness to invest in a country's joint ventures, too, demonstrates financial credibility. But to prove that the world believes in a country's future—that outsiders have confidence in the stability of its government and the productive potential of its internal economy—that country must be able to borrow by issuing long-term bonds.

It is this principal form of borrowing that, for so many years, the Soviet Union was unable to effect for itself. Part of the problem was that Soviet bloc countries in general were not deemed to have sufficient credit standing to make them eligible to launch issues in the bond market. Of the seven countries customarily considered to compose the Soviet bloc (Yugoslavia is not among them), only Hungary was able to borrow from the West in recent years by offering sovereign bonds.[1] Even at that, a 1986 offering for $250 million in floating rate notes had to be collateralized by zero-coupon U.S. Treasury bonds in order to appeal to Euromarket investors.[2]

For the Soviet Union, the main obstacle has been the legal barriers erected to prohibit defaulting governments from using the
world's primary capital markets to raise additional monies from
private investors. As we know, those barriers for the most part
stem from debts incurred before Lenin took control of the Soviet
government.

For the Soviets, getting into the long-term bond market means
facing historical facts recent enough to be painful and, perhaps,
embarrassing. The cause of present-day Soviet unity would not
be served if anyone were to officially reexamine the time when
a number of groups rose in opposition to Lenin. Nor would it do
to highlight the fact that while outside nations were channeling
money, supplies, and armed forces to Russia to stave off the Germans, Lenin was taking advantage of chaotic wartime conditions
to stage his own revolutionary coup against the government. If
the Soviet government is accepted as having begun on the first
day of the Revolution, November 7, 1917, then one would expect
that, in accordance with generally accepted notions of sovereign
obligation, the Soviet Union would accept responsibility for all
debts outstanding as at that date, including monies received to
support the war effort, unless the Soviets are prepared to say that
the Bolsheviks felt no compulsion to fend off German invaders or
that the Soviet ascendancy to power marked the end of Russia's
existence.

Compounding the matter of historical embarrassment is a long-
standing Soviet reluctance to divulge financial information and
technical data of the sort normally required by investors before
they will make long-term commitments. In the United States, securities for public offering are registered with the Securities and
Exchange Commission and normally rated by credit analysts. In
the Euromarkets, regulators are more inclined to waive certain
disclosure requirements. But the Soviets nevertheless are vulner-
able to two questions: What rate must be paid to entice investor
interest, and what terms must be attached to secure investor confidence? In other words, just how much value do Western financial markets attach to long-term bonds backed by the full faith
and credit of the Soviet government?

Prerevolutionary Ties

The State Bank organized under Tsar Alexander II after the Russian financial crisis in the late 1850s had the same name as its

modern Soviet counterpart, Gosbank.[3] Coinciding with the liberation of serfs in 1861—and preceding by just a few years the creation of the national banking system in the United States—the tsarist State Bank took a very active role in the economic development of the country by dispensing credits and subsidies in keeping with national priorities. Other central banks in Europe, which were all privately owned (except for that of Sweden) prior to World War I, made loans that contributed to the development of their own countries' economic growth. But economic development in the national interest was merely incidental to decisions about the commercial viability of individual loans. Tsarist Russia's State Bank was the only institution that

> . . . consistently undertook credit operations in the interest of
> economic development and in this connection frequently took
> credit risks incompatible with normal business practice. It made
> loans under conditions that, in some cases, were equivalent to
> subsidies, and occasionally waived repayment, effectively
> transforming loans into grants, in order to nurse through
> enterprises judged essential from the national standpoint. It even
> supplied capital indirectly to industry through loans collateralized
> by new securities, and provided part of the initial capital for some
> new banks.[4]

It is curious that the banking system established by Lenin after the failure of the revolutionary People's Bank would come to resemble the earlier state-controlled tsarist organization. The Gosbank system of the late nineteenth century sought to improve the economy of Russia; it provided capital to spur industrialization and supported agricultural expansion. The Farmers Bank, founded by the state as a mortgage bank under Gosbank in 1883, was established to furnish credit to the former serfs who had become peasant farmers. The Noble Agricultural Bank, also founded by the state, was established two years later for the benefit of the large landowners.

Beyond allocating its own resources to advance national objectives, the state exerted influence over the private banks that began to proliferate after the establishment of the first privately owned commercial bank in Russia in 1864, the Petersburger Private Commercial Bank.[5] The growing needs of commerce and industry for Russian development spawned the creation of "mixed" banking, financial institutions that carried on the traditional function of accepting savings deposits while at the same time engaging in securities underwriting. Many of the equities held in private bank portfolios represented shares in corporations that were sponsored or otherwise supported by the tsarist government. As the number of private banks in Russia rapidly increased, foreign capital began to pour in, supplementing domestic resources and giving outsiders a financial stake in the lucrative process of Russian industrialization. Ultimately, some 74 percent of the capital shares of private banks came to be held in foreign hands.[6] Of the banks in St. Petersburg at the beginning of the twentieth century, one foreign observer writes that they were "Russian in appearance, foreign with regard to their resources, and ministerial as to risk bearing."[7]

Risk bearing by the tsarist government was assumed in the form of state guarantees. Foreign money to fund industrial corporations and to pay for the construction of railroads was solicited with promises from the tsarist government that all loans would be repaid, that there was no possibility of default. Indeed, the maturity dates of some of the bonds issued during the 1880s and 1890s assumed that the tsarist succession would extend well into the future. External bonds on behalf of the Russian government carrying a 4 percent rate of interest and denominated in gold rubles were issued in 1894 with a maturity date of 1975—a period of eighty years. Railway bonds guaranteed by the government and denominated in francs, pounds, and marks were considered just as safe and were likewise issued with extremely long maturities; pound-denominated bonds sold in 1913 to finance the building of the Black Sea–Kuban railway will not come due until 1992.[8]

Russian bonds were extremely popular with foreign investors in France, Britain, and Germany. During the last decade of the nineteenth century, other favored regions for international investment had suffered from a variety of problems. Latin American governments had defaulted on their loans. American railroad companies had gone bankrupt. Australia had been hit by drought. South Africa, popular earlier with British investors who had rushed in with capital to develop the gold mines, was now beset with political problems.[9] Russia appeared to be the one "safe haven" in the world. Offering attractive returns on projects guaranteed by the Tsar himself, it presented the best apparent opportunities for foreign investors.

France, in particular, was attracted to Russian investment. Encouraged by their government, French banks were looking beyond their own borders for productive investment, and they hastened to make loans to such relatively unexploited areas as North Africa and Eastern Europe.[10] The Russian situation was especially appealing because the tsarist government was promoting a grand vision of economic development and progress. French money poured into such major projects as the Trans-Siberian Railway, begun in 1891 under Tsar Alexander III. Russian industry flourished thanks to the steady infusion of foreign capital being channeled through private banks. With the assumption to the throne of Tsar Nicholas II in 1894, the alliance between France and Russia gained strength as French investors proceeded to develop a heavy vested interest in preserving the tsarist regime.

Russia's war with Japan in 1904–5 did little to discourage French investors; if anything, they became even more determined to support the tsarist government as well as Russian economic and political influence in East Asia. Financing the war was itself a profitable venture for the banks, which solicited foreign funds with war bonds issued by the Tsar to pay for armaments and strategic railroads. Even when Russia lost the war, and with it, much of its perceived creditworthiness, the French government continued to persuade banks to raise new loans, to support the Franco-Russian political alliance that had been formed.[11]

But as French investors aligned themselves with the Tsar, they put themselves at odds with the revolutionary movement beginning to spread among the Russian population. It was clear that the tsarist regime would not accommodate socialist sentiments. But pressed by liberal intellectuals, as well as peasant hordes, to abolish the autocracy and establish a parliament, Tsar Nicholas II initially displayed some willingness to tolerate a degree of self-government for the people. On the advice of his Finance Minister, Count Witte, the Tsar in October 1905 approved the establishment of a State Duma, or parliament, to be elected on a wide basis. Composed of both Bolsheviks and Mensheviks, the Duma well represented the revolutionary segment of the population:

When it opened in May 1906 it immediately became the scene of violent demands for the government's resignation, for a political amnesty, for a democratic electoral system and for the right to strike. By July the Czar had had enough and dissolved it, saying it had exceeded its competence.[12]

As conflict intensified, the revolutionaries began to regard the foreign investors, primarily French, as in league with the Tsar, holding them equally responsible for perceived acts of tyranny against the peasants. When the tsarist government, shortly after the Russo-Japanese War, raised new money from private banks and the French public with the help of the French government, it was seen as aggression against the Russian workers, who at the time were striking for more civil liberties. "Every French citizen who buys the loan," Maxim Gorky proclaimed, "is an accomplice in the organized murder of a people."[13] But French investors had more at stake than ever in tsarist rule, because by this point, one-quarter of all French foreign investment was linked to Russia and France faced the prospect of a banking collapse should the Tsar be overthrown.[14]

During the years of industrial expansion and wartime expenditures from 1885 to 1914, the number of private banks operating in Russia had increased by some 35 percent and the aggregate banking capital had gone up by some 700 percent—the vast majority of it from foreign sources.[15] The stability of the Russian financial system rested with Gosbank, which in 1914 had ten main offices in the most important Russian cities. The main offices were linked to 124 subsidiary offices and a network of 791 subscription offices in smaller towns and villages.[16] The entire Gosbank system was part of the Treasury, which in turn was part of the tsarist government.

When Russia entered World War I, the interests of private investors were seconded by the governments of Britain, France, and the United States, all of which wanted to help Russia against Germany. In 1916 American investors purchased $75 million in dollar-denominated securities issued by the Imperial Russian Government; shortly thereafter, the U.S. government sponsored the Liberty Bonds Act of 1917, out of which some $187.7 million was advanced to Russia between July and November of 1917, followed by $4.9 million worth of foodstuffs and supplies furnished on credit in July 1918 and February 1919. The democratic provisional government, formed after rioting and strikes in Petrograd, ruled briefly during the transitional period between the collapse of autocracy in March 1917 and the Bolshevik takeover in November 1917. Turmoil between reformists and reactionaries—Social Democrats and Bolsheviks, Bolsheviks and Social Revolutionaries—made it difficult for outside governments to determine who was in charge of fighting the war with the Germans. The

Russian Soviet Federated Socialist Republic, an interim government, was not established until July 1918, four months after British troops had landed in Murmansk to protect Russian supply depots from the Germans, who, promptly after the Bolshevik coup, had occupied the Baltic states and had landed troops in Finland.[17]

What was clear, however, following the signing of the Allied armistice with Germany in November 1918, some eight months after Russia signed a separate peace treaty with Germany, was that the Russian authorities the allies thought they were helping at the onset of World War I were not the same people who seemed to hold power in Russia when the war ended. After Lenin successfully assaulted both the weakened tsarist empire and the moderate Social Democrats represented by the provisional government, he proceeded to lay claim to the financial resources of Gosbank, dispatching an armed Bolshevik detachment of workers and soldiers to occupy the main office of the State Bank in Petrograd on the first day of the coup.

Bank employees resisted and went so far as to attempt to sabotage Lenin's efforts to take over financial and banking operations. All private commercial banks immediately closed down in concerted action with the State Bank to thwart Lenin and the revolutionary forces. Bank officials worked to protect existing shareholder claims to financial assets, yet they also sought to bring about economic paralysis to cripple the revolutionary movement. Employees were given three months' advance salary on the condition that they refuse to serve the Soviet regime. Those actions presented obstacles for Lenin, but his immediate goal was to empty the vaults of their currency; this he managed to do.[18]

When it became clear that bank officials and employees could not be persuaded to embrace the cause of the Soviet revolution, Lenin moved quickly to bring in armed Bolshevik representatives again, this time placing them in the offices of the commercial banks. On December 27, 1917, the Soviet government decreed that all commercial banks were nationalized without compensation to shareholders, domestic or foreign.[19] Earlier claims were null and void; what had formerly belonged to private investors was now the property of the new Soviet government. Claiming the banks, of course, did not mean taking responsibility for the obligations of Russian financial institutions, either public or private. Creditors were simply dismissed. Claims for monies due to foreign governments as well as private foreign investors were ignored, including the claims of the U.S. government for bonds slated to mature in 1921.

Spurned Creditors

In retrospect, outside investors should have perhaps anticipated that the tsarist regime was ripe for revolution, but the actual coup did come very quickly with World War I acting as the catalyst. Since 1894, Tsar Nicholas II had reigned as the legitimate head of the Russian government, presiding over a period of tremendous economic development and industrial expansion. Going into World War I, he was still the recognized head of Russia and the official guarantor of the innumerable debt obligations that had been issued to private investors in the name of the Imperial Russian Government. But after the war, the financial claims represented by shares in Russian banks and by bonds issued with the Tsar's double-headed eagle insignia, including the newly issued war bonds, turned into just so much paper.

The amounts involved were staggering. Because so many of the bonds issued under the tsarist government carried maturity dates extending eighty years and more into the future, Lenin's refusal to honor the commitments of the prior government meant a series of Russian defaults would continue until the very end of the twentieth century. Interest payments on sovereign debt obligations were suspended in 1917, just one year after the Imperial Russian Government had issued $75 million in dollar bonds; $50 million, carrying a 6.5 interest rate, was payable in 1919 while the other $25 million, paying 5.5 percent interest, was set to mature in 1921. All the national bonds issued in the name of Russia to fund the process of industrialization throughout the last half of the nineteenth century, all the railway bonds guaranteed by the tsarist government to build an internal transportation system, all the debt obligations to finance armaments and strategic supplies for the Russo-Japanese War and for the war against the Germans—all were disclaimed by the new Soviet government, all defaulted. Many of the bonds had been denominated in the currencies of the lending countries, so that foreign investors held Russian debt defined in British pounds, French francs, German marks, or Dutch guilders. In total, defaulted Russian bonds to private investors, not counting interest but merely principal, amounted to 176 million pounds in British debt, 6.1 billion francs in French debt, 1.8 billion marks in German debt, and 5.3 million guilders in Dutch debt.[20] A further billion in debt denominated in gold rubles, and 4 billion more in regular rubles, were also held by investors and were likewise dismissed by the new Soviet government.

The immediate financial effect on the lending countries was devastating, particularly for France, where the Soviet cancellation led to that country's greatest banking catastrophe. The United States was perhaps more confused than financially affected by the turn of events in Russia. Some 7,500 U.S. Marines had been sent to Vladivostok in September 1918 to assist Admiral Aleksandr Kolchak, head of the All-Russian government, in his battle against German forces. But the American soldiers were evacuated from Russia the following year during the height of the civil war there. The Union of Soviet Socialist Republics would not officially come into existence until 1923.[21] It seemed that private American investors and the U.S. government had been supporting a country that no longer existed.

By the acknowledged principles of international law, the Soviets did not have the right to ignore the obligations of the prior government—not without violating the most basic precepts of national responsibility. As stated in the *International Law Digest*, quoting Secretary of State John Quincy Adams (August 10, 1818):

> No principle of international law can be more clearly established than this: That the *rights* and the *obligations* of a nation in regard to other States are independent of its internal revolutions of government. It extends even to the case of conquest. The conqueror who reduces a nation to his subjection receives it subject to all its engagements and duties toward others, the fulfillment of which then becomes his own duty.[22]

And with specific reference to financial obligations: "Public debts, whether due to or from the revolutionized State, are neither cancelled nor affected by any change in the constitution or internal government of a State."[23]

Asked to issue an opinion on the applicability of the Johnson Debt Default Act to the Soviet Union, U.S. Attorney General Homer Cummings ruled in 1934 that the Soviet government was indeed in default, that the U.S. government held the Soviet government responsible for the obligations incurred by prior Russian governments, and that the position of the U.S. government in this respect accorded with accepted principles of international law.[24] The position that the Soviet Union is in default on its payments to the United States was upheld in 1967 by an opinion issued by Attorney General Ramsey Clark. Clark said that financing arrangements on behalf of the Soviet Union directly tied to specific export transactions, with terms based on bona fide business considerations, were permitted under the act. But he was careful to point out:

> On the other hand, as the same opinion suggests, if the financial form of a transaction is a subterfuge to conceal what is, in effect, a general purpose loan, it would violate the act. Nor does the act permit any arrangement that contemplates the marketing of foreign government obligations to the American public.[25]

The punishment imposed on the Soviet government was to bar it from ever being able to borrow through U.S. securities markets by issuing bonds; it is also illegal for anyone in the United States to purchase such bonds or other sovereign obligations of the Soviet Union, unless, of course, the Soviets choose to pay back the amounts owed to the U.S. government for wartime debts. The principal amount connected with World War I of $192.6 million has been accruing interest for some seventy years. According to officials at the U.S. Treasury, the total accumulated interest on this amount as of the end of March 1988 is $675.9 million. If the Soviets wanted to settle their account with the U.S. government, if they wanted to move beyond the original sanctions of the Johnson Debt Default Act and open the way toward selling bonds to the American public, the up-front costs from World War I would total $868.5 million. Outstanding World War II debt adds up to another $674 million.

For the British, not only did private investors lose the value of the tsarist-backed bonds, but other Britons had their commercial property and assets in Russia seized by the Bolsheviks and nationalized without compensation by the Soviet government. In all, some 36,000 claimants in Britain were denied some 250 million pounds' worth of financial claims represented by the face value of Russian bonds and property holdings in Russia.[26] On top of that were loans extended by the British government to aid in the war effort against Germany. When the Soviets reneged on Russia's foreign debt, they offended the British Crown. In retaliation, the Exchequer requested that funds being held in the name of the Tsar in an account at Barings Bank in London be turned over to the British government. Fearing a potential Soviet counterclaim, Barings demurred at releasing the funds but agreed to freeze the account. As a further indication of Britain's displeasure, the Bank of England resolved to forbid the Soviet government from issuing sovereign bonds through London capital markets until the matter of repayment to Britons on Russian debts was settled.

At one point, in 1934, members of the British cabinet argued among themselves about whether to use the disputed balances at Barings to work out some kind of settlement between British claimants and the Soviet government. Anthony Eden, the Foreign Secretary, admitted that the 6 million pounds being held at Barings was a trivial sum measured against the 250 million pounds in outstanding Russian debts owed to Britons. He pointed out, however, that "some of the creditors were in a very bad way and it would be better to obtain this than nothing at all."[27] Neville Chamberlain, Chancellor of the Exchequer, said that it would be "humiliating" to accept such a minuscule amount of money. According to the minutes of the British cabinet meeting, it was declared that the money in the Barings account rightfully "should be paid to the British taxpayer since, broadly speaking, it represents money advanced to the former Russian Government for the prosecution of the War, but not used for this purpose.[28] Unable to resolve the grievances of creditors and the refusal of the Soviets to drop their claim to tsarist assets unless that action relieved the Soviet government of all former claims of Britons against Russia, the British cabinet meeting ended in 1934 on a note of resignation:

> The conclusion seems to be that no action can usefully be taken about the Baring Balances until negotiations with Russia about claims and debts generally can be undertaken with some hope of being less a fiasco than the abortive negotiations of 1924 and 1929.[29]

Ready to Settle

The ban imposed by the Bank of England against allowing the Soviet Union to float sovereign bonds in London markets stayed in effect until July 15, 1986, when the United Kingdom and the Soviet Union settled the claims. Signed by British Foreign Secretary Sir Geoffrey Howe and Soviet Foreign Minister Eduard

Shevardnadze, the agreement stipulates that the money held at Barings be released to the British government, which then becomes solely responsible for meeting the claims of British investors involving debt instruments issued or guaranteed by any pre-Soviet government before November 7, 1917. That same amount from Barings is also to be used to meet any postrevolutionary claims by Britons for the loss of property, rights, or interests confiscated in the territory of the former Russian empire.

The agreement is described as a "final settlement of mutual financial and property claims" and addresses the counterclaims of the Soviet Union against Britain as well. Those claims include a charge of intervention between November 7, 1917, and March 16, 1921, which involved armed operations and hostile measures against the fledgling Soviet government. The agreement also takes into account transfers of gold to the British government under pre-Soviet governments and gold given to Germany by the Soviets in war reparations subsequently turned over to the Allies when the Germans later signed a peace treaty with them. Finally, the Soviets waived their claims to any tsarist assets that may yet remain in the United Kingdom.[30]

The terms would probably be denounced once more by Neville Chamberlain as too humiliating to accept. The Baring balances, which had grown with interest to about $75 million, were to be used to cover $203 million in bonds plus claims registered by Britons totaling $598 million on property seized during the revolution.[31] If interest and appreciation are included, the British government is forgiving $69 billion in debts defaulted as the result of the Bolshevik takeover.[32]

At the news of the settlement, bonds printed in Russian, French, and German began to pour in to Price Waterhouse in London, the accounting firm chosen to administer the compensation fund. According to Price Waterhouse sources, the firm had been contacted by 3,319 claimants and expected to receive perhaps 500,000 bonds, most of them from the $1.75 billion in face value bonds that the tsarist government had issued to finance building projects. In a letter to Price Waterhouse, one Englishman described how he had obtained the bonds in 1949 from his dying father and now hoped to collect some amount of repayment on them. According to the letter, the father had thrown the bonds at his son in disgust, saying: "I have never been able to do anything with these swindling Soviet SOBs. See if you can do any better."[33]

What may have been an unexpected opportunity for the British was no mere whimsical gesture on the part of the Soviet Union. The Soviets were willing to compromise because it seemed the only way to get around the prohibition against borrowing through the issuance of bonds in London capital markets— another example of pragmatism triumphing over ideological posturing under Gorbachev's administration. Financially, the agreement was extremely advantageous to the Soviet Union. By relinquishing a claim to monies that the Soviet Union could never use, and that had never physically left Britain, the Kremlin paved the way for increased borrowing—in new, much more efficient ways—from the West. Responding to the agreement, an official at the Bank of England declared that the settlement "has removed an obstacle" to new Soviet issues in the sterling capital markets and that the Bank of England no longer had any objection to such issues by the Soviet government.[34]

Investment banks were reportedly quick to respond to the Soviet Union's newly gained access to the Euromarkets. According to the managing director of First Chicago Ltd. in London: "If anybody in the capital markets has not yet presented the Soviets with any interesting ideas, they will now."[35] A Rand publication likewise reported that Soviet financial authorities were being approached by a steady stream of merchant banking organizations offering proposals for structuring and managing debt issues.[36] The Soviet Union would represent a plum for any London investment banking firm, because the Soviet Union is positioned to become a major player in the bond markets. Its syndicated loans have been rapidly oversubscribed by Western commercial banks in recent years. Eurobonds are the logical next step, and big British, Japanese, West German, and U.S. banks are battling to lead anticipated Soviet Eurobond issues in London.[37]

In a surprise move, however, the Soviets opted not to go with a London firm for their first foreign bond offering but rather with a little-known Swiss unit of a state-owned West German bank. In January 1988, the Bank fur Kredit und Aussenhandel A.G., a subsidiary of Westdeutsche Landesbank, served as lead manager for the syndicate of seventeen banks that underwrote the Soviet Union's maiden entry into the Eurobond markets. The Soviet bond offering, issued in the name of the U.S.S.R. Bank for Foreign Economic Affairs, was for 100 million Swiss francs ($78 million). It carried an interest rate of 5 percent with a ten-year maturity, callable after five years.

The 5 percent coupon was considered tight by financial analysts; the Soviet Union is a relatively unknown borrower, after all, and ten years is a long time. Just prior to the offering, the Soviet Union agreed to pay off Russia's tsarist debts to Switzerland. Although the details of the debt settlement agreement were not announced, banking officials said that the controversy over old tsarist debts had been resolved in principle in late 1987 during an exchange of state visits between Switzerland and the U.S.S.R.[38] The purpose for the latter-day loan was to raise funds "for general financing purposes." Speculation was that Swiss investors would be too conservative to buy paper from a communist country.[39] But as it turned out, the issue was very successful. According to Holger Bahl, general manager of the bank that handled the Soviet offering, the issue had met with considerable interest from Swiss and other banks and institutional investors and was quickly oversubscribed by the underwriting syndicate. It had also generated interest from a "surprising" number of private investors, he said.[40]

Following the successful first offering, Victor Gerashenko, deputy chairman of the Bank for Foreign Economic Affairs, indicated that the Soviet Union was looking at the possible "further use of this form of financing in various currencies on international and national capital markets" and that it had received numerous offers from banks in different countries.[41] One of those offers came from the Dresdner Bank, A. G. in West Germany and involved the much larger issuance of a $294 million Eurobond. One possible hurdle connected with the offering was a West German stock exchange rule requiring that bond issuers disclose their debt and foreign exchange reserves. However, the Soviets managed to have the disclosure requirement waived by Swiss officials, and it was expected that they would be able to exact the same concession in West Germany.[42]

The main advantage of borrowing through bonds is that the Soviets end up paying a lower rate of interest, other things being the same, than they would have to pay on syndicated commercial bank loans. In addition to lower rates, bonds generally carry longer maturities. By issuing sovereign bonds, the Soviet Union locks in long-term financing for nebulous pursuits that might otherwise have to be defined for purposes of obtaining specific funding. Most importantly, by issuing Eurobonds, the Soviet Union demonstrates its status as a first-class participant in international credit markets.[43] The prestige factor continues to exert a decisive influence over Soviet actions toward the West. The Soviets have approached the markets very cautiously, limiting the amounts of bonds issued and optimizing the timing, to ensure that these initial efforts are successful.

Moscow Narodny Bank in London had earlier tested the waters by launching two note issues of its own. The offerings by Moscow Narodny, as a chartered bank in the United Kingdom, were not sovereign obligations, nor were they officially backed by the full faith and credit of the Soviet government. However, since the bank is 100 percent owned by various Soviet banking and foreign trade organizations—which are, in turn, owned by the Soviet government—the notes floated in London represented a surrogate for a Soviet offering. The results were gratifying. The Kremlin had also paid attention, no doubt, to the hospitable reception granted by the West to note offerings issued by Hungary. Bankers Trust International, along with the Dai-Ichi Kangyo Bank and First Chicago, had sponsored one such offering in December 1985 for a $400 million loan to the National Bank of Hungary.[44] Commercial banks seemed willing enough to purchase Soviet bloc offerings for their own portfolios. Enthusiasm on the part of private investors, while it remains to be seen on future Soviet offerings, may turn out to be an unexpected bonus.

Poised for Participation

Soviet officials have displayed their eagerness to pursue opportunities in the Eurobond market that might lead to American participation. In the advertising supplement that appeared in the *Wall Street Journal* in August 1987, a special article was directed at U.S. banks about the prospects for expanded cooperation in the future. Alluding to the market for Euronotes and Eurobonds, the message declared:

> There are opportunities for developing relations with banks and other financial institutions in the area of international capital markets, including the new instruments of these markets. It goes without saying that due to the relative novelty for the U.S.S.R. of such operations, the U.S.S.R. Vneshtorgbank is cautious in developing them. However, there is potential for cooperation in this field.[45]

If U.S. banks would purchase—through their foreign branches—bond obligations issued in Western Europe, the Soviets would receive a tremendous boost in international capital markets. The same loophole in the Johnson Debt Default Act that allows U.S. banks to issue untied loans to the Soviet Union might well be extended to cover purchases of Soviet securities by foreign branches of U.S. banks. As with the untied loans, the U.S. branch could act as a lead manager of a syndicate, turning around and selling off the issue to participating foreign banks. A U.S. bank could thus facilitate a Soviet bond offering presumably without violating the Johnson Debt Default Act, as long as the funds were sourced from the Eurodollar market, which would mean they did not represent domestic American deposits.

The Soviets, naturally, would like to see the Johnson Debt Default Act rescinded. Barring that, however, they could take the practical action to meet the conditions of the act: For a total of $1.54 billion, they could pay off their debts to the U.S. government. Perhaps they could work out a much less expensive settlement, as they did with the British government, and merely pay the principal amount due on the World War I debt—$192.6 million—rather than principal plus interest. Or they could get around the Johnson Act prohibition altogether by being accepted as members of the IMF and the World Bank. Whether that would be cheaper than paying off the wartime debts owed to the U.S. government would depend on the amount the Soviet Union was assessed as its required quota to join the IMF and the World Bank.

Those financial options are undoubtedly being analyzed by Soviet officials. Gaining access to U.S. investors via a bond offering not only increases the supply of qualified investors but also maximizes the competition for any Soviet issue in Western markets. And if American banks were allowed to hold Soviet securities in their portfolios and sell them off to their own investment clients, the Soviets could go a long way toward driving down the cost of Western capital while expanding available international resources.

In the meantime, one innovation in the bond market the Soviets should perhaps consider taking up is a gold-linked securities offering. Linking gold with Eurobonds is one way of luring conservative Eurobond investors who might otherwise be leery of Soviet issues. Gold-linked bonds normally include a warrant to buy gold at a fixed price at some time in the future, but such an offering might also include interest payments fixed to the price of gold. For the issuer, the advantage is that investors are willing to pay significant premiums for gold options in debt securities. A flurry of gold-linked securities offerings in April 1987 enabled such borrowers as the government of Belgium and France's Saint-Gobain S.A. to raise money at a cost well below prevailing Euromarket interest rates.[46] For instance, Saint-Gobain's $110 million Eurobond offering paying 4.5 percent and carrying three-year gold warrants was priced, according to its underwriter, Salomon Brothers International, at 45 percent above the combined underlying value of the bonds and warrants.[47] Of course, to benefit from the hybrid bond instrument, the issuer must be perceived as having the gold so that there is no question that the warrants will be honored. Here, the Soviet Union has a unique advantage in international credit markets. What it lacks in financial sophistication, as judged by global investors, it makes up for in reputed gold reserves.

Borrowing in the Eurobond market gives the Soviets one particular advantage that will become increasingly important to them as they continue to build up their indebtedness to the West: It allows them to circumvent the monitoring process. Many financial underwriters are independent from commercial banks and are not required to report country lending exposure to regulatory authorities or to the Bank for International Settlements. There is currently pressure, mostly from British officials, on the Association of International Bond Dealers to require Eurobond dealers to achieve "transparency" in financial transactions, but tremendous resistance also exists.[48] Bond traders prefer to negotiate prices over the telephone, away from the scrutiny of supervisory authorities. Accordingly, they do not want a computerized trade confirmation system publicly listing Eurobond trades on a real-time screen. The bond dealers are sharply critical of regulatory proposals advanced by British authorities, which the dealers feel would threaten the long-standing freedom that has made London the center of Eurobond operations.[49] If the bond dealers prevail, it will be extremely difficult to track Soviet offerings held by nonbank entities.

Even among commercial banks, some of the financial practices of recent years threaten the ability of banking authorities to monitor the risk exposure of banks involved in off-balance sheet transactions. As commercial banks have begun to underwrite notes and bonds, they have taken to selling them off as quickly as possible to avoid having to raise capital ratios to cover portfolio exposure. But banks are increasingly dealing in "swaps" whereby loans are essentially arbitraged—an activity based on differences in currency demand or interest rates in different countries—and they often take positions on one side or the other of a swap without setting aside adequate capital reserves to cover the risk. About 70 percent of all Eurobond issues are now swapped,[50] and regulators worry that banks may unwittingly pile up large credit risks to a single customer, because when an underwriting bank carries a Eurobond offering as an off-balance sheet commitment, it is hidden from public view.

Assuming those sophisticated swaps are included among the "new instruments" referred to by the Soviets in their message to commercial Western bankers, it appears that the problem of transparency and monitoring by Western financial authorities poses no great moral dilemma for the Kremlin. Indeed, the ability to raise large sums of money through Eurobond offerings is no doubt enhanced by the fact that it is not easily monitored. The statistics published by the BIS/OECD on the external indebtedness of individual countries specifically omit purchases of international securities by nonbank financial institutions, so figures for Soviet indebtedness to the West do not include Soviet bonds sold to private investors or even specialized underwriting subsidiaries of banks. That works to Soviet advantage: Although Kremlin officials are eager to impress the West with the level of popular demand for their debt instruments, they do not want to be perceived as taking on unmanageable financial commitments.

9

Joining the Club

For decades, the Soviet Union made no secret of its disdain for the International Monetary Fund (IMF), characterizing it as a sham organization, a front for carrying out the imperialist objectives of the United States under the guise of international financial cooperation. Imitation, however, is the sincerest form of flattery. The Soviet Union attempts to exert the same sort of influence through the Council for Mutual Economic Assistance (CMEA), which it established to facilitate trade among socialist nations. The CMEA does not, of course, carry the economic clout of the IMF; it is less a system for eliminating international barriers to trade than a vehicle for extending the Soviet model of centralized planning to satellite nations. But the Kremlin has always construed its role in the CMEA as one prompted by a purely benevolent motive—to share its economic achievements with political allies—the morally superior alternative to joining the "capitalist club."

One might suppose that the absence of the Soviet Union, the country that for so long was presumed to have the second largest economy in the world, would leave a conspicuous and embarrassing hole in the IMF's make-up. But the analysts and economists of mainstream global organizations seem to have grown accustomed to the Soviet Union's absence. The vast land mass that covers a considerable portion of Europe and Asia is simply blanked out. Politicians and businessmen worry endlessly about the relationship of the dollar to the mark, the yen, the pound, or the franc but give not a thought to the relationship between the dollar and the ruble. Not part of the international monetary system, Moscow is ignored on matters requiring international economic cooperation and is not present at world monetary conferences.

For a long time this state of affairs suited the Soviets just fine. They were only too happy to stay away from the corrupting influence of capitalists as they threw their collective financial weight around the world. Indeed, Moscow has shown far greater interest in competing militarily with the West than in attaining the same degree of financial sophistication. As long as their own country's economy was booming, it was all the Soviets could do to employ internal resources efficiently and fulfill the ambitious tasks laid out by central planning authorities. While the rest of the world clamored to join world trade and financial organizations to reap the benefits of international cooperation, the Soviet Union persisted in its efforts to become relatively autarkic or self-sufficient. Why bother to establish traditional ties with capitalist countries and adapt to their monetary system when the socialist model was expected to emerge as the economic answer of the future?

For a while it almost looked as if Soviet claims about the efficiency of a state-managed economy would turn out to be correct. For the Soviet Union, at least, socialism provided the ideological foundation for a period of tremendous economic progress. After World War II, the country moved to build huge factories and construct massive dams and railroads. Projects were built to take advantage of huge supplies of natural resources and to increase manufacturing output. By the 1960s the Soviet Union was starting to close the gap with the United States—not just in terms of economic productivity, but in military armaments as well.

With increasing military power came a newfound respect in the West for the U.S.S.R. as a global force. That was no doubt heady for the Soviets, who had struggled so long to pull themselves out of economic backwardness and to stake out a place in the modern world. The Soviets had clinched their claim to superpower status by building up a nuclear force to rival that of the United States. By the early 1970s, Soviet political influence was so great that an American president was willing to travel to Moscow to meet with his counterpart. The Soviets could afford to feel proud, even smug, about their economic and military accomplishments. But when Soviet productivity began to drop after the mid-1970s, Moscow was confronted with a difficult choice: to cut back on defense expenditures and maintain spending for fixed investment and consumer welfare, or to support the military sector at all costs.

In an ironic postscript to détente, the Soviets opted to maintain and even strengthen their military forces, even while a larger and larger proportion of total resources was being devoted to the military out of a stagnating economic base. In the end, Kremlin authorities could not bring themselves to cut back on the Soviet Union's nuclear arsenal, their main claim to global status and the source of Soviet influence around the world. To build up the military, the other sectors of the Soviet economy were being squeezed harder and harder. Fixed capital investment was slashed, and consumer needs were given short shrift. By the early 1980s, defense was claiming more than one-fifth of total Soviet production and soaking up an inordinate proportion of Soviet talent and technological capabilities.

Politically speaking, a strong defense may be deemed a necessity. Economically speaking, it is a luxury. To support its military habit through the end of the 1980s and into the 1990s, Moscow is being forced to compromise on other desired objectives. One of the most painful of the necessary compromises may well turn out to be the goal of self-sufficiency, for Gorbachev has clearly reconciled himself to the fact that outside capital is crucial to the survival of the Soviet economy. Having accepted the notion that additional money is required to keep all of Moscow's balls in the air, Gorbachev now finds himself having to persuade Western lenders that the Soviet Union is a safe investment haven. He needs, in short, to convince businessmen and bankers that Moscow is willing to abide by the rules of the Western financial community. One of the most effective ways to convince them would be for the Soviet Union to become a member of the IMF—the very symbol of Western economic and financial cooperation. For Gorbachev, the advantages of membership overwhelm any blow to the Soviet Union's sense of autonomy. It is time to join the capitalist club.

The Bretton Woods Split

Despite all the criticism the Soviets have since leveled at the IMF, they were initially enthused about joining the organization when it was first being put together in the mid-1940s. With World War II still raging, representatives of seventeen countries were invited to Atlantic City, New Jersey, in June 1944 to work out a preliminary draft for a new international monetary system to encourage cooperation and mutual advancement in the postwar world. Besides the United States, the countries invited to participate were Australia, Belgium, Brazil, Canada, Chile, China, Cuba, Czechoslovakia, France, Greece, India, Mexico, the Netherlands, Norway, the United Kingdom, and the Soviet Union. Thus the Soviets were part of the select group of countries in on the ground floor of a new global monetary organization.

Delegates from the core planning session subsequently went on to meet the following month with a wider group of representatives at the remote mountain village of Bretton Woods, New Hampshire. There they worked to draft the Articles of Agreement for establishing what would be called the International Monetary Fund and the International Bank for Reconstruction and Development, later the World Bank. Negotiations among the delegates from forty-five countries were intense and, according to John Maynard Keynes of the United Kingdom, one of the key architects of the new world economic order, mentally exhausting:

> It is as though . . . one had to accomplish the preliminary work of many interdepartmental and Cabinet committees, the job of the . . . draftsmen, and the passage . . . of two intricate legislative measures of large dimensions, all this carried on in committees and commissions numbering anything up to 200 persons in rooms with bad acoustics, shouting through microphones, many of those present . . . with an imperfect knowledge of English, each wanting to get something on the record which would look well in the press down at home, and . . . the Russians only understanding what was afoot with the utmost difficulty. . . . We have all of us worked every minute of our waking hours . . . all of us . . . are all in.[1]

What Keynes meant by his reference to "the Russians" is not entirely clear. He seems to suggest that painstaking effort was required to explain the proceedings of a monetary conference to Soviet representatives, perhaps because they were accustomed to a closed economic system and had only the vaguest concept of currency convertibility. Frustrations about Soviet naïveté were no doubt heightened, too, by Soviet suspicions about American motives. Not particularly flattered at being asked to become a leading sponsor of the envisioned postwar international monetary system, which featured the U.S. dollar as the monetary anchor, the Soviets began to act as if everything were some sort of trap.

But if Keynes found it trying to work with the Russians, the other key architect of the system, Harry Dexter White, may have been predisposed to help the Soviets acquire a strong voice in it. White was the American counterpart to Keynes at the Bretton Woods conference; indeed, as chief adviser to the U.S. Secretary of the Treasury, White was the reigning expert on international monetary affairs, having devised his own blueprint for the postwar financial system. According to Whittaker Chambers, White was very sympathetic to the communist cause and routinely allowed information to be passed to Soviet agents about Treasury affairs. Chambers later testified, when asked whether or not White was a communist, before the House Committee on Un-American Activities: "I can't say positively that he was a registered member of the Communist Party, but he certainly was a fellow traveler so far within the fold that his not being a Communist would be a mistake on both sides."[2]

White exerted enormous influence in laying out the foundations of the IMF. Given his intellectual sympathies, it is probably no coincidence that the Soviet Union was slated to play a significant role in the envisioned new system. A country's impact on IMF decisions is determined by the number of votes it is allowed to cast; that number in turn is determined by the size of that country's quota, the amount it is assessed to contribute to the fund. In the original Articles of Agreement for the IMF adopted at Bretton Woods in 1944, the United States' quota was set at $2.75 billion and the United Kingdom's at $1.3 billion. The Soviet Union's quota was set just slightly below the United Kingdom's at $1.2 billion. None of the other forty-two nations at the conference had an assessment even half the amount of the Soviet Union's.[3] If the Soviet Union had decided to join by December 31, 1945, the most powerful communist country in the world would have been positioned as the third most powerful member of the IMF.

It is now ironic that the Soviets chose to walk away from a

monumental opportunity. At the time, the Soviets were the beneficiaries not only of the political leanings of White (who, according to Chambers, even offered the Soviet government a plan for
reforming the Soviet monetary structure) but also of the spirit of
good feeling that flourished briefly between the United States
and the Soviet Union—allies together against Germany—following World War II. A strong feeling existed that the countries that
had won the war together should now win the peace by building
an international monetary system together. As Fred Vinson, later
U.S. Secretary of the Treasury, put it: "We march to victory together; we move on the path of peace together."[4]

Stalin, however, became more and more irked with the U.S.
refusal to provide loans to the Soviet Union on the same scale as
those being made to Britain. The Soviet Union, Stalin argued,
had been hurt much worse than Britain by the Germans. Accordingly, the Soviet Union was entitled to special consideration
from the United States. Specifically, the Soviets wanted $10 bil-
lion, ten times the newly expanded resources of the U.S. Import-
Export Bank. The U.S. government was willing to lend the entire
$1 billion that had been allocated to the Eximbank to the Soviet
Union, but to Stalin this amount was so small as to be insulting.

The Soviet delegates to Bretton Woods, who earlier had shown
a positive attitude toward joining the new system, now began to
openly resent the preeminent role assigned to the United States.
Observers from the Soviet Union continued to sit in on the meetings where arrangements for the IMF were being fine-tuned by
the participating countries. By the end of 1945, however, it was
clear that the Kremlin had reversed its original position and
would not be joining after all.[5]

Meanwhile, White, who was expected to be named the first
managing director of the IMF, had come under FBI scrutiny because of his suspected cooperation with Soviet agents. In 1946,
shortly before the inaugural meeting of the IMF Board of Gover-
nors was to be held, President Truman was informed by the FBI
that White had been passing secret information about Treasury
business to sources who made it available to the Soviet government. Truman decided that White would be named not managing director of the IMF but rather one of the twelve executive
directors, and that he should be surrounded by carefully
screened assistants.[6] Two years later, White himself was called
before the House Committee on Un-American Activities to refute
charges that he was working with the communists. White sweep-

ingly denied all charges, affirming his patriotism and responding to Representative Richard Nixon's questions with high indignation. A few days later, White died of a heart attack.

Setting Up a Rival Organization

Despite all the factors working in their favor, then, the Soviets made a deliberate decision to forgo an influence in steering the course of global economic development. Instead, they immediately set about creating a rival economic organization in which the Soviet Union would become the dominant member, able to dictate the terms of trade and financial relations between members. So within two years after they turned down the invitation to join the IMF, the Soviets were structuring the CMEA for the purpose of uniting socialist allies and steering them away from developing financial ties with the West.

In January 1949, Moscow issued a Tass communiqué that said the Soviet Union, Bulgaria, Czechoslovakia, Hungary, Poland, and Romania had formed a multinational organization for the purpose of "organizing broader economic cooperation."[7] Poland had actually been a founding member of the IMF, but at Stalin's insistence it left the organization. Albania and East Germany joined the CMEA a short time later, although Albania chose not to actively participate in the CMEA after its dispute with the Soviets in 1961. Even though the CMEA was heralded as the socialist alternative to the IMF, a vehicle for spawning progressive economic development, it more or less languished for the first few years of its existence. Meetings were held only infrequently, and the various member countries proceeded to stake out separate paths to industrialization.

After Stalin's death in 1953, however, Soviet authorities realized that the members of the socialist fraternity would have to work more closely together if they were to triumph over capitalism. The objectives of the CMEA were redefined, and new arrangements were instituted requiring a higher degree of cooperation among members. The purposes of the economic alliance, besides allocating resources to maximize the welfare of the entire socialist community, were (1) to stimulate economic and technical development, (2) to eliminate the gap between richer and poorer CMEA members, and (3) to strengthen the overall defense capacity of the group.[8] Those objectives in fact bolstered Moscow's economic control over satellite nations, as well as enlisting them in the struggle against the West.

As membership in the CMEA was enlarged to include less developed nations, its objectives began to conflict with one another. If the goal was to eliminate the gap between richer and poorer members, poorer newcomers would have to be subsidized by the relatively prosperous East European member countries. For example, Mongolia, invited to join in 1962, immediately became a net drain on the economies of the other CMEA members. On a per capita basis, Mongolia continues to receive the most economic aid, including trade subsidies, of all the member countries. The next in line is Cuba, which joined in 1972 and absorbs, in addition to CMEA aid, some $3 billion in direct military assistance from the Soviet Union. Meanwhile, Vietnam, a member since 1978, has the second largest population among all the CMEA countries and requires a $20 per capita annual subsidy from the organization, supplemented by a billion yearly in military assistance from Moscow.[9]

Mongolia, Cuba, and Vietnam were recruited by the Soviet Union not only to cultivate further their socialist leanings, obviously, but to make them part of the Soviet defense network against the West. As they all offer excellent bases for carrying out military operations, they play an important role in the Soviet Union's global strategy. To keep them happy, the Soviet Union extends special CMEA financial privileges. In addition to the economic aid, Mongolia, Cuba, and Vietnam are permitted to borrow from the CMEA's investment bank at interest rates of only 0.5 to 2 percent instead of the 2 to 5 percent paid by other CMEA members. They also enjoy preferential prices on Soviet energy supplies. Together, the three countries absorb about 75 percent of the CMEA's total overseas economic aid.[10] The latest potential recruit appears to be Nicaragua, which Moscow has invited to attend CMEA council sessions. That is usually the precursor to an invitation to join the organization.

The East European members of the CMEA have long resented the burden of having to carry the economies of the poorer members. They understand perfectly well that less developed countries have been brought into the CMEA largely for the political and military benefit of the Soviet Union. The fact is that the Soviet Union foots most of the bill. Nevertheless, other CMEA members are periodically assessed to pay for the subsidies and transfer payments going to so-called fraternal economic allies. Chagrin has surfaced a number of times, as wealthier individual CMEA members have tried to assert independence from the organization and the centralized economic authority exercised by the Soviet Union.

The resentment felt at the pursuit of Soviet foreign policy aims through the CMEA has developed into outright rejection of the Soviet economic model by some of the East European members. Hungary and Poland, in particular, have moved to scrap the centralized administrative approach in their domestic economies. They have requested that the CMEA similarly reorganize its trading rules to allow for the free exchange of goods among socialist countries. Rather than use the bureaucratic, government-to-government system established in Stalin's day, these dissident members want to set prices and transact business according to the law of supply and demand.[11] Mostly, they would like to abolish the cumbersome annual exchange agreements, which require a full year's buildup of potential trade arrangements to be handled through inefficient official government channels.

Any inclination on the part of East European countries to buck the CMEA system, however, must be tempered because of their overall dependence on the Soviet Union. The most vital economic link to Moscow is the flow of Soviet oil. Until the mid-1980s, Soviet-supplied oil was a bargain for other CMEA members, available to them at subsidized prices. While the rest of the world had to contend with prices set by OPEC, CMEA members could buy at discount rates thanks to prior arrangements with Moscow. The Soviets make oil available to CMEA members using a five-year moving average pricing formula. However, the tables turned when the price of oil dropped in 1986 and CMEA members found themselves having to pay more for Soviet oil than they would have to pay on world markets. Not only did Moscow insist that its allies continue to abide by the formula, but additional pressure was put on them to pay for the fuel with their highest-quality foodstuffs, consumer goods, and machinery—precisely those items the East European countries would normally export to the West to cover their own hard currency needs.

Since 1985, the Soviets have also begun to press their fellow CMEA members to repay the debts they have accumulated through years of running trade deficits with their economic benefactors in Moscow. Rough estimates set total East European ruble debt to the Soviet Union at approximately 13 billion rubles in 1985; while it is not clear what kind of repayment terms have been laid down, indications are that the Soviets expect most of the East European countries to repay their debt by 1990.[12] Poland has been granted an extension because of its especially distressing economic circumstances, but the obligation has in no way been waived. Zdzislaw M. Rurarz, who served as Poland's Ambassador to Japan before defecting to the West in December 1981, explains:

> What does appear certain right now is that Poland is to provide the U.S.S.R. with credits amounting to about 900 billion zlotys over the years 1986 to 2000. What this translates to in dollars is difficult to say, because one of the quirks of the artificially set currencies of the U.S.S.R. and its Eastern European satellites is that it costs more to buy U.S. dollars with Polish zlotys than it does with Russian rubles. But a reasonable estimate would put these credits' real worth at about $10 billion.[13]

Moscow thus has an effective way to keep members from breaking away from the CMEA alliance. The countries of Eastern Europe may not like having to prop up Third World newcomers, and they may object to interference with their attempts to trade directly with the West. But the East European countries have piled up debts at the Soviet company store and cannot escape from them. So in the end the CMEA is not the mutually beneficial gathering of equals it is touted to be, but rather an oppressive guild dominated politically and economically by the Soviet Union—a situation that foments mutinous inclinations.

Gorbachev is acutely aware of potential rebellion among CMEA members. While oil remains an important way to control Eastern Europe, the Soviets would really prefer to divert energy to Western Europe, where it can be sold for hard currency. Putting the bite on Poland and other debtors to make good on past debts amounts to scraping the bottom of the barrel for foreign capital. What Gorbachev really wants out of the CMEA is more high-quality imports for the Soviet Union; East Germany, for example, produces sophisticated technology and consumer products. But it is not clear, given the politically sensitive nature of the Soviet relationship with the East European countries, whether the carrot or the stick offers the best approach.

Soon after Gorbachev came to power in 1985, he chose to use the stick. He asked for strict obedience from CMEA members and issued a warning through *Pravda* to avoid displays of nationalism that hinted at "Russophobia and anti-Sovietism."[14] He also

dashed hopes that individual members would be permitted to develop their own links to the West without express Soviet approval. But East European leaders apparently were not wholly
intimidated. During the next two years, member countries continued to buy new industrial machinery from the West even as
they resisted exhortations to expand trade with the Soviet Union.
Self-interest, it seems, was more important than fulfilling CMEA
objectives.

Ever the pragmatist, Gorbachev has recently begun to mod-
ulate the Soviet Union's position to accommodate the mood of
its socialist allies. Speaking in Prague in early 1987, Gorbachev
made this somewhat startling declaration: "No party has a mo-
nopoly on truth. Some problems that are now priorities in the
Soviet Union have already been solved in other socialist countries, or they are solving them in their own way."[15] Gorbachev
has been especially complimentary toward East Germany, which
he cites as a model of socialist economic efficiency. He even
seems prepared to tolerate the kind of hybrid system that has
developed in Hungary, so long as it fulfills certain roles important to Moscow in the broader context of East–West relations;
Hungary, after all, is a useful conduit for obtaining Western capital and goods. The bottom line is that the CMEA must be re-
formed to accommodate current economic circumstances.
Otherwise, the organization first established to rival the IMF will
continue to impress Western observers as the "council for the
mutual exchange of inefficiency."[16]

New Ties

The fact that individual East European countries were strongly
discouraged from developing links with the West did not mean
the Soviet Union felt likewise constrained. Gorbachev's assessment of CMEA prospects apparently prompted him to look beyond the socialist fraternity for the benefits of international
trade. The expedient way to tap the economic energy of other
countries seemed to lie in developing ties with more successful
economic clubs. The nearest was right next door: the European
Economic Community (EEC). Little time was lost in cultivating
possible links. In June 1985 the president of the EEC received a
short letter from the head of the CMEA proposing that the two

organizations get together and issue a joint declaration about their relationship.[17]

Economic performance within the EEC offers a startling contrast to the CMEA. With about 10 percent of the world's population, CMEA members annually export about $50 billion worth of goods outside the CMEA. EEC members, meanwhile, account for just 6 percent of the world's total population, yet manage to export some $275 billion yearly to buyers outside EEC territory.[18] The two organizations operate under very different mandates. The CMEA, as we know, is a vehicle for pressuring the rest of Eastern Europe to adhere to the central planning objectives defined by Moscow; the EEC works to eliminate trade barriers between individual countries to create a common market in which private companies have greater opportunity and incentive to pursue profitable business operations.

The design of the EEC is obviously appealing to Gorbachev. It conforms to his own ideas about the inefficiency of rigid bureaucracies and the effect of competition on incentives. Indeed, developing strong ties with the EEC would go a long way toward validating the principles of perestroika, on top of providing substantial benefits for the domestic Soviet economy. Gorbachev has already signaled that he is willing to compromise on long-held Soviet positions in order to establish a relationship with the EEC. Though EEC authorities generally liked the idea of opening an informal dialogue with the CMEA, proposed in June 1985, they balked at Moscow's initial refusal to acknowledge the supranational authority of the EEC over its individual members. Gorbachev immediately capitulated, indicating in a speech that the CMEA was ready to make concessions on the supranationality issue.[19] In January 1986 the EEC issued a statement saying that it accepted in principle the notion put forward by the CMEA calling for a joint declaration by the two groups about their future relationship.[20]

As vague as the statement was, it represented an important first step in the mutual recognition by each of the legitimacy of the other—required, of course, if any future trade agreements were to be worked out between the two organizations. For its part, the CMEA has even been willing to admit that it is not the EEC's equal in trade competence. But as its chief pointed out, an EEC–CMEA declaration "could create more favorable conditions" for bilateral trade negotiations between the EEC as a whole and individual CMEA member states.[21] Gorbachev apparently figures that the potential economic benefits to the bloc as a whole are worth the political risk of allowing individual CMEA members to operate under their own arrangements with the EEC. Romania has had such an agreement with the EEC since 1980. Hungary and Czechoslovakia have been chafing to conduct negotiations to gain better access to the EEC market for their domestic goods, and permission here from Moscow might relieve tensions. Poland and Bulgaria are cooler about EEC relations, since their formal contacts so far have been limited to reluctantly accepting EEC quotas on their steel and textile exports.[22] East Germany in effect already has access to the EEC, because its relations with West Germany are considered domestic transactions and are thus tariff-free. Not surprisingly, East Germany's trade with West Germany is three times higher than its trade with all other members of the EEC.[23]

So the biggest change that would come from substantive ties between the EEC and the CMEA would not impact the satellite countries so much as it would improve trade prospects for the Soviet Union itself. Ironically, up to now the Soviet Union has been exceedingly hostile to the EEC. Gorbachev is demonstrating once again that he is willing to sacrifice Soviet pride in exchange for gaining increased Soviet access to Western goods. To explain his sudden cozying up to the EEC, some observers have suggested that with the move Gorbachev hopes to drive a wedge between America and its EEC allies. Another motive cited by Western analysts is a desire to counter American-inspired restrictions on high-technology trade with the Soviet bloc.[24] Those may well be peripheral objectives, but the main thrust behind Gorbachev's effort is to seek relief from Moscow's more immediate economic and financial problems.

Toward that end, Gorbachev has recently scored yet another triumph. In June 1988, the EEC and the CMEA ended thirty-one years of hostility by finally signing a declaration of mutual recognition.[25] Negotiations had stalled a few months earlier when the Soviet Union refused to acknowledge that West Berlin was part of the EEC.[26] But CMEA officials ultimately decided to come around and make concessions on the West Berlin issue for the sake of concluding an agreement. Signing the accord, one of the CMEA representatives observed: "The signing of the joint declaration . . . is another proof that with good will and realistic attitudes, states having different social systems can reach agreement on major international issues."[27]

It was, perhaps, in this vein that the Soviet Union sought to approach another organization, the General Agreement on Tariffs and Trade (GATT). GATT, which has ninety-four member countries, is intended to resolve specific tariff disputes among its members and to set the general rules for world trade. Poland, Hungary, Czechoslovakia, and Romania have long been members of the organization, but the Soviet Union has traditionally spurned the group as yet another global organization perceived to be dominated by Western interests. Early in the 1980s, however, the Soviets quietly began to approach a number of GATT members to test the waters about eventual Soviet participation. Still, the initiative had no force until Gorbachev came to power. Then, suddenly, an outright request from Moscow: The Soviet Union would like to be granted observer status to attend the 1986 annual GATT meetings.

The United States instantly became a potential spoiler. What was behind the Soviet request? Reagan administration officials wondered. Were the Soviets genuinely interested in joining an organization dedicated to free market principles, or did they just want to eavesdrop? China had already received permission to sit in on the meetings, the Soviets pointed out, and was working toward full GATT membership. Besides, the Soviets insisted, based on their own poll, a majority of GATT members had no real objection to allowing the Soviet Union to attend.[28] But, U.S. Trade Representative Clayton Yeutter explained:

> China has moved much more toward a market-oriented kind of economy than has the Soviet Union. . . . I don't see much indication at the moment that the Soviet Union is moving its economy in that direction. If that changes in the future, we'd be delighted with that, of course, and if it looks like some day we can begin to more nearly mesh the functions of these economies—West versus East—that might be a good thing for everybody. I don't think we're there yet.[29]

The United States thus took the position that the Soviet Union could not become a useful member of GATT because it did not have a market-oriented economy. So the application for observer status was rebuffed by GATT, with the United States taking the lead in opposing it. Gorbachev, though, was undeterred. On the heels of the Yeutter statement, an official from the Soviet Ministry of Foreign Trade announced that the Soviets were indeed reforming their economy in the direction of free market principles.

He cited the Kremlin's decision to allow certain state enterprises to conduct business directly with foreign companies, and he added that the role of the state would be significantly reduced to allow Soviet enterprises to "freely enter into markets."[30]

That was not enough, however, to persuade GATT members to include the Soviet Union in the 1986 annual meetings. Still, Gorbachev remained undaunted. A few months later, in August 1987, the Soviet Union applied for membership in the Multifiber Arrangement, a fifty-four-nation organization that establishes the rules for trade in textiles. Administered by GATT, the group offers an indirect route for eventual GATT membership. China had used that approach, becoming first a member of the Multifiber Arrangement before seeking observer status in GATT. Now the Soviets were looking to do the same.[31]

Even more disturbing to the United States, Moscow began to drop hints that it was thinking about making a bid to join the IMF and the World Bank as well. In August 1986 several Soviet officials, including Ivan Ivanov, deputy chairman of the newly created State Commission for Foreign Economic Relations, met in Moscow with a group of American economists to exchange views on future political and financial relations. The U.S. participants were informed that the Soviet leadership had begun to rethink its long-standing position toward the IMF and the World Bank and was now contemplating joining the organizations. According to Herbert Levine, an expert on Soviet affairs who has helped organize the U.S.–U.S.S.R. economic seminars over the last thirteen years, this was the first time the Soviets expressed a definite desire to become a member.[32] Later, Ivanov would muddy the message by telling a delegation representing European and American business interests that the Soviet Union was ready to restructure its approach to foreign trade to meet with GATT requirements but was less interested in joining the IMF, because that organization "improperly runs the international monetary system."[33]

High-Level Dithering

If the Soviets waffled on the IMF and the World Bank, U.S. government officials responding to the prospect of Soviet membership were even more confused. In earlier opposing Soviet participation in GATT, the United States asserted that the Soviet economic system was fundamentally at odds—in both philosophy and practice—with the aspirations of GATT. But according to some Reagan administration officials in the summer of 1987, the State Department was now trying to steer policy toward a favorable response at least to Soviet entry into the Multifiber Arrangement.[34] A change of heart within the administration had been at the center of a still earlier dispute about statements made by Deputy Secretary of State John Whitehead at a forum on U.S.–Soviet trade. When asked about Soviet attempts to join GATT, the IMF, and the World Bank, Whitehead replied: "We would like to see the Soviet Union become a member of all these international bodies."[35]

A week after Whitehead spoke, Secretary of State George Shultz insisted at a congressional hearing that what his deputy had actually said was that the administration would *not* like to see the Soviet Union become a member of all those international bodies. But Representative Jack Kemp (R.—N.Y.) questioned the assertion that the number two official at the State Department had simply been misquoted. Transcripts of the meeting, as well as reporters' tapes and notes, indicated that Whitehead had indeed been quoted correctly. Kemp wanted to know if the administration was signaling a policy shift on Soviet membership. Shultz, however, stayed with his explanation that the transcript was wrong: "They've missed a word."[36]

There had been a similar flap just a few months earlier, in October 1986. Here also an apparent change in U.S. policy was announced by one administration official, only to be retracted by another shortly afterward. Responding to Gorbachev's desire for more financial contact with the West, World Bank President Barber Conable told reporters that the bank "would be happy to explore" a membership bid from the Soviet Union. Conable noted that the World Bank was designed to encourage cooperation among all countries. He also pointed out that Soviet membership in the bank would be difficult and would take time "because it will require an openness that the Russians haven't shown in the past." He did say, however, that he would not want to discourage Soviet interest in joining the IMF and the World Bank. "We should seek a more cooperative and less confrontational environment," Conable asserted.[37]

Kemp took exception at the time, sending a letter to Treasury Secretary James Baker asking if the United States was preparing to change its position on Soviet membership in the World Bank.

Kemp made it clear that he believed Soviet membership would serve the interests of neither the United States nor the World Bank. He suggested that if the Soviet Union joined the bank, it might attempt to distract developing member countries from moving toward market-oriented economic systems. There was a strong possibility, Kemp said in his letter, that the Soviet Union would seek to disrupt the bank by acting as the ringleader of an antidemocratic coalition. Kemp wanted clarification of the Reagan administration's position. He contended that silence would only produce confusion about U.S. intentions and might encourage the Soviets to move forward.[38]

Baker, seeing a need to quell any suspicion that there had been any fundamental shift in the administration's position, wrote back that Soviet membership would not be in the best interests of the United States or the World Bank. He also noted that the Soviets had not officially applied for World Bank membership, nor had they applied to join the IMF; a country must first qualify to be a member of the IMF before it can apply to the World Bank. But the administration was prepared to state in advance, Baker asserted, that it "would oppose Soviet membership in the IMF and the World Bank and would work actively within their respective executive boards to this end. . . . I hope this clarifies the Administration's position."[39]

Baker's remarks were meant to be the final word on the U.S. position. Yet journalists continued to speculate that the Reagan administration was preparing to offer trade and monetary concessions to Gorbachev to promote a détente in superpower relations. In November 1987 the columnists Rowland Evans and Robert Novak hinted that early drafts of an accommodating U.S. economic policy toward the Soviet Union were being kept under wraps. " 'This is one of the administration's best-kept secrets, but it's the Democrats who are trying to scout it out,' one hard-line administration official told us."[40] In January 1988 ambiguous wording in the National Security Council's annual report suggested once again that Reagan was willing to open the door to Soviet membership in GATT, the IMF, and the World Bank, provided that Moscow made good on its internal economic reforms. Vigilant political observers challenged the notion, and, within days, the White House was forced to issue another clarification: "The Treasury Department and the administration remain opposed to Soviet membership."[41]

In a repeat of the early 1970s, when Democratic Senator Henry

Jackson challenged the Republican Nixon's approach to détente, a number of prominent Democratic leaders are now pushing for a firmer U.S. position against granting credits to the Soviet Union. Senator Bill Bradley (D.—N.J.) wrote in the *New York Times* in October 1987:

> In the absence of Western capital and technology, the Soviets can increase domestic investment only by decreasing military spending. I question the wisdom of helping the Soviets avoid the choice between civilian investment and military buildups—especially while we force harsher decisions on struggling democracies where people are starving.[42]

Bradley asserted that the investment capital needed to reverse Soviet declines in productivity "must come from a reduction in Soviet military spending or from Western financial markets." He also asserted that access to Western capital is crucially important to Gorbachev's plans for economic reform, especially as opposition to the radical aspects of perestroika grow within the Soviet inner political circles. "That is why the West," he wrote, "while not overstating its importance should treat its capital as a strategic asset and develop a plan for its flow eastward."[43]

Another powerful Democrat, Senator William Proxmire, went so far as to send a personal letter to Gorbachev in October 1987. He said that, as chairman of the Joint Economic Committee's panel on National Security Economics, he was concerned that Moscow's interest in trade and monetary concessions from the United States was aimed at establishing "a stronger foundation for a new military buildup" tied to internal economic reform.[44] Proxmire wrote after learning that Gorbachev had publicly criticized specific remarks made by a Pentagon official who was testifying at a subcommittee hearing chaired by Proxmire on the national security implications of Soviet economic reform. Proxmire wanted to clarify the Pentagon official's point that perestroika in itself posed no threat to the West, but if the Soviet military were to become the chief beneficiary of the economic dividends produced by Gorbachev's reforms, NATO and the Western defense community would find themselves facing a more powerful and dynamic adversary.[45] It was of course highly significant that Gorbachev himself had taken enough interest in the hearings to monitor the testimony of Proxmire's witnesses.

Concern among both conservative Republicans and some individual Democrats has tended to center on Reagan's Commerce

Secretary, William Verity, whose earlier position with the U.S.–U.S.S.R. Trade and Economic Council suggests an enthusiasm for increased trade relations. Verity has clearly been aware that, for the Soviet Union, international trade is inextricably tied in with international finance, because credit arrangements are traditionally part of any Soviet decision to buy Western goods. Some observers fear that Verity has been too willing to accommodate Soviet credit requests in the interests of fostering expanded trade relations between the superpowers. Evans and Novak summed up in November 1987, just before Gorbachev's summit visit to Washington:

> Verity is playing a major role in shaping the postsummit trade policy that will decide Soviet requests for most-favored-nation treatment, membership in the International Monetary Fund, World Bank and GATT (the international trade agreement) and easier government and commercial credit to finance perestroika. . . . Democrats Bradley and Proxmire want Gorbachev to come to Washington without illusions. The problem is, ironically, that so far President Reagan is not helping.[46]

What Gorbachev Wants

What would the Soviets have to gain by joining the IMF and the World Bank? Clearly they would become borrowers, not contributors. Although they would have to ante up the necessary quota (as yet undetermined) as a membership fee, this burden is more than offset, because members can draw on IMF resources up to six times the amount of their quota.[47] Meanwhile, World Bank loans can amount to much more, especially in the short term, than IMF assistance. Experience has also shown that a country can parlay IMF support into expanded access to commercial credits; for every dollar borrowed from the IMF, an IMF member can borrow six more from the private markets.[48] Quota requirements can be revised every five years (total quota subscriptions for the IMF's 146 member countries in 1983 were at $99 billion). But the membership fee is an inconsequential cost, given the tremendously enhanced borrowing opportunities that would be made available for the Soviet Union.

Private financial markets are partial to IMF members, because membership shows a borrower's willingness to cooperate with global monetary authorities to resolve any debt dispute. The IMF will not assume the debts of a defaulting member, but it does stand ready to work out agreements with commercial banks and governments to satisfy concerned parties and to supply bridge financing if necessary. Accordingly, IMF membership reduces the risk of making loans to a particular country, which in turn means the borrower can negotiate lower interest charges on commercial loans than otherwise possible. Not that the Soviet Union would necessarily abide by IMF counseling in the event of a pending default. As a *Wall Street Journal* editorial put it in January 1988:

> How, for example, would the IMF go about setting up an adjustment program for the Soviet Union? Would it require the Soviets to cut back on the already paltry supply of foodstuffs and consumer goods, thus risking hunger? Would it dictate less spending on tanks and missiles, and, if so, how would it enforce that edict? Would it require a devaluation of the ruble, and, if so, what exactly would that mean? Would it insist on privatization of state enterprises? It would, of course, do none of those things.[49]

The Soviet Union would obviously have far greater leverage for resisting IMF pressures than more typical members. But to size up the advantages of joining the IMF and the World Bank, the Soviets have evaluated the experiences of their East European allies, Poland, Romania, and Hungary (and Yugoslavia). Khrushchev reluctantly agreed in 1957 to let Poland join GATT but refused to grant it permission to rejoin the IMF, which he denounced as a "class enemy."[50] In 1981, however, in the midst of the Solidarity movement, Poland's circumstances were desperate, its economy torn apart. After the Soviet invasion of Afghanistan, there had been a massive withdrawal of Western capital from the region. When the Poles applied once more to join the IMF, Moscow did not try to stop them. Rurarz has surmised: "The Soviet approval is probably explained by the fact that the Poles were pressing the Soviets for financial assistance. Moscow may have found it more convenient to let the troublesome country look to the West for support."[51]

Moscow is undoubtedly looking now to pick up support for itself from the West. One of the unique advantages for the Soviet Union if it were to join the IMF and the World Bank would be instant exemption from the Johnson Debt Default Act. The Soviet Union could stay in default on its World War I and World War

II loans from the U.S. government and yet no longer be prohibited from receiving untied loans through U.S. credit markets. The Soviets would not have to endure the embarrassing and potentially expensive exercise of settling with the U.S. government, not to mention the heirs of private American investors. Moreover, the Soviet Union would be exempt from the current restrictions that prohibit it from selling its bond obligations to purchasers in the United States. American commercial banks would no longer be forced to fund Soviet loans through their foreign branches but would be permitted to make Soviet loans using American domestic deposits.

The possible disadvantages of membership for the Soviet Union are relatively minor. They involve two stipulated requirements for IMF membership: (1) Members are asked to make certain economic information available, and (2) they are expected to move toward currency convertibility. The first requirement is softened by the words in the IMF Articles of Agreement: "In requesting information the Fund shall take into consideration the varying ability of members to furnish the data requested."[52] Romania has been able to get around the stipulation by saying that it does not have sufficient computational and statistical resources to supply accurate economic data. Soviet authorities have no doubt figured out that the information requirement poses no great obstacle.

As for currency convertibility, Moscow has recently indicated that the Soviet leadership wants to adopt a long-range plan for reforming the CMEA that would include the creation of the Soviet bloc's first convertible currency. With it, trade between CMEA members would no longer be a matter of balancing imports against exports with paper debits and credits; instead, trade would reflect the competitiveness of individual member countries and provide an incentive to maximize exports, because the funds generated could be used to purchase goods from any one of the CMEA members rather than just the Soviet Union. The plan calls for phasing in a convertible currency over a period of ten years, starting in 1991.[53]

An even longer-term goal would be to develop a ruble convertible into foreign currencies outside the CMEA. "Obviously as a big industrial power, we would prefer to have our currency freely convertible," said senior Soviet official Ivan Ivanov, speaking before some seven hundred top business leaders at the World Economic Forum in Davos, Switzerland, in February 1988. "But we have to make several steps first. We have to stabilize money supply and product supply. We have problems in these two areas.''[54]

For the Soviet IMF bid there is no need to rush the timetable. The currency convertibility requirement has already been well compromised; of the 151 current IMF members, sixty countries have convertible currencies, while ninety-one do not.[55]

In short, Gorbachev has little to lose and everything to gain financially by getting the Soviet Union into the IMF and the World Bank. The about-face in Moscow's attitude is yet another telling sign that the Soviet internal financial situation has reached a crisis point. It is, furthermore, an implicit acknowledgment that the CMEA has been a failure, that the alliance established among socialist countries decades ago has yielded very little in terms of genuine trade benefits. Accordingly, the Soviet Union's interest in joining the IMF and the World Bank at this time is an admission that the socialist giant needs to tap into the cooperative strength and financial resources of the Western monetary system to survive. Gorbachev may portray his approach to the West as a sign of progressive Soviet thinking, but it is in fact an attempt to correct a mistake the Soviet Union made forty years ago when it decided to turn its back on Bretton Woods.

PART
THREE
Guidelines for the West

10

Proper Perspective

Under Gorbachev, the Soviets are moving so quickly to pick up Western credits that it is difficult for Western analysts to keep up with them. The increase in the sheer volume of Soviet borrowing from Western commercial banks is disquieting enough, going from about $11 billion at the beginning of Gorbachev's tenure to nearly $26 billion by the end of June 1987. The Soviets owe an additional $12 billion to Western governments. But even more startling is the array of new borrowing options Gorbachev has established. He has begun to permit foreigners to channel capital into the Soviet Union through joint ventures. He settled with Britain and Switzerland on outstanding tsarist debts and floated the Soviet Union's first public bond offering on international capital markets in January 1988. Gorbachev is making determined efforts to win IMF and World Bank membership for his country, and he may very well succeed, further enhancing the ability of the Soviet Union to tap into the capital resources of the West.

Western governments so far seem dazzled by all the fancy Soviet footwork in the financial markets. Torn between a desire to encourage economic and ideological reform in the Soviet Union and a reluctance to contribute directly to strengthening Soviet military capacity, they have become paralyzed observers of international commerce. So by default, bankers and businessmen have been granted the power to make strategic policy decisions. In government circles, the big worry over Soviet access to Western credit is its use to procure restricted technology. The fact that capital is ultimately fungible is seldom acknowledged. Nor is it generally recognized that most of what the Soviet Union stands to gain from stimulating economic output does not require getting around the COCOM list or paying off Western traitors with cash. The Soviets have discovered a much easier way to get the imports they need from the West. They buy them on credit.

The important thing Western policymakers should realize is that the Soviets intend to *keep on buying*. It is absolutely critical to bring in more and more consumer goods and technology from the outside. What Moscow cannot pay for by selling Soviet products on world markets, it will pay for with borrowed funds. That is a decision the Kremlin has already made. So much has been clear since late 1984, when the Soviet Union suddenly began pursuing commercial credits after a virtual five-year hiatus from the markets. In general, it is now apparent that Gorbachev is prepared to maximize Soviet indebtedness to the West as part of the price of perestroika.

Does Gorbachev's vigorous campaign to borrow from the outside, in itself a radical departure from socialist ideals, signal the scope of Soviet economic vulnerability? Unquestionably, yes. But Gorbachev has tried to offset what would normally be a considerable strategic disadvantage by getting the jump on his targeted financial benefactors in the West.

It is time to start responding to Soviet maneuvering in international credit markets. The West must shake off the stupor that has so far characterized official reaction to Gorbachev's financial initiatives. The first thing we should grasp is that Gorbachev is exhibiting such daring precisely because there is so much at stake for the Soviet economy. His willingness to take the risks he has taken is a measure of the desperation behind current Kremlin efforts to address the internal budget crisis and to forestall financial collapse. In turning to the West, Gorbachev has perhaps handed us all the cards; after all, it is the Soviets who are asking us for economic assistance, not the other way around. But Gorbachev can be expected to portray any political transaction that involves trade or financial concessions from the United States as part of a mutually beneficial exchange. U.S. policymakers should thus keep in mind that the Soviet concept of U.S.–U.S.S.R. trade is like the recipe for horse-and-rabbit stew: one horse plus one rabbit.

Becoming aware that the Soviet internal economy is in critical condition and that Gorbachev is out to maximize Soviet options in Western financial markets is the first step toward structuring an appropriate Western response. Maintaining proper perspective in the face of diplomatic thrusts and parries by the Kremlin is key. To understand the driving force behind Soviet overtures toward the West, we need to develop an appreciation for the Soviet Union's economic position vis-à-vis the West as Gorbachev perceives it. We need to analyze his motives and comprehend precisely what he seeks to accomplish. In other words, we need to evaluate Soviet borrowing opportunities from the Kremlin's perspective so that we can anticipate how Gorbachev will move to exploit them.

At all times we need to guard against losing our basic understanding of the Soviet Union's economic circumstances that shape its need to deal with the West and limit its political options. Otherwise, the chances are that we will misread Soviet initiatives or misinterpret events, and perhaps respond with inadequate or inappropriate measures. To formulate judgments about the future of financial relations with the Soviet Union, there are key points that should be remembered and mental traps that must be avoided by Western policymakers.

1. Don't lose track of Moscow's fundamental problem.

The biggest threat to the continued global authority of the Soviet Union and its status as a working model of socialism is the massive budget deficit it is carrying. For years, the Kremlin has had to resort to printing money to paper over chronic revenue shortfalls. That is a recipe for inflation, no matter what the ideological tenets of the system. The Soviet Union is not, of course, the utopia where money doesn't matter; under perestroika, it matters very much indeed. Money defines the profitability of firms and determines wages for workers based on performance. Yet inflation has rendered the ruble all but worthless. So the internal financial situation threatens the very foundation of economic restructuring; productivity can hardly be improved with a monetary system on the verge of breakdown.

Gorbachev's radical actions should thus be understood in terms of a drastic need to reduce the budget deficit. What he is trying to do is *increase* budget revenues by raising the productivity and profitability of Soviet enterprises, but to an even greater extent he is trying to *decrease* budget expenditures. He is prepared to go to extremes to accomplish both, even if it means testing the absolute limits of social and political acceptance: pushing to reduce overall wages even as workers are being exhorted to work harder, cutting subsidies from the government on consumer goods and allowing prices to rise, firing bureaucrats en masse. Concepts formerly anathema to the doctrine of socialism are now being promoted as the way to perfect the socialist mechanism: bankruptcy and unemployment, perhaps even the forced relocation of workers.

Meanwhile, Western observers should understand that Gorbachev has decided to extract the budget savings from consumption, not from fixed investment or defense spending. Gorbachev has declared, in fact, that expenditures for fixed capital investment are going to be substantially increased. He has also made it clear that any escalation on the U.S. side in the level of technological sophistication in the military competition with the Soviet Union will be countered in full. The Kremlin's priorities have thus been made clear: first, maintain a strong defense; second, invest in the facilities that are necessary for future economic gains; third, attend to the consumer needs of the population.

In considering any proposal submitted by Gorbachev to the West, the potential impact on the Soviet budget should be considered first and foremost. That goes for arms control negotiations as well as for economic relations. Gorbachev contends, for example, that the Strategic Defense Initiative (SDI) could be countered very easily by the Soviet Union. In his book *Perestroika*, he asserts that "a tenth of the U.S. investments would be enough to create a counter-system to frustrate SDI."[1] That seems highly unlikely, but the important thing is whether or not the Soviets believe it. Nuclear warheads themselves are not especially expensive to produce; in terms of "bang for the buck," they are very efficient military investments. So if arms control agreements are not really expected to deliver much in the way of budget savings to the Soviet government, why are they being pursued so vigorously by Gorbachev? That is, if pacts to destroy existing nuclear weapons won't significantly reduce the burden of military out-lays for the Soviet government, and a spending war with the United States over SDI would produce negative consequences for the U.S. internal budget, why is Gorbachev so interested in summits and signings?

The answer is that arms control negotiations are aimed not at reducing military spending so much as they are at promoting a political atmosphere conducive to cooperative East–West rela-tions, and "cooperative" here means the United States will do nothing to dissuade Western allies from proffering financial and economic assistance to the Soviet Union and perhaps will even go so far as to extend trade benefits itself. Given Moscow's fun-damental problem, the budget deficit, talks to reduce nuclear stockpiles merely serve as a captivating diversion to shift atten-tion away from Gorbachev's more immediate set of economic and financial objectives in negotiating with the West.

2. Don't underestimate the importance of trading with the West for the Soviet Union.

An opinion commonly expressed among Western observers is that Soviet domestic economic problems are so overwhelming that trade with the West is a trivial matter. Accordingly, financial and economic assistance from the West can have little impact on the economic destiny of the Soviet Union. The ensuing policy advice is that we might as well provide the Soviet Union with consumer goods and technology—and the credits to pay for them—because that will not affect the outcome of perestroika one way or the other.

The problem with the theory is that it reverses the comparative importance of trade for the parties concerned, downplaying the significance of Western purchases for the Kremlin while elevat-ing the significance of Soviet sales for Western businessmen and bankers. What is dismissed as being only marginally useful for the Soviet economy is proclaimed as having great impact on the domestic health of exporting countries. Contained within such an outlook, moreover, is the implicit value judgment that the sanctity of private commerce overrides national security consid-erations as they relate to the strength of the Soviet economy.

It may be a more comfortable policy position to assert that trad-ing with the Soviet Union doesn't really matter; after all, no one wants to undermine the principles of free trade. But it is irresponsible to ignore the reality of the Soviet economic situation. The fact is, consumer goods and technology from the West are needed as catalysts for perestroika. Gorbachev cannot get Soviet workers to be more productive unless he offers them some reward for their efforts. Rubles in themselves are no great prize. They can't even buy a place in line. But Western consumer goods are worth having and thus provide the means for restoring incentive power to the ruble. Technology, if it can be imported from the West, offers the dual bonus of saving internal resources and accelerating Soviet efficiency overnight.

Gorbachev needs help from the West to get perestroika off the ground. Bringing in Western-produced goods is a way to provide budget relief through enhanced revenues and reduced expenditures for the Soviet government. Sophisticated technology, in particular, permits Moscow to avoid costly outlays for research and development. Then there is the ultimate irony: High-quality Western products can be carefully copied, reproduced in quantity, and the knockoffs sold to foreign buyers as Soviet products, all of which generates additional hard currency revenues for Moscow. From Gorbachev's perspective, this is a money machine.

The point is, expanded trade with the West, particularly with the United States, is a high-priority objective for the Kremlin and should not be treated lightly by American policymakers. U.S.–Soviet trade should be regarded as an issue in itself, not something to be given away as a goodwill gesture or a display of mutual cooperation incidental to some other aspect of the superpower relationship, like arms control. Gorbachev is willing to go to tremendous lengths to increase the Soviet Union's access to the Western imports necessary to attain the objectives of perestroika. And timing is critical. As Gorbachev is discovering, the switch from central planning to self-financing and autonomous management has fostered confusion and disruptions in production. As a result, the internal economic situation is destined to get worse before it gets better. For the next few years, then, during this crucial period of transition for the Soviet Union, trade with the West takes on vital significance.

3. Don't be excessively flattered by Soviet moves toward capitalism.

There is a tendency in the West, especially among Americans, to view some of Gorbachev's initiatives as a move away from social-

ism toward capitalism. We flatter ourselves that the Soviets have
finally come around to our way of thinking. And we assume that
by the seeming embrace of capitalist values, the Kremlin has softened its attitude toward us as adherents of free market practices.
Naturally, our first impulse is to encourage the Soviets in their
newfound ways, and we find ourselves willing to promote en-
lightenment by providing the best our system can offer in the
way of consumer goods, financial capital, management expertise, and technology.

But it is important to remain clearheaded about recent changes
in the Soviet Union. What Gorbachev is doing is not capitalism.
Capitalism is not something that can be imposed from the top
down; it works from the bottom up through individual people
working to promote their own welfare. It can survive only where
there is sanctity attached to the ideal of personal freedom—indeed, it would seem impossible to separate economic freedom
from political freedom. What Gorbachev is doing is wringing
more output from the Soviet economy by temporarily changing
the rules, pulling the rug out from under Soviet citizens who
have long believed that personal sacrifice was the price of social
justice.

It is of course this very citizenry that has supported the Soviet
government for so long, keeping its vast program of expenditures
for industrial and military development afloat with revenues
taken from the manufacturing and consumer sector. Now Soviet
citizens are simply being asked to row faster. Far from enjoying
expanded economic freedoms under perestroika, the average Soviet worker will find himself caught in an economic squeeze between lower wages and higher prices. He will be subjected to the
harshest elements of capitalism—bankruptcy and unemployment—while experiencing few of its advantages. In short, Gorbachev has introduced certain free market mechanisms into the Soviet economy for reasons having little to do with individual
liberty and much to do with expediency.

Some Western observers feel that Gorbachev is a closet capitalist. They read too much into concepts like glasnost, which does
not connote openness so much as publicity (coming from the
Russian word for "voice"). Under glasnost, Soviet citizens are
supposedly encouraged to question the wisdom of government
authorities and to criticize official policies freely. But the limits
of glasnost may have already been reached. In February 1988 the
Soviet government ordered a halt to the creation of independent
printing shops and publishing houses, even though the action

flies in the face of perestroika and the right of individuals to establish private businesses. So much for free enterprise and so much for freedom of the press, both fundamental to genuine capitalism.

Why is it that we cheer Soviet initiatives and look disapprovingly upon what is happening in Poland? The selfsame initiatives hailed as splendid realism and pragmatism when taken by Gorbachev are regarded as part of a brutal program of subjugation when advanced by General Wojciech Jaruzelski. We don't see price hikes in Warsaw as part of a broader program for economic restructuring and liberalization. And we don't regard a government referendum asking the Polish people to endorse radical reform and difficult years of austerity to achieve "democratization" as an indication of a popular shift toward free market principles. In fact, the communist version of capitalism here is so distorted as to be blasphemous, amounting to nothing more than a set of stopgap measures instituted by desperate officials in the face of extreme economic circumstances. And if that is true of Jaruzelski's reforms, it is no less true of Gorbachev's.

What we think of as the positive features of capitalism now surfacing in the Soviet Union—managerial discretion, independence from the state, reliance on profitability—are being touted by Gorbachev as part of the logical next step in the evolution of *socialism*. According to Leonid Abalkin, Gorbachev's economic adviser, most Soviets do not even understand such basic free market concepts as the relationship between prices and supply.[2] So they haven't developed any sudden fraternal ideological bond with the United States just because certain features of a capitalist system have been adopted for use in their country. Why should they? We do not see ourselves growing closer to socialists when Medicare benefits are increased.

So we need objectivity as we assess Gorbachev's new initiatives. For example, there is talk now of allowing Soviet citizens to purchase shares in Soviet enterprises. Nikolai Shmelyov, a leading Soviet writer and a member of Gorbachev's economic brain trust, was quoted in February 1988 as complaining that vast amounts of rubles were lying idle in low-interest savings accounts while Soviet industry cried out for finance. "If we allowed enterprises to issue and sell and the population to buy shares with a sufficiently high yield," Shmelyov suggested, "then manufacturing companies and collective farms could mobilize in addition to their own resources tens of millions of rubles."[3]

But exactly what would this mean in a socialist economic system whose internal budget is in desperate straits? Gorbachev wants not to create private ownership of the means of production but to remove excess purchasing power from the consumption sector. Accordingly, the trick is to tie up savings so that they are effectively unspendable. If Soviet enterprises are allowed to offer shares that potentially pay higher dividends than the interest rate on savings deposits, it would be an insidious way to absorb excess purchasing power and keep it out of circulation. Those are not "savings" in the sense that they represent voluntary decisions to forgo current consumption; they represent instead accumulated inflation. Gorbachev needs to keep that money out of the hands of consumers to reduce the demand for goods.

The Soviet version of shareholding, we can well imagine, would be a far cry from Western-style capital markets. Individuals would be allowed to "invest" their savings in the enterprise where they work to demonstrate patriotic support of perestroika. But people almost certainly would not be allowed to invest in other enterprises. They would not be permitted to trade their shares, diversify their portfolios, or even redeem their holdings in cash on short notice. Moreover, the size of the dividend would be directly related to the firm's profitability; thus workers now being exhorted to work harder to earn a bonus would be asked in the future to work harder to increase their return on investment. In short, it is doubtful that shareholding would amount to anything more than a sham to permit the Soviet government to exercise even more control over the discretionary spending of the population.

4. Don't promote a personality cult for Gorbachev.

It is perhaps a vestige from tsarist times that the Soviet people have a tendency to exhalt the wisdom of their leaders, to make them larger than life, even to deify them. At any rate, personality cults typically develop around Soviet leaders while they are in power, only to be repudiated and dismantled after the leader is removed or dies. Except for Lenin, virtually every Soviet leader has been disparaged by his successors and has had numerous offenses subsequently attributed to him.

Gorbachev may have this in mind when he admonishes toadying political comrades not to invoke his name too often, as if he wants to limit in advance the steepness of the fall from grace. Plenty of unemployed bureaucrats on the streets of Moscow today have no desire to sing the praises of Mikhail Sergeyevich. Their ranks may soon be swelled by thousands of harried enterprise managers and millions of displaced workers. Then too, the forthcoming price increases will result in unhappy consumers throughout the country. And there are always rival politicos in the Kremlin ready to pounce on a misstep. Gorbachev could soon enough turn out to be a very unpopular figure in the Soviet Union.

Even as Gorbachev risks the support of comrades back home, who may like perestroika in the abstract but very much don't like paying more than $1.50 a pound for meat, he is successfully cultivating his popularity in the West. His maverick style plays especially well in the United States. Americans are inclined to cheer on the individual willing to take on the establishment— Gorbachev as the Lee Iacocca of the Politburo. Clearly, Gorbachev's personal popularity fuels much of the American public opinion in favor of a positive response to Soviet proposals. That should cause us to ask ourselves: Would we be so enthusiastic about summits and treaties with the Soviet Union if Gorbachev were suddenly replaced by, let us say, the current Soviet Minister of Defense? Would corporate chiefs be as eager to sit down with that minister to set up U.S.–U.S.S.R. joint ventures?

Some might respond by saying that U.S. interests are best served by seeing that Gorbachev *does* remain in power, so we should support him by giving him the kind of trade and financial benefits he wants. But imagine this scenario: Gorbachev's program for economic restructuring is implemented in full in the Soviet Union, then fails miserably. Enterprises, having grown to rely on government procurement, cannot support themselves financially under free market conditions, and when the umbilical cord to the state-run banking system is cut, they go bankrupt. Widespread unemployment follows. Workers denied their bonuses for not meeting production targets go on strike at one plant after another. There is a run on goods in anticipation of fewer consumer products and rising prices. Black market activities explode. The government imposes currency reform and cracks down on hoarders to stem the rise in illegal transactions. It then eliminates state subsidies on foodstuffs, fuel, and housing. That brings on more strikes, civil disobedience, and pervasive social unrest throughout the Soviet Union. What is the United States left to contend with? A country that has become another Poland—only with nuclear warheads.

There is another scenario: Perestroika turns out to be a great success, and the Soviet Union starts to grow much faster than the United States. The Soviets begin processing their vast raw materials at a much higher level of efficiency, thanks to expert design and managerial input from American and Japanese companies. The U.S.S.R. becomes a major competitor on world markets, selling manufactured goods and materials, perhaps even technology. Its gross national product begins to rival that of the United States. The Kremlin continues to allocate the same proportion of the national economy to the defense sector, and Soviet military capabilities quickly dwarf U.S. forces. That is not something we want either.

Obviously, we must plan our future relationship with the Soviet Union not on the basis of who is currently in charge but on the underlying economic, political, and social circumstances beyond the influence of any single individual. Gorbachev could be gone tomorrow, or he could be around for a long time. Either way, we must avoid emotional responses that cloud our objectivity about whether or not to finance perestroika and thus help to prop up, if not save, the Soviet internal economy. False hopes and an appealing persona may set us up for something less than pleasant. The Soviet emigré dissident Vladimir Bukovsky prophesies:

> Five to seven years down the line the whole herd of socialist cows, now well-fattened by their Western keepers, will answer the call of the Soviet cowherd and desert the rich pastures of capitalism. At that point, Western bankers and businessmen will be setting out to cut their losses, exactly as they are doing today with their Third World loans. They may make angry speeches and threats, but taxpayers and stockholders will bail them out.[4]

5. Don't trade economic and financial assistance for Soviet political concessions.

An example would be awarding the Soviet Union most-favored-nation trade status in exchange for Soviet cooperation on human rights. This tradeoff has been pursued for so long it has become politically enshrined as an appropriate *quid pro quo* to be achieved. In the United States, many are prepared to extend trade benefits to Moscow if the Kremlin permits increased Jewish emigration and exercises leniency toward dissidents. The problem is, in our desperation to pressure the Soviets into acts of basic human decency and to provide relief to victims of discrimination and political intolerance, we are prepared to give away too much, not just economically and financially, but by way of moral principle.

From the beginning, the Kremlin has refused to tolerate what it considers "interference" in internal policy matters. The United States could thus rest easy with the Jackson–Vanik Amendment, adopted in 1975, which stipulates that most-favored-nation trade treatment is not extended to countries that deny their citizens the right to emigrate freely. Under Gorbachev's leadership, however, there has been a decided shift in Soviet priorities. Thanks to severe internal economic pressures, Moscow has become newly flexible on human rights issues. The Soviets, for their part, seem ready to make good on the inherent contractual arrangements of the amendment. Prominent dissidents are being released from prison camps, and emigration levels are up.

The ball is now in our court. Does the United States fulfill its side of the bargain and provide economic and financial benefits to the Soviet Union? Do we permit Moscow to earn U.S. dollars by selling Soviet-manufactured goods (most likely, the ones produced through joint ventures with Western private companies) in the United States no longer subject to high tariff rates? Do we grant eligibility to the Soviet Union to receive U.S. government-backed trade credits from the Export-Import Bank—credits, by definition, subsidized by American taxpayers? What we have effectively agreed to do is pay ransom in return for the release of hostages. Indeed, to the extent that economic assistance from abroad is fungible and contributes to the overall resources available to the Kremlin to fund military activities, extending trade benefits is akin to trading arms for hostages—a policy that has been shown to have disastrous consequences.

If Gorbachev can get the United States to waive the Jackson–Vanik Amendment, he will enhance the Soviet Union's ability to pick up hard currency by selling its goods here and by stepping up its borrowing. The United States is potentially a much greater market for the Soviet Union than the much-touted Soviet market is for Western businessmen. U.S. producers generally find it difficult to compete against goods that utilize cheap foreign labor, and Soviet wages are abysmally low by Western standards. Items that require heavy inputs of iron or steel can be produced at lower cost in the Soviet Union and then shipped to the United States to compete against their American counterparts. The big advantage for Moscow, too, in selling its goods here is that the Soviets end up with something valuable, U.S. dollars, whereas Western manufacturers that attempt to sell their products in Soviet markets are left wrangling with the Soviet government over the exchange rate for turning in unwanted rubles.

Waiving the Jackson–Vanik Amendment would give a green light to U.S. bankers who may have not yet made loans to the Soviet Union for fear of higher levels of government scrutiny or public disapproval. The Soviet Union's status in the business and financial community would change drastically if it received most-favored-nation trade status and gained eligibility to borrow from the Eximbank. If a U.S. president is willing to vouch for Moscow by asking for a waiver, and if the Congress ratifies the administration's position, how can bankers and businessmen be criticized for doing business? And how can other Western countries be faulted for selling goods and technology and for granting credits to the Soviet Union once the United States puts a stamp of approval on such activity?

Neutralizing the Jackson–Vanik Amendment is thus a high-stakes matter for Gorbachev. He needs to accommodate those in the United States who have set the political price to be paid by the Kremlin in order to receive U.S. economic and financial assistance. For some it is human rights. For others it is Soviet withdrawal from regional conflicts. For still others it is arms control. Gorbachev's strategy will be to explore all three as he negotiates with U.S. officials. His best approach is to come across as reasonble and willing to compromise: Continue to release emigrants, begin scaling back Soviet activities in Angola and Nicaragua, keep the arms control process going. So, because Gorbachev is giving us what we want by addressing American preoccupations regarding Soviet behavior, it seems incumbent on us to give Gorbachev what he wants. And what Gorbachev wants is U.S. dollars.

The glaring error in that kind of thinking is the lack of symmetry in the tradeoff. Basic human values and matters of life and death on one hand, tariff policy and trade credits on the other.

It's indecent, really. Remember that whenever the subject of human rights comes up, Gorbachev responds huffily that the United States has political prisoners of its own and denounces the United States for not showing proper respect and compassion toward its Native American population. Yet he does not volunteer to help us with our deficit as a reward to induce better treatment for American Indians. He does not, in short, offer to lend us money. Put another way, if the Kremlin is genuinely concerned about the way the U.S. government treats its citizens, why doesn't it propose a more appropriate tradeoff? In exchange for Soviet improvement on human rights issues, perhaps the United States could agree to improve its own performance on human rights. In exchange for Soviet withdrawal from regional conflicts, we might well agree to curtail our own activities in sensitive areas. In exchange for Soviet reduction of military forces, we respond in kind by reducing our own military forces.

When money is part of the deal on one side only, we are no longer talking about mutual agreement between equal parties. It becomes extortion. Such an arrangement does not foster feelings of cooperation but instead breeds resentment. In the case of the Soviets, hostility toward condescending American diplomacy is accompanied by sardonic derision. The very courses of action that the United States is willing to pay them to take are already in keeping with Soviet national interests: getting rid of refuseniks, limiting geopolitical exposure, reducing military expenditures. Those are policies completely in line with long-term Kremlin objectives. In the meantime, though, Gorbachev exploits their political leverage to elicit the maximum payoff from the West. He invokes them to press for trade concessions from the United States, all the while begging us not to throw him, Br'er Rabbit, into the briar patch.

Finally, keep in mind that there is nothing new about linking financial benefits to what we call "human rights." This has long been part of the patronizing Western approach to Russia. Recall when French banks were eagerly pouring money into Russia just after the turn of the century, assisting the Tsar by financing industry and building up the Russian infrastructure. Rothschilds, one of the largest of the global banking networks, was managing a syndicate to raise a large loan for Russia but then suddenly withdrew to protest the persecution of Russian Jews. Crédit Lyonnais took over as chief agent on the loan.[5]

6. Don't get confused over labels—it's all a transfer of capital.

When a Western commercial bank makes a loan to Moscow, it is clear enough that financial resources are being withdrawn from the West and made available to the Soviet Union; it is the most straightforward way a West-to-East capital transfer is executed. There are many other mechanisms, however, for accomplishing the same thing. In some cases restrictions are involved that specifically limit what goods can be purchased with particular funds, but they are easily circumvented in an overall Soviet plan for obtaining Western products. The key concept here is fungibility.

The Soviets can obtain hard currency by selling their own goods abroad—oil, gold, weapons—or by taking out loans denominated in Western currencies. In the past the Soviets relied chiefly on syndicated commercial bank loans, but they now have started floating Eurobond offerings, which they are likely to do more and more often, allowing them to borrow in greater amounts at lower interest rates for longer periods. Whether hard currency is gained by selling Soviet goods or by issuing Soviet sovereign bonds, Moscow has the right to spend it as it sees fit. No one can dictate to the Soviet Union how to use the money it earns through the sale of Soviet products in the West. Likewise, there are no strings attached to funds received through sovereign bond offerings.

When the Soviet Union receives trade credits arranged through commercial banks or granted directly from Western governments, it can no longer spend the funds as it pleases. The credits are specifically tied to the goods being purchased. Not that this poses any real problem for Moscow; it is something Soviet foreign procurement officials can work around. Whenever trade credit financing is made available in conjunction with the purchase of Western exports, the Soviets do well to take advantage of the opportunity. The goal, of course, is to maximize access to unlimited credits and leave all options open. But even the most tightly restricted financing is useful if the purchase in question is on the Soviet wish list. In short, there is little difference between tied credits and general purpose loans.

The analysis can be taken further to argue that for Soviet central planning authorities there is no real qualitative difference between being supplied with Western washing machines and Western machine guns. If the production of so many washing machines is part of Moscow's plan for the domestic economy, being able to pick them up from the West means that the internal resources that *would* have been spent by the Soviet government to manufacture the washing machines on its own can now be used instead to produce more machine guns. Indeed, given comparative advantage, the Soviets would be better off importing the washing machines; domestically, they can probably produce machine guns much more efficiently than consumer durables.

Joint ventures with Western firms offer the best of all possible worlds for the Soviets, because they provide financial capital without imposing a debt obligation. Not only do the Soviets avoid having to pay interest, they also enjoy access to hard currency that does not show up in the debt statistics. The lower the figure for total debt, the more inclined Western bankers are to make additional loans. But whether funds are obtained through untied commercial loans or government-backed trade credits or Eurobonds, whether they are received in the form of debt or equity, the effect is to deliver benefits to Moscow. They all represent transfusions of capital from the West that go toward propping up the Soviet economy.

7. Improve monitoring capabilities.

As we know, Western capital can be transferred to the Soviet Union in a number of different ways, some of them currently not subject to surveillance. Obtaining accurate statistics is obviously the first step toward understanding the nature and extent of Soviet borrowing. But getting good numbers, unfortunately, is a very difficult task. Neither the Bank for International Settlements (BIS) nor the Organization for Economic Cooperation and Development (OECD) pays particular attention to Soviet borrowing; the information they provide for Western commercial bank loans and government trade credits to the U.S.S.R. is merely incidental to the larger task of aggregating debt statistics for some 160 countries. No multinational authority exists whose explicit function is to compile in a comprehensive way the transfer of Western capital to the Soviet Union.

Even for those forms of Soviet borrowing that are subject to global monitoring, there are distressing gaps in the coverage. The

BIS cannot track commercial loans that go across certain borders. Soviet-owned banks operating in the West are not segregated from other domestic banks. Certain Western countries, such as Switzerland, do not provide the BIS with information on credits made available to the Soviet Union through the *à forfait* market, even when they are provided by a specialized financial subsidiary of a reporting bank. That may well be the reason that the Soviets have stepped up their use of this little-known type of financing. According to the February 1988 issue of *Financial Market Trends:*

> The *à forfait* market has proven highly receptive to Eastern Europe in the past two years. According to market estimates, whereas in 1984 the East Europeans only accounted for 10 percent of the market, by 1986, when the credit standing of the region was in question, the East Europeans had increased their share to 25 percent. In 1987 the East Europeans reportedly account for 35–40 percent of activity.[6]

To monitor government-backed trade credits to the Soviet Union, the problems the OECD faces stem from the fact that information is provided by Western governments on a voluntary basis, and those same governments are not especially eager to publicize the extent to which they violate principles of free trade to promote their own exports with easy credit arrangements. Some international trade covered by government financing involves the transfer of military weaponry and is presumably omitted from reports for security reasons. Occasionally credits are left out because they are difficult to classify; for example, an OECD report for 1985 overlooked over $3 billion in Western loans to CMEA banks because it was impossible to determine how the money was distributed among Soviet bloc member countries.[7]

One might expect the United States to regulate its own financial dealings with Moscow more prudently. But our own central bank, the U.S. Federal Reserve, follows the same general procedures as the BIS in its treatment of loans from U.S. banks to Soviet-owned banks operating in Western countries. And even though it is expressly prohibited—a violation of the Johnson Debt Default Act—to use American deposits to fund general purpose loans to the Soviet Union, U.S. officials make little attempt to verify that American banks indeed use only their foreign deposits for such loans. Technology has complicated the intent of the original law; in these days of electronic funds transfer, where money can be held in New York on one day and wired in a split second to a branch office in London, how does one determine where the deposits are coming from?

The statistics on Soviet borrowing offered by the CIA are not particularly reassuring, either. They lack any kind of useful format and are far from comprehensive in their coverage. The CIA follows the time-honored but misleading practice of reducing the total figure for Soviet debt to the West by the amount of Soviet assets held in the West. "Soviet assets" means funds kept on deposit with Western banks. Thus the original gross figure is significantly offset to obtain a net figure for Soviet debt. That net debt figure conveys the impression that the Soviets have borrowed much less than they actually have; in 1985, the difference between the two figures amounted to more than $13 billion.[8]

What the CIA approach overlooks is that those deposits can be withdrawn by the Soviets at any time; the net debt figure could conceivably go up by $13 billion overnight. Whatever the timing of withdrawal, the deposits represent hard currency reserves that should be included to assess the financial resources available to Moscow and to calculate total Soviet indebtedness. There is another point to consider, too. We don't know exactly which Western banks are holding the deposits on behalf of the Soviets. The combined deposit base of the five Soviet-owned banks operating in the West exceeds $10 billion. How much of that represents money borrowed from Western banks? Using the CIA's approach, it is possible for the Soviet Union to borrow $30 billion from the West, keep $10 billion of it on deposit in its own banks—which qualify as Western banks—and register a net debt figure of just $20 billion.

The worrisome problem is that the BIS, the OECD, and the CIA are not set up to keep track of Soviet borrowing beyond commercial bank loans and government trade credits. Credits granted through nonbank forfaiting companies escape the scrutiny of monitoring authorities, as do private credits offered by Western companies that deal directly with the Soviet Union. Financial capital channeled through joint ventures is shielded in the course of private commerce—and this is likely to increase in the future as a source of funding for the Soviets. There is at present no method, either, for tracing the source of money that goes into purchasing Soviet bond offerings.

Admittedly, it is difficult to monitor financial transactions across international borders because of the sophisticated and complex procedures involved. Also working against monitoring is a certain traditional tendency toward secrecy, call it "discretion," in the banking and financial industry. But a lot is at stake in keeping track of Western capital flows to the Soviet Union. The United States, in particular, should initiate efforts to establish a specialized on-line monitoring authority, if not out of prudent business considerations or even national security interests, then because of the law on the books that prohibits private parties from making American domestic financial resources available to the Soviet government for unspecified purposes.

8. The United States must lead.

It is clearly in the overall interest of the West to put together a coordinated response to Soviet financial and economic initiatives. Because seepage undercuts the effectiveness of any program to restrict the transfer of capital, members of the Western alliance should cooperate to forge a united front on this issue. But the United States finds itself in the position of having to persuade its own allies to refrain from indiscriminately funding the Soviet Union. Those allies have separate agendas defining their political and economic relationship with Moscow. In this particular instance, we can concede the benefits of central planning; Gorbachev is able to run his campaign to obtain financial and economic assistance from the West with a single-mindedness that is most effective, while competitive forces in the West foment diversity and internal bickering to the point of precluding any definitive policy of response. Nations do not like to be told with whom they can trade or do business. Money is a sensitive issue, and money is what Gorbachev's foray into the West is all about.

The United States needs to convince its allies that making capital available to the Soviet Union constitutes the transfer of a strategic Western asset. It is ironic that the country most loath to impose capital controls must now ask other members of the Western alliance to support such a policy. But this is an area where national security interests should take precedence over the profit motives of businessmen and bankers. The sanctity of unfettered commerce has already been compromised, with extremely worthwhile results, by the prohibition on the transfer of

Western technology that can be used by the Soviets for military purposes. What the United States needs to do now is initiate a joint effort among Western allies to impose parallel restrictions to limit the transfer of financial capital.

The effectiveness of the COCOM (Coordinating Committee) program to restrict technology has come about because of a comprehensive effort by the United States to inform its allies about the problem and to persuade them that their cooperation was needed. The United States has put on well-informed demonstrations showing that technology transfers to the Soviet Union were directly used to strengthen Soviet military capabilities. To meet enhanced Soviet capacity, the West was forced to bear higher defense expenditures, which, of course, primarily affects the United States. Allies were made to acknowledge their own responsibility to mitigate the cost of the common defense and to concede that the national security interests of the Western alliance superseded the economic self-interest of individual nations. There are still problems to be resolved about the length and specificity of the restricted technology list, but there now seems to be an overall willingness among Western allies to abide by COCOM regulations, especially since the United States has also demonstrated its resolve to penalize nations that do not exercise sufficient control over technology transfers across their borders.

To make its case that the transfer of capital to the Soviet Union also results in higher defense costs for the West, the United States must provide an equally compelling demonstration that such transfers improve Soviet economic performance, which in turn enhances Soviet military capabilities. As a good first step toward cooperation, the United States should persuade its allies to help establish a comprehensive monitoring system to track financial flows to the Soviet Union. Information is inherently neutral, but revealing the scope of Soviet borrowing would underscore the potential impact of Western capital on the Soviet economy and convince allies of the need to oversee its transfer jointly. The eventual goal for the United States should be to structure a coordinated allied effort to restrict the flow of Western capital to the Soviets, to set up a financial COCOM of sorts.

In its appeal for support, the United States can point out that there are not just security risks but economic and financial risks as well. Because of inadequate monitoring, no one knows precisely how much Western capital has already been transferred to the Soviets and what obligations have been incurred by the So-

viet government toward Western creditors. Every bond obligation sold through the Eurobond markets is an additional claim
on the same hard currency reserves of the Soviet Union, and the
Kremlin cannot back up its full-faith-and-credit obligations by extracting additional revenues (denominated in rubles) from its
population. There is thus great potential for issuing numerous
claims to the same collateral without notifying investors.

If oil revenues plummeted or the price of gold dropped significantly, the Soviets would have little choice but to supplement
their hard currency reserves by floating additional debt in the
West. In other words, to pay off interest and principal obligations
coming due on past borrowings, the Soviets would have to borrow more from Western sources. The practice of soliciting additional loans to pay off existing debt obligations has proved disastrous in the past, not only for Third World borrowers but for the
international financial community caught in a trap of its own
making.

The West has so far made little effort to penetrate the Soviet
penchant for secretiveness about its internal budget situation
and its economic prospects. There was nary a protest when, on
the prospectus that accompanied its Eurobond offering, the Soviet government claimed that it was running a surplus in its state
budget.[9] One wonders what will happen when Gorbachev
presses his bid for Soviet membership in the IMF. Who will insist
that the Soviet government publish its internal accounting procedures and submit its statistics to Western financial analysts?
Which IMF member country will be willing to claim that Moscow's interest in joining the IMF and the World Bank is to sap
credit away from other potential recipients and buoy up the
standing of the Soviet Union in the eyes of private creditors?

The duty to expose misleading Soviet financial data and to
question Soviet motives behind its appeal to the West for economic and financial support falls to the United States. This country is not only the chief defender of the West, it is also the last
bastion of resistance Gorbachev must confront to open up Soviet
access to Western financial resouces. He has already settled with
the British and the Swiss on tsarist debts. Meanwhile, West Germany has a strong incentive to cultivate its business and banking
ties with Moscow; in seeking closer ties to East Germany, West
Germany seems willing to placate the Kremlin with financial favors. France has always taken a contrary path, unwilling to deny
credits to the Soviets even during the Siberian pipeline dispute,

and the largest of the Soviet-owned banks operating in the West is located in Paris. Whether or not Japan can be persuaded to redline the Soviet Union is an open question, but its banks now dominate world lending.

One thing, however, is certain. As Western financial flows provide sustenance to the Soviet economy, the United States will bear the brunt of the expense of having to contend with a stronger Soviet military threat. And if Moscow ultimately defaults on its debt to the West, the rest of the world will look to the United States to stabilize the financial markets and the international lending organizations. Americans thus have every right to assert their interests and assume leadership in the matter of providing credits to the Soviet Union.

In implicit acknowledgment of that right, other members of the Western alliance now appear to be waiting to see what the Americans will do. The foreign press is alert to every nuance that suggests the United States might be willing to accommodate Gorbachev's request for trade benefits. If we show that we are amenable to providing financial and economic assistance to the Soviet Union, the countries that earlier were willing to do business with Moscow will now be eager. If most-favored-nation trade status is requested by the U.S. president and granted by Congress, the power of America's entire banking network and business community will be unleashed to pursue arrangements with the Soviets. The United States is thus the linchpin that will determine the extent of Western cooperation with the Kremlin.

The policy implications vary widely, depending on whether the United States prefers to live with a sick bear or a rejuvenated one. But it is hard to argue with one very basic point: It doesn't make sense to provide financial aid to the Soviets when we are spending billions to defend ourselves from the military threat they pose. American citizens should not be asked to work against themselves as taxpayers, and bailing out the Soviet economy is anathema to our own economic priorities as well as our political sensibilities.

This does not mean that the Soviet Union is to be forever ostracized from the international financial markets. It just means that if it wishes to participate, it must behave as a responsible economic power and display maturity in its financial dealings with other countries. It cannot isolate itself with an unconvertible currency and expect to be embraced as a trading partner by the

West. It cannot orient its economy to building up a war machine and expect the rest of the world to treat it with civility and trust.

It has now been over seventy years since the Tsar was overthrown and the Russian people sought to run their own country. It is time for the Soviet Union as a nation to get beyond past grudges and take responsibility for its own failings as well as its achievements. If the Soviets aspire to become reputable members of the international financial community and the global economy, they should not come begging for handouts. If they want to be accepted as trading partners, they should work to have something worthwhile to trade. If they want to acquire hard currency, they should concentrate on developing ways to earn it. There is more to superpower status than sheer military might, because the world of global finance requires a more sophisticated kind of expertise. If the Soviets are prepared to change venue, they must demonstrate it. It is time for them to grow up and play by the rules.

Notes

CHAPTER 1. **The Internal Budget Mess**

1. George Garvy, *Money, Financial Flows and Credit in the Soviet Union* (Cambridge, Mass.: Ballinger, 1977), p. 83.
2. O. Kuschpeta, *The Banking and Credit System of the USSR* (Leyden and Boston: Martinus Nijhoff Social Sciences Division, 1978), pp. 118–19.
3. Tsentral'noye Statisticheskoye Upravleniye SSSR, *Narodnoye Khozyaistvo SSSR v 19.. g.: Statisticheskiy Yezhegodnik* (National Economy of the U.S.S.R. in 19..: A Statistical Yearbook), Moscow, *Finansy i Statistika*, for various years.
4. Ministerstvo Finansov SSSR, *Gosudarstvennyy Byudzhet SSSR 19..–19..: Statisticheskiy Sbornik* (State Budget of the U.S.S.R. 19..–19..: A Statistical Handbook), Moscow, *Finansy i Statistika*, for various years.
5. Igor Birman, *Secret Incomes of the Soviet State Budget* (The Hague: Martinus Nijhoff, 1981), pp. 10–11.
6. *Ibid.*, p. 315.
7. *Ibid.*, p. ix.
8. *Ibid.*, p. 34.
9. *Ibid.*, pp. 8–9.
10. Z. V. Atlas, ed., *Denezhnoye Obrashcheniye i Kredit SSSR: Uchebnik* (Money Circulation and Credit in the U.S.S.R.: A Textbook), Moscow, Gosfinizdat, 1957, pp. 168–69. Quoted in Birman, *Secret Incomes*, p. 118.

11. Birman, *Secret Incomes*, p. 25.
12. *Ibid.*, p. x.
13. Mark D'Anastasio, "Soviets Said to Distort Data to Show Improved Economy," *Wall Street Journal/Europe*, March 11, 1987, p. 2.
14. V. A. Yevdokimov, "O Klassifikatsii Dokhodov i Raskhodov Gosudarstvennovo Byudzheta SSSR" (On the Classification of the Revenues and Expenditures of the U.S.S.R. State Budget), *Finansy SSSR*, no. 8, 1976, p. 37. Quoted in Birman, *Secret Incomes*, p. 205.

CHAPTER 2. **Economic Fallout**

1. Vladimir I. Lenin, *Collected Works* (Moscow, 1960), 26: 106. Quoted in George Garvy, *Money, Financial Flows and Credit in the Soviet Union* (Cambridge, Mass.: Ballinger, 1977), p. 21. Emphasis in original.
2. Garvy, *Money, Financial Flows and Credit*, p. 121.
3. *Ibid.*, pp. 131–33.
4. Alexander Guber, "Price Stability," *Soviet Life*, January 1985, p. 10.
5. Celestine Bohlen, "Polish, Soviet Shoppers Hear the Footsteps of Price Reform," *Washington Post*, October 23, 1987, p. A34.
6. Elena Klepikova, "A View from the Queue," *Newsweek*, December 8, 1986, p. 18.
7. Serge Schmemann, "Queues in Soviet Persist As Scourge of Daily Life," *New York Times*, February 6, 1985, p. 6.
8. Mark D'Anatasio, "Soviet Media Admit Inflation's Existence," *Wall Street Journal*, May 22, 1987.
9. *Ibid.*
10. Klepikova, "View from Queue, p. 19.
11. O. Kuschpeta, *The Banking and Credit System of the U.S.S.R.* (Leyden and Boston: Martinus Nijhoff Social Sciences Division, 1978), p. 44.
12. D'Anatasio, "Soviet Media Admit."
13. Igor Birman and Roger A. Clarke, "Inflation and the Money Supply in the Soviet Economy," *Soviet Studies*, XXXVII, no. 4 (October 1985): 501–502.
14. Klepikova, "View from Queue," p. 19.

CHAPTER 3. **Perestroika to the Rescue**

1. Mikhail Gorbachev, *Perestroika: New Thinking for Our Country and the World* (New York: Harper & Row, 1987), p. 23.
2. *Ibid.*, p. 17.
3. Mikhail Gorbachev, report to the Communist Party Central Committee on June 25, 1987, entitled "On the Party's Tasks in Funda-

mentally Restructuring Management of the Economy," as distributed in translation by Tass, reprinted in "Excerpts from Gorbachev's Report on Restructuring the Soviet Economy," *New York Times*, June 26, 1987, p. A8.

4. Nikolai Shmelyov in *Novy Mir*, June 1987, translated by John Glad of the University of Maryland, excerpts reprinted in "Toward a Soviet Market Economy," *Wall Street Journal*, August 26, 1987.

5. Celestine Bohlen, "Soviet Leadership Endorses Sweeping Economic Restructuring," *Washington Post*, June 27, 1987.

6. Celestine Bohlen, "Hunkering Down for Perestroika," *Washington Post*, January 1, 1988, p. A26.

7. *Ibid.*

8. Peter Galuszka, "A Tractor Factory Tries to Pull its Own Weight," *Business Week*, December 7, 1987, p. 79.

9. Gorbachev, *Perestroika*, p. 100.

10. Stephen Sestanovich, "Gorbachev's Secret Foe: The Workers," *Washington Post*, November 1, 1987, p. C1.

11. *Ibid.*, p. C2.

12. Bohlen, "Hunkering Down."

13. Mikhail Gorbachev, "In His Words," *U.S. News & World Report*, November 9, 1987, p. 71.

14. Gorbachev, "On Party's Tasks."

15. Peter Galuszka and Bill Javetski, "Reforming the Soviet Economy," *Business Week*, December 7, 1987, p. 76.

16. Gorbachev, *Perestroika*, p. 91.

17. Merrill McLoughlin, "Gorbachev's Challenge," *U.S. News & World Report*, October 19, 1987, p. 36.

18. Gorbachev, *Perestroika*, p. 91.

19. Celestine Bohlen, "Soviet Press Campaign Hits Party Old Guard in Provinces," *International Herald Tribune*, January 28, 1988, p. 2.

20. Charles Hodgson, "Gorbachev's Agricultural Gamble," *Financial Times*, January 26, 1988, p. 30.

21. *Ibid.*

22. Peter Galuszka, "On the Farm, Ma and Pa Pyatayev Are Raising Some Cash Cows," *Business Week*, December 7, 1987, p. 80.

23. "Nothing to Lose But Your Queues," *The Economist*, December 19, 1987, p. 46.

24. Alexander Guber, "Price Stability," *Soviet Life*, no. 1 (340) (January 1985): 10.

25. Gorbachev, "On Party's Tasks."

26. Peter Gumbel, "Soviet Aides Press Plan to Cut Subsidies Despite Concern About Public's Reaction," *Wall Street Journal*, December 8, 1987, p. 33.

27. Bohlen, "Soviet Leadership Endorses."
28. Celestine Bohlen, "Polish, Soviet Shoppers Hear the Footsteps of Price Reform," *Washington Post*, October 23, 1987, p. A25.
29. *Ibid.*, p. A34.
30. "Oh Brother," *The Economist*, October 24, 1987, p. 56.
31. Bohlen, "Hunkering Down."
32. *Ibid.*
33. Philip Taubman, "Gorbachev Urges 'Radical' Changes to Spur Economy," *New York Times*, June 26, 1987, p. A8.
34. Charles Hodgson, "Moscow to Shed 20m Jobs Under Gorbachev Reform Plan," *Financial Times*, January 22, 1988.
35. *Ibid.*
36. Gorbachev, *Perestroika*, p. 52.
37. Bohlen, "Polish, Soviet Shoppers Hear Footsteps," p. A25.
38. "3 Key Supporters of Gorbachev Elevated to Politburo," *Washington Post*, June 27, 1987.

CHAPTER 4. How the West Fits In

1. Merrill McLoughlin, "Gorbachev's Challenge," *U.S. News & World Report*, October 19, 1987, p. 37.
2. Mark D'Anatasio, "Gorbachev Economic Plan Called Radical," *Wall Street Journal*, June 29, 1987, p. 2.
3. Anders Aslund, "Soviet Economy: Worse than the CIA Says," *International Herald Tribune*, May 21–22, 1988, p. 6.
4. Henry S. Rowen, "Living with a Sick Bear," *The National Interest*, 2 (Winter 1985/86): 14.
5. Mikhail Gorbachev, *Perestroika* (New York: Harper & Row, 1987), pp. 18–19.
6. Peter Galuszka, "A Tractor Factory Tries to Pull its Own Weight," *Business Week*, December 7, 1987, p. 79.
7. Igor Birman, *Secret Incomes of the Soviet State Budget* (The Hague: Martinus Nijhoff, 1981), p. 156.
8. Gorbachev, *Perestroika*, p. 92.
9. *Ibid.*, pp. 93–94.
10. Jonathan P. Stern, "Soviet Oil and Gas Production and Exports to the West: A Framework for Analysis and Forecasting," Study Papers, *Gorbachev's Economic Plans*, vol. 1, Joint Economic Committee, Congress of the United States (Washington, D.C.: Government Printing Office, 1987), p. 512.
11. Joan F. McIntyre, "The U.S.S.R.'s Hard Currency Trade and Payments Position," Study Papers, *Gorbachev's Economic Plans*, vol. 2, *ibid.*, p. 475.

12. Paul Kennedy, "What Gorbachev Is Up Against," *Atlantic Monthly*, June 1987, p. 33.
13. McIntyre, "The U.S.S.R.'s Hard Currency Position," p. 481.
14. *Ibid.*, p. 483.
15. "Soviet Polished Gem Sales Ease," *Financial Times*, November 1, 1984.
16. Carol Fogarty and Kevin Tritle, "Moscow's Economic Aid Programs in Less-Developed Countries: A Perspective on the 1980s," Study Papers, *Gorbachev's Economic Plans*, vol. 2, *ibid.*, p. 534.
17. Anthony Sampson, *The Money Lenders* (Harmondsworth, Middlesex, U.K.: Penguin Books, 1983), p. 46.
18. Mikhail Gorbachev, report to the Communist Party Central Committee on June 11, 1985, entitled "A Fundamental Issue of the Party's Economic Policy," as translated in "Gorbachev Speaks on Economic Progress, Planning," *Foreign Broadcast Information Service; U.S.S.R. National Affairs*, June 12, 1985, p. R4.

CHAPTER 5. The Role of Banks

1. Judy Shelton, "Would U.S. Banks Like a Loan Market in Moscow?" *Wall Street Journal*, January 8, 1985, p. 32.
2. Frederick Kempe, "Soviets Get $250 Million Loan; U.S. Banks Stay Out," *Wall Street Journal*, May 11, 1984, p. 35.
3. *Ibid.*
4. "Kremlin Calling," *Time*, December 9, 1985, p. 68.
5. William J. McDonough, executive vice president and chief financial officer, First Chicago Corporation, testimony before the United States Senate, Committee on Banking, Housing, and Urban Affairs, hearing on S. 812, the Financial Export Control Act, Washington, D.C., September 26, 1985.
6. Karen Riley, "Soviets Turning to Western Banks for Loans with No Strings Attached," *Washington Times*, April 20, 1987, p. 1A.
7. *Ibid.*
8. *Ibid.*, p. 10A.
9. George J. Clark, executive vice president, Citibank, N.A., testimony before the United States Senate, Committee on Banking, Housing, and Urban Affairs, hearing on S. 812, the Financial Export Control Act, Washington, D.C., September 26, 1985.
10. McDonough testimony.
11. Roger W. Robinson, Jr., "Soviet Cash & Western Banks, *The National Interest*, 4 (Summer 1986): 38.
12. *Ibid.*, p. 41.
13. Transcript (original) of hearing on S. 812, the Financial Export Control Act, United States Senate, Committee on Banking, Housing,

and Urban Affairs, Washington, D.C., September 26, 1985, pp. 111–12.

14. Moscow Narodny Bank Limited, Annual Report 1985, p. 15.
15. Vladimir I. Lenin, *Imperialism, the Highest Stage of Capitalism,* 1917, Chapter VII. Quoted in Anthony Sampson, *The Money Lenders* (Harmondsworth, Middlesex, U.K.: Penguin Books, 1983), p. 48.
16. O. Kuschpeta, *The Banking and Credit System of the U.S.S.R.* (Leyden and Boston: Martinus Nijhoff Social Sciences Division, 1978), p. 71.
17. Sampson, *The Money Lenders,* p. 330.
18. *Wall Street Journal,* August 8, 1981. Quoted in Darrell Delamaide, *Debt Shock* (Garden City: Anchor Books, 1985), pp. 70–71.
19. Wharton Econometric Forecasting Associates, *Centrally Planned Economies Outlook for Foreign Trade and Finance,* 1, no. 1 (December 1985).
20. Inter-American Development Bank, *External Debt and Economic Development in Latin America: Background and Prospects* (Washington, D.C., January 1984). Cited in Benjamin J. Cohen, *In Whose Interest* (New Haven and London: Yale University Press, 1986), p. 206.
21. Delamaide, *Debt Shock,* pp. 73–74.
22. Cohen, *In Whose Interest,* pp. 189–90.
23. *Ibid.,* pp. 195–96.
24. *Ibid.,* pp. 3–4.
25. McDonough testimony.
26. Transcript of hearing on S. 812, September 26, 1985, p. 4.
27. David C. Mulford, assistant secretary of the Treasury for International Affairs, testimony before the United States Senate, Committee on Banking, Housing, and Urban Affairs, hearing on S. 812, the Financial Export Control Act, Washington, D.C., December 4, 1985.
28. Judy Shelton, "Reagan Signals Business-as-Usual," *Wall Street Journal,* December 26, 1985, p. 6.
29. Kevin Maler, "Bill Would Curb Some Soviet Loans," *Washington Times,* August 5, 1987.
30. Stephen Green, "Moscow's Banking Scheme," *Washington Times,* March 20, 1986.
31. *Ibid.*
32. Maler, "Bill Would Curb."
33. Gerald M. Boyd, "U.S. Agrees to Aid Poland with Debt as Bush Pays Visit," *New York Times,* September 28, 1987, p. 1.
34. "U.S. Defense Chief Opposes German Credit for Soviets," *Wall Street Journal/Europe,* May 11, 1988, p. 11.
35. David Marsh, "Bonn Cool to U.S. Attack on Credit for Moscow," *Financial Times,* May 12, 1988, p. 6.

CHAPTER 6. **Government Lending**

1. "Subsidizing the Soviets," *Wall Street Journal*, May 14, 1984, p. 26.
2. *Ibid.*
3. *Ibid.*
4. *Ibid.*
5. Stephen W. Salant, "Export Subsidies as Instruments of Economic and Foreign Policy," *The Rand Corporation*, June 1984, p. 1.
6. Daniel F. Kohler, "Economic Cost and Benefits of Subsidizing Western Credits to the East," *The Rand Corporation*, July 1984, p. v.
7. Daniel F. Kohler, "Economic Cost and Benefits of Subsidizing Western Credits to the East: Executive Briefing," *The Rand Corporation*, February 1985, p. 10.
8. Kohler, "Economic Costs and Benefits," July 1984, p. vi.
9. "Technology and East–West Trade: An Update," Office of Technology Assessment, Congress of the United States (Washington, D.C., May 1983), p. 63.
10. Constantine C. Menges, "Détente's Dark History," *Wall Street Journal*, January 9, 1987.
11. Joseph Finder, "Trading with an Adversary Won't Soften Him," *Wall Street Journal/Europe*, June 3, 1985.
12. Zdzislaw M. Rurarz, "Poland Gives Credit Where It's Due: to Russia," *Wall Street Journal*, June 19, 1985, p. 31.
13. Daniel F. Kohler and Peter H. Reuter, "Honor Among Nations: Enforcing the Gentlemen's Agreement on Export Credits," *The Rand Corporation*, December 1986, p. 2.
14. *The Export Credit Financing Systems in OECD Member Countries* (Paris: OECD, 1987), p. 7.
15. Office of Technology Assessment, "Technology and East–West Trade," p. 104.
16. *Ibid.*
17. Kohler, "Economic Costs and Benefits," July 1984, p. 40.
18. I. M. Destler, "Congress," from *The Making of America's Soviet Policy*, edited by Joseph S. Nye, Jr. (New Haven and London: Yale University Press, 1984), p. 46.
19. Suzanne F. Porter, *East–West Trade Financing: An Introductory Guide*, U.S. Department of Commerce, September 1976, pp. 53–54.
20. Marshall Goldman and Raymond Vernon, "Economic Relations," from Nye, *America's Soviet Policy*, p. 163.
21. "Gorbachev Rules Out Rise in Trade with U.S." *Wall Street Journal*, December 11, 1985.
22. Celestine Bohlen, "Gorbachev Describes Obstacles to Trade with U.S.," *Washington Post*, December 11, 1985.
23. *Ibid.*

24. John M. Goshko, "Soviets Pledge Exit for 117, U.S. Says," *Washington Post*, May 28, 1986, p. A1.
25. John M. Goshko, "Jewish Leader Says Soviets May Let Thousands Emigrate," *Washington Post*, March 31, 1987, p. A1.
26. John Pearson, "Gorbachev Opens the Border for Jews—with Good Reason," *Business Week*, April 20, 1987, p. 28.
27. Neal Sandler, "Why the Doors Could Open Wider for Soviet Jews," *Business Week*, September 16, 1985, p. 49.
28. Robert B. Cullen, "Soviet Jewry," *Foreign Affairs*, 65, no. 2 (Winter 1986–1987): 260–61.
29. David Remnick, "Shcharansky Meets Reagan; 'Quiet Diplomacy' Unchanged," *Washington Post*, May 14, 1986, p. A1.
30. Sandler, "Why Doors Could Open."
31. "Ivan the Credit Seeker," *Wall Street Journal*, April 1, 1985.
32. Ralph Z. Hallow, "Dole Urges Removal of Soviet Trade Restrictions," *Washington Times*, April 28, 1986, p. 1A.
33. Anne Swardson, "Verity Tells of Doubts About Trade Law," *Washington Post*, September 11, 1987, p. D1.
34. Joan Mower, "Trade Restrictions May Ease, Dole Tells Gorbachev," *Washington Times*, June 2, 1988, p. A7.

CHAPTER 7. Access to Private Capital

1. V. Malkevich, "A Message from the First Deputy Minister of Foreign Trade of the U.S.S.R.," advertisement in *Wall Street Journal/ Europe*, August 24, 1987, p. 5.
2. "Perestroika on Wall Street," *Time*, September 7, 1987, p. 34.
3. N. V. Zinovyev, Director, Department of Trade with the Countries of America, U.S.S.R. Ministry of Foreign Trade, "The Soviet Union Is Willing to Expand Trade with the U.S.A.," special supplement in *International Herald Tribune*, November 7, 1986, p. 12.
4. I. Ivanov, "Ventures Made Easier," advertisement in *Wall Street Journal*, August 24, 1987, p. 6.
5. Mark D'Anatasio, "Soviet Union," *Business Week*, April 21, 1986, p. 41.
6. *Ibid.*
7. "Foreign Trade Rights?" *Soviet Business & Trade*, newsletter published by Leo G. B. Welt, Welt Publishing Company, Washington, D.C., June 23, 1987, p. 2.
8. Ivanov, "Ventures Made Easier."
9. *Ibid.*
10. Peter Keresztes, "How Moscow Makes Its Pitch," *Wall Street Journal*, July 2, 1987.
11. Gary Lee, "Moscow Woos Westerners for Joint Ventures," *Washington Post*, January 28, 1987, p. F1.

12. Mark D'Anastasio, "Capitalists Wary of Moscow's Hard Sell to Invest in Joint-Venture Enterprises," *Wall Street Journal*, April 6, 1987, p. 25.

13. Keresztes, "How Moscow Makes Its Pitch."

14. D'Anastasio, "Capitalists Wary."

15. "Venturing Jointly into the Russian Unknown," *The Economist*, June 6, 1987, p. 69.

16. Roon Lewald, "Ivan Starts Learning the Capitalist Ropes," *Business Week*, November 2, 1987, p. 154.

17. *Ibid.*

18. Keresztes, "How Moscow Makes Its Pitch."

19. Lewald, "Ivan Starts Learning the Ropes."

20. "Comrade Capitalists, Come Make Money in the Soviet Union," *U.S. News & World Report*, January 19, 1987, p. 39.

21. Rose Brady, "Fast Food Is Coming, Fast Food Is Coming," *Business Week*, December 1, 1986, p. 50.

22. Gary Lee, "U.S. Entrepreneurs Hope Perestroika Translates into Profits in Soviet Union," *Washington Post*, April 17, 1988.

23. "How About a Big Mcski?" *U.S. News & World Report*, June 22, 1987, p. 43.

24. David Remnick, "Moscow's Big Mac Attack," *Washington Post*, April 30, 1988, p. C1.

25. Axel Krause, "French Bank, Moscow Sign Soviet Venture," *International Herald Tribune*, March 21, 1987, p. 9.

26. *Ibid.*

27. "Venturing Jointly," p. 70.

28. "Pizza-Hut in the U.S.S.R." *Soviet Business & Trade*, newsletter published by Leo G. B. Welt, Welt Publishing Company, Washington, D.C., September 23, 1987, p. 1.

29. Gary Lee, "Gorbachev Prods and Dines American Business Leaders," *Washington Post*, April 14, 1988, p. A1.

30. *Ibid.*, p. A26.

CHAPTER 8. **Issuing a Eurobond**

1. OECD, *Financial Statistics Monthly*, January 1987.

2. Peter Montagnon, "Hungary Launches Unique Floater," *Financial Times*, March 20, 1986.

3. O. Kuschpeta, *The Banking and Credit System of the USSR* (Leyden and Boston: Martinus Nijhoff Social Sciences Division, 1978), p. 17.

4. George Garvy, *Money, Financial Flows and Credit in the Soviet Union* (Cambridge, Mass.: Ballinger, 1977), p. 14.

5. Kuschpeta, *Banking and Credit System*, p. 17.

6. *Ibid.*, p. 18.
7. E. Aghad, *Grossbanken and Weltmarkt* (Berlin: 1914), pp. 136–37. Quoted in Garvy, *Money, Financial Flows and Credit*, p. 18.
8. Foreign Bondholders Protective Council, Inc., *Report 1962 Through 1964*, New York, pp. 123–24.
9. Anthony Sampson, *The Money Lenders* (Harmondsworth, Middlesex, U.K.: Penguin Books, 1983), p. 46.
10. *Ibid.*, pp. 46–47.
11. *Ibid.*, p. 47.
12. Graham Webb, "History of the Soviet Union," *Fodor's Soviet Union 1985* (New York: Fodor's Travel Guides, 1984), p. 96.
13. Sampson, *Money Lenders*, p. 47.
14. *Ibid.*, p. 46.
15. Kuschpeta, *Banking and Credit System*, p. 18.
16. *Ibid.*, p. 20.
17. Dennis R. Papazian, "When the Allies Intervened in Russia," letter to the editor, *Wall Street Journal*, February 25, 1987.
18. Garvy, *Money, Financial Flows and Credit*, pp. 23–24.
19. *Ibid.*, p. 24.
20. Foreign Bondholders Protective Council, Inc., *Report*, p. 126.
21. Papazian, "When the Allies Intervened."
22. Moore, *International Law Digest*, vol. 1, sec. 96. Cited in opinion of Attorney General Homer Cummings to the Secretary of State, May 5, 1934. Emphasis in original.
23. Halleck, *International Law*, 3d ed. 1: 90. Cited in opinion of Attorney General Homer Cummings to the Secretary of State, May 5, 1934.
24. Opinion of Attorney General Homer Cummings to the Secretary of State, May 5, 1934 [37 Op. A.G. 505 (1934)].
25. Opinion of Attorney General Ramsey Clark to the Secretary of State, May 9, 1967 [42 Op. A.G., May 9].
26. "In Britain's Cabinet Files—Seeds of a Sellout," *Wall Street Journal/ Europe*, July 17, 1986, p. 6.
27. Minutes from British Cabinet Meeting, January 17, 1934, quoted in "Beyond the Baring Balances," *Wall Street Journal/Europe*, July 17, 1986, p. 6.
28. "In Britain's Cabinet Files."
29. *Ibid.*
30. Agreement between the Government of the United Kingdom of Great Britain and Northern Ireland and the Government of the Union of Soviet Socialist Republics concerning the Settlement of Mutual Financial and Property Claims arising before 1939, London, July 15, 1986.

31. Craig Forman, "Soviets, British Reach Accord on Czarist Debt," *Wall Street Journal,* July 16, 1986.

32. "From Russia with Love," *U.S. News & World Report,* July 28, 1986.

33. Barbara Toman, "After 70 Years, Russian Czarist Bonds Translate into Some Hope for Holders," *Wall Street Journal,* April 1, 1987.

34. Forman, "Soviets, British Reach Accord."

35. *Ibid.*

36. C. R. Neu and John Lund, "Toward a Profile of Soviet Behavior in International Financial Markets," *The Rand Corporation,* August 1987, p. 30.

37. Stephen D. Moore, "Major Soviet Bond Issues Are Expected Despite Requirements to Disclose Secrets," *Wall Street Journal,* January 8, 1988.

38. "Czars' Debts to Switzerland to Be Paid by Soviet Union," *Wall Street Journal/Europe,* January 19, 1988, p. 10.

39. "Soviet Bank Taps Eurobond Market for $78 Million," *Wall Street Journal,* January 6, 1988.

40. John Wicks, "Soviet Bank May Borrow More," *Financial Times,* February 9, 1988.

41. *Ibid.*

42. "Soviet Bond Offering," *Soviet Business & Trade,* newsletter published by Leo G. B. Welt, Welt Publishing Company, Washington, D.C., June 9, 1988, p. 1.

43. Neu and Lund, "Toward a Profile of Soviet Behavior," p. 31.

44. Tombstone ad for National Bank of Hungary in *Financial Times,* March 4, 1986, p. 26.

45. Victor Gerashchenko, First Deputy Chairman of the Board, U.S.S.R. Bank for Foreign Trade, "Cooperation with U.S. Banks: Prospects for the Future," advertisement in *Wall Street Journal/Europe,* August 24, 1987, p. 13.

46. "Several Eurobonds Are Linked to Gold in Bid to Revive Interest in New Issues," *Wall Street Journal,* April 21, 1987.

47. *Ibid.*

48. "No Let-Up Expected in Eurobond Market Regulatory Pressure," *Financial Times,* May 26, 1987.

49. Stephen D. Moore, "Resistance Lingers to Eurobond Regulation," *Wall Street Journal/Europe,* May 25, 1987, p. 10.

50. Charles Grant, "A Survey of the Euromarkets," *The Economist,* May 16, 1987, p. 14.

CHAPTER 9. Joining the Club

1. J. Keith Horsefield, *The International Monetary Fund, 1945–1965: Twenty Years of International Monetary Cooperation* (Washington, D.C.: International Monetary Fund, 1969), vol. I, p. 92. Quoted in

Margaret Garritsen de Vries, *The IMF in a Changing World, 1945–85* (Washington, D.C.: International Monetary Fund, 1986), p. 11.

2. Whittaker Chambers, *Witness* (Chicago: Regnery Gateway, 1952), p. 544.

3. *Articles of Agreement of the International Monetary Fund,* adopted at the United Nations Monetary and Financial Conference, Bretton Woods, New Hampshire, July 22, 1944 (Washington, D.C.: International Monetary Fund, 1944), Schedule A, "Quotas," p. 81.

4. Anthony Sampson, *The Money Lenders* (Harmondsworth, Middlesex, U.K.: Penguin Books, 1983), p. 87.

5. *Ibid.,* p. 88.

6. *Ibid.,* p. 89.

7. Daniel Franklin and Edwina Moreton, "Comecon Survey," *The Economist,* April 20, 1985, p. 3.

8. *Ibid.,* p. 4.

9. *Ibid.,* p. 7.

10. *Ibid.*

11. Jackson Diehl, "Soviet Trade with COMECON Lagging," *International Herald Tribune,* June 2, 1987, p. 8.

12. Wharton Econometric Forecasting Associates, *Centrally Planned Economies Outlook for Foreign Trade and Finance,* 1, no. 1 (December 1985): 1–2.

13. Zdzislaw M. Rurarz, "Poland Gives Credit Where It's Due: to Russia," *Wall Street Journal,* June 19, 1985, p. 31.

14. "With a Friend Like Him?" *The Economist,* July 13, 1985, p. 16.

15. Jackson Diehl, "Kremlin Decides It Can Learn from Its Allies," *Washington Post,* October 13, 1987, p. A1.

16. Franklin and Moreton, "Comecon Survey," p. 3.

17. "Red Letter Day," *The Economist,* June 22, 1985, p. 71.

18. Franklin and Moreton, "Comecon Survey," p. 1.

19. "Soviet Signal Renewed Interest in EC-Comecon Cooperation," *Wall Street Journal/Europe,* May 31, 1985, p. 1.

20. "More Comradely," *The Economist,* January 25, 1986, p. 46.

21. David Buchan, "Comecon Plays Hard to Get with EEC Suitor," *Financial Times,* March 7, 1986.

22. "More Comradely."

23. Buchan, "Comecon Plays Hard to Get."

24. "Red Letter Day."

25. Robert J. McCartney, "Comecon, EC End Hostilities," *Washington Post,* June 26, 1988, p. A22.

26. Thomas Netter, "EC, Comecon End Talks Still Blocked on Berlin," *International Herald Tribune,* March 21, 1987.

27. McCartney, "Comecon, EC End Hostilities."

28. "Soviet Move Linked to Membership Attempt," *Financial Times,* September 10, 1986.

29. "Yeutter Cool on Soviet Entry," *Wall Street Journal/Europe,* September 4, 1986, p. 2.

30. "Soviet Move Linked."

31. Clyde H. Farnsworth, "Moscow Asks to Join Textile Pact," *New York Times,* August 28, 1987.

32. S. Karen Witcher, "Soviets Consider Joining IMF, World Bank," *Wall Street Journal,* August 15, 1986.

33. Peter Keresztes, "How Moscow Makes Its Pitch," *Wall Street Journal,* July 2, 1987.

34. Farnsworth, "Moscow Asks to Join."

35. *Ibid.*

36. Joanne Omang, "Deeper Meanings at the State Dept.," *Washington Post,* March 13, 1987.

37. Hobart Rowen, "Conable Receptive to Soviets," *Washington Post,* October 17, 1986.

38. Hobart Rowen, "Baker: U.S. Would Oppose Soviet IMF Bid," *Washington Post,* November 22, 1986.

39. Bill Gertz, "U.S. Clarifies Stance on Soviet Financial Role," *Washington Times,* March 13, 1987.

40. Rowland Evans and Robert Novak, "The Democrats Give Gorbachev a Signal," *Washington Post,* November 11, 1987.

41. "Who's Minding the NSC?" *Wall Street Journal/Europe,* January 21, 1988, p. 6.

42. Bill Bradley, "West's Economy: Gorbachev's Stake," *New York Times,* October 15, 1987.

43. *Ibid.*

44. Evans and Novak, "The Democrats Give a Signal."

45. David G. Wigg, deputy assistant secretary of defense policy analysis, testimony before the Joint Economic Committee, Subcommittee on National Security Economics and Trade, concerning the national security implications of Soviet economic reforms, Washington, D.C., September 10, 1987.

46. Evans and Novak, "The Democrats Give a Signal."

47. Edmund Pietrzak, "Warsaw Counts Cost of Joining IMF," *Financial Times,* September 10, 1986, p. 2.

48. *Ibid.*

49. "Who's Minding the NSC?"

50. Zdzislaw M. Rurarz, "Poland May Not Want in the IMF Now," *Wall Street Journal,* January 23, 1985, p. 35.

51. *Ibid.*

52. *Articles of Agreement of the International Monetary Fund,* p. 32.

53. Diehl, "Kremlin Decides It Can Learn," p. A15.
54. "Soviet Union Aims for Convertible Ruble," *International Herald Tribune*, February 4, 1988, p. 13.
55. Pietrzak, "Warsaw Counts Cost."

CHAPTER 10. **Proper Perspective**

1. Mikhail Gorbachev, *Perestroika* (New York: Harper & Row, 1987), p. 234.
2. Peter Fuhrman, "'The Soviet Economy Is in a Grave State,'" *Forbes*, October 19, 1987, p. 110.
3. "Soviet Economics Writer Backs Shareholding System," *Wall Street Journal/Europe*, February 4, 1988.
4. Vladimir Bukovsky, "Gorbachev's Reforms: Where's the Beef?" *Wall Street Journal*, December 22, 1987.
5. Anthony Sampson, *The Money Lenders* (Harmondsworth, Middlesex, U.K.: Penguin Books, 1983), p. 47.
6. Organization for Economic Cooperation and Development, *Financial Market Trends* (Paris: OECD, February 1988), p. 32.
7. Compare *Statistics on External Indebtedness* (Paris and Basel: BIS/OECD, July 1987, p. 15) for the end of 1985, which includes the debt of the two CMEA banks under U.S.S.R. debt, with *External Debt Statistics* (Paris: OECD, 1987, p. 19) for total Soviet debt at the end of 1985.
8. *Handbook of Economic Statistics, 1987* (Washington, D.C.: Central Intelligence Agency, September 1987), p. 75.
9. Haig Simonian, "Moscow Plans More Borrowing," *Financial Times*, January 21, 1988.

Index